DEVELOPMENT, SOCIAL CHANGE AND ENVIRONMENTAL SUSTAINABILITY

PROCEEDINGS OF THE INTERNATIONAL CONFERENCE ON CONTEMPORARY SOCIOLOGY AND EDUCATIONAL TRANSFORMATION (ICCSET 2020), MALANG, INDONESIA, 23 SEPTEMBER 2020

Development, Social Change and Environmental Sustainability

Edited by

Sumarmi, Nanda Harda Pratama Meiji,
Joan Hesti Gita Purwasih & Abdul Kodir
Universitas Negeri Malang, Indonesia

Edo Han Siu Andriesse
Seoul National University, Republic of Korea

Dorina Camelia Ilies
University of Oradea, Romania

Ken Miichi
Waseda Univercity, Japan

CRC Press is an imprint of the
Taylor & Francis Group, an **informa** business

A BALKEMA BOOK

CRC Press/Balkema is an imprint of the Taylor & Francis Group, an informa business

© 2021 selection and editorial matter, the Editors; individual chapters, the contributors

Typeset in Times New Roman by MPS Limited, Chennai, India

The Open Access version of this book, available at www.taylorfrancis.com, has been made available under a Creative Commons Attribution-Non Commercial-No Derivatives 4.0 license.

Although all care is taken to ensure integrity and the quality of this publication and the information herein, no responsibility is assumed by the publishers nor the author for any damage to the property or persons as a result of operation or use of this publication and/or the information contained herein.

Library of Congress Cataloging-in-Publication Data
A catalog record has been requested for this book

Published by: CRC Press/Balkema
Schipholweg 107C, 2316 XC Leiden, The Netherlands
e-mail: enquiries@taylorandfrancis.com
www.routledge.com – www.taylorandfrancis.com

ISBN: 978-1-032-01320-6 (Hbk)
ISBN: 978-1-032-06730-8 (Pbk)
ISBN: 978-1-003-17816-3 (eBook)
DOI: 10.1201/9781003178163

Development, Social Change and Environmental Sustainability – Sumarmi et al (Eds)
© 2021 Taylor & Francis Group, London, ISBN 978-1-032-01320-6

Table of contents

Preface	ix
Acknowledgments	xi
Organizing committee	xiii
Scientific committee	xv

The effect of the Problem Based Service Eco Learning (PBSEcoL) model on student environmental concern attitudes
Sumarmi — 1

Community conservation in transition
W. Dressler — 5

Sociology and geography of growing seaweed in the Philippines
E. Andriesse — 8

History of the Ludruk Rukun Famili in Sumenep Madura Island, 1943–1997
R. Ridhoi, A.N.A. Utama & J. Sayono — 14

Promoting moderatism, countering radicalism: Religious discourse of high school students in Malang
A.A. Widianto, J.H.G. Purwasih, N.H.P. Meiji & R.P. Prabawangi — 18

The female terrorism: Victimization in the striving for family
E. Malihah, S. Nurbayani, P. Wulandari & Wilodati — 23

Legal culture in cockfighting games in east Java communities, Indonesia
Sudirman & R. Umar — 29

"Sumberawan water site": History, sustainable preservation and use as a learning source
W.D. Sulistyo & M.A. Dewanti — 34

Coping strategy based on socio-agriculture approach in Landslide Prone Area in the Gede Catchment, Malang Regency
N. Muddarisna, H. Masruroh, E.D. Yuniwati & A.R. Oktaviansyah — 39

Utilization of new media as a promotion facility in entrepreneurship development for students at SMAN 1 Torjun
E. Kurniawati, J.H.G. Purwasih, P.P. Anzari & D.W. Apriadi — 44

Plague in Malang 1910–1916
S.S.P. Jati, A. Subekti, W.D. Sulistyo & M.N.L. Khakim — 50

The problems of COVID-19 waste management in East Java
A. Tanjung, A. Kodir, I.K. Astina, M.Y. Affandi & M.G. Rosyendra — 53

The dynamics of community response to the development of the New Capital (IKN) of Indonesia
A. Kodir, N. Hadi, I.K. Astina, D. Taryana, N. Ratnawati & Idris — 57

Geo-ecological interaction: Community based forest management in Karanganyar, Indonesia
A.S. Fibrianto, A.D. Yuniar, I. Deffinika, A. Azzardina & D. Afrianty — 62

The development of application for child care services in facilitating distance learning 66
R.A. Rahma, M. Ishaq, Sucipto & Y. Affriyenni

Educators' professional ability to manage online learning during the COVID-19 pandemic 70
S.S. Pratiwi, I.H. Al Siddiq, P.P. Anzari, M.N. Fatanti & D.F.V. Silvallana

Learning style from face-to-face to online learning in pandemic COVID-19
(the case study at East Java) 74
D.S. Rozakiyah, I.Y. Suhanti & S.S. Pratiwi

Private school reform through learning community: Evidence from Muhammadiyah School 79
L.A. Perguna, H. Sutanto & J.H.G. Purwasih

Women in education: A review of Indonesian feminism 83
Yuliati, M.N.L. Khakim & Idris

The woman's international migration: Controlling rural land by women workers 87
M. Zid & A.R. Casmana

Analysis of population vulnerability towards the spread of COVID-19 in
Malang Raya from a spatial perspective 92
Purwanto, I.S. Astuti, A. Tanjung & F. Rohman

The distribution problem of social safety net program in Surabaya and
Gresik during pandemic 98
I.H. Al Siddiq, A. Kodir, I. Mukhlis, F.K. Aditya & S. Paramanandana

Capturing the dual role of female medical workers during the COVID-19
pandemic in Surabaya 102
D.W. Apriadi, D. Mawarni & M. Saputra

Environmental health behavior of fishing communities during COVID-19 pandemic 107
S. Susilo, Budijanto & I. Deffinika

Social media management as optimization of tourism potential in Osing Kemiren,
Banyuwangi Regency 113
N. Hadi, E. Kurniawati & P.P. Anzari

From pandemic to infodemic: Bias information of covid-19 and ethical consideration
among Indonesian youtuber 118
R.P. Prabawangi & M.N. Fatanti

How virtual fancy things build self-presentation? consumer's acceptance and
use of e-commerce 123
A.D. Yuniar & A.S. Fibrianto

Assessing the role of mass media in information mitigation on COVID-19
pandemic issues in Indonesia: A discourse analysis on *KOMPAS* daily newspaper 128
M.N. Fatanti & C. Anggraini

The levels of empowerment of forest farmer group in coastal village development in
South Malang, Indonesian 132
K.M. Raharjo, Sucipto, Zulkarnain, Hardika & M. Widyaswari

Digital activism through online petition: A challenge for digital public sphere in Indonesia 136
K.S. Ananda & M.N. Fatanti

Philanthropy movement's response to government policy in negotiating COVID-19
in Indonesia 141
N.H.P. Meiji, A. Kodir, Sumarmi, A. Tanjung, A.F. Dianah & M.A. Al Kindy

Facilitating communities to identify local potential and hazards through P-GIS and FGD 145
L.Y. Irawan, Sumarmi, S. Bachri, M.M.R. Devy, R. Faizal & W.E. Prasetyo

Optimizing village assets for rural tourism development in South Malang 151
J. Sayono, L. Ayundasari, Nasikh & F.K. Aditya

Zoo management for animal welfare through sustainable tourism principles 157
A. Demartoto

Development strategy sustainability of historical and cultural tourism in Pacitan 162
L. Ayundasari, A. Sapto, W.D. Sulistyo, R. Ridhoi & U. Nafiah

Author index 167

Development, Social Change and Environmental Sustainability – Sumarmi et al (Eds)
© 2021 Taylor & Francis Group, London, ISBN 978-1-032-01320-6

Preface

The SDGs (Sustainable Development Goals) concept has replaced the MDGs (Millennium Development Goals). The topic of today's environment becomes an essential issue for the development of humanity. Furthermore, we saw that the development of technology and modernity is faster than before. We have come into a risk society which made us more flexible and adaptive to face the problems even though the issues change with the changing time. The world is becoming more uncertain than the previous one. Therefore, cooperation and participation from all elements and stakeholders are needed to overcome various late modernity society problems.

The first International Conference on Contemporary Sociology and Educational Transformation (ICSSET) 2020 was held on September 23, 2020, in Universitas Negeri Malang in East Java, Indonesia. The Conference was held online due to the corona pandemic, which occurred globally. Sociology Department, Social Science Faculty, Universitas Negeri Malang managed this Conference for the first time. There were four main speakers at this Conference, including Prof. Kosuke Mizuno, CSEAS Kyoto University/SIL UI, Prof. Wolfarm Dressler, University of Melbourne, Asc. Prof. Edo Han Siu Andriesse, Seoul National University, and Prof. Dr. Sumarmi M.Pd, Universitas Negeri Malang.

The participants of this Conference came from various universities in Indonesia and some other countries. This Conference tried to compile the discourses from anywhere and everywhere. The committee received about 122 articles, and there were 99 articles accepted to be presented. There were 36 articles carried in the book series published by CRC Press Balkema, Taylor and Francis Group from the total number. With full support from Universitas Negeri Malang, this Conference could be placed for the presenters to collaborate on the topic. Hopefully, this Conference could enrich the discourses about the topic area.

Development, Social Change and Environmental Sustainability – Sumarmi et al (Eds)
© 2021 Taylor & Francis Group, London, ISBN 978-1-032-01320-6

Acknowledgments

All articles in this book are the final version of the paper presented at the International Conference on Contemporary Sociology and Educational Transformation (ICCSET) which was held on 23rd September 2020 through a virtual meeting in Malang, Indonesia. We would like to thank the Chancellor and Dean of the Faculty of Social and Political Sciences, Universitas Negeri Malang who have supported to this event. On behalf of the committee, writers and readers, we would also like to thank all keynote speakers and reviewers for their hard work, time and dedication to this conference. Their efforts to maintain good quality articles deserve the highest appreciation. We do not forget to thank all the speakers and conference participants who have participated in this event. Finally, we would like to thank the committee and all peoples who have helped and supported this conference.

The committee would like to apologize to all the speakers who could not publish their writings in the proceedings of this conference. Our apologies also to all participants for any shortcomings during the conference. See you at the next 2nd ICCSET at the Universitas Negeri Malang.

Stay Safe!

Malang, January 25 2021

Organizer of ICCSET
Universitas Negeri Malang
INDONESIA

Development, Social Change and Environmental Sustainability – Sumarmi et al (Eds)
© 2021 Taylor & Francis Group, London, ISBN 978-1-032-01320-6

Organizing committee

Advisory Board
Prof. Dr. Ah. Rofi'uddin
Universitas Negeri Malang, Indonesia

Chairman
Nanda Harda P.M. M.A.
Universitas Negeri Malang, Indonesia

Secretary
Deny Wahyu Apriadi M.A.
Seli Septiana Pratiwi M.Pd.
Universitas Negeri Malang, Indonesia

Treasury
Elya Kurniawati M.M.
Desy Santi Rozakiyah M.Pd.
Universitas Negeri Malang, Indonesia

Technical Chair
Luhung Achmad M.A.
Alan Sigit Fibrianto M.Sos
Ahmad Arif W. M.A.
Ananda Dwitha Y. M.A.
Prawinda Putri A. M.Si.
Imamul Huda A. M.Sosio
Anggaunitakiranantika M.Sosio
Drs. Irawan M.Hum
Dr. Abdul Latif Bustami M.Si
Universitas Negeri Malang, Indonesia

Publication
Joan Hesti G.P. M.Si.
Abdul Kodir M.Sosio
Kun Sila Ananda M.A.
Megasari Noer F. M.I.Kom
Universitas Negeri Malang, Indonesia

Development, Social Change and Environmental Sustainability – Sumarmi et al (Eds)
© 2021 Taylor & Francis Group, London, ISBN 978-1-032-01320-6

Scientific committee

Prof. Dr. Myrtati Dyah Artaria M.A.
Universitas Airlangga, Indonesia

Inaya Rakhmani Ph.D
Universitas Indonesia, Indonesia

Rachmad K. Dwi Susilo M.A. Ph.D
Universitas Muhammadiyah Malang, Indonesia

Prof. Dr. Ely Malihah M.Si
Universitas Pendidikan Indonesia, Indonesia

Yuti Ariani Ph.D
Nanyang Technological University, Singapore

Dr. Suryo Adi Prabowo
Institut Pertanian Bogor, Indonesia

Kvestoslava Matlovicova Ph.D
University of Prestov, Slovakia

Oki Rahadianto Sutopo Ph.D
Universitas Gadjah Mada, Indonesia

Azmil Tayeb Ph.D
Universiti Sains Malaysia

Development, Social Change and Environmental Sustainability – Sumarmi et al (Eds)
© 2021 Taylor & Francis Group, London, ISBN 978-1-032-01320-6

The effect of the Problem Based Service Eco Learning (PBSEcoL) model on student environmental concern attitudes

Sumarmi*
Universitas Negeri Malang, Malang, Indonesia

ABSTRACT: This research aims to determine the effect of the Problem Based Service Eco Learning (PBSEcoL) model on disaster awareness and environmental concern attitudes. The research design is a quasi-experiment. The research subjects were students of the Department of Geography and Faculty of Social Sciences in the State University of Malang. The sample was taken from class A and class B with homogenous features in the Environmental Geography course. The data was collected using an attitude questionnaire and then analyzed by comparing the questionnaire gain score of the control and experimental groups. The result showed that the PBSEcoL model had an effect on students' environmental concern attitudes with an average value in the experimental group of 86.53, while the control group was 75.94. The research is expected to provide information about the application and benefits of the PBSEcoL model in learning geography for students.

1 INTRODUCTION

Problem Based Service Eco Learning (PBSEcoL) integrated the educational process and direct community service. The learning objective is to improve critical thinking, analytical, and responsibility. The program is used to develop students' active participation in services and other activities related to the environment (Ardani et al. 2016; Irfianti et al. 2016). Students can apply their knowledge from the classroom to solve problems in real life.

Lecturers can use PBSEcoL to integrate learning with real-life by applying knowledge to answer students' problems while participating in learning in the classroom. PBSEcoL is a learning model that is fully integrated with services to the community related to the environment. PBSEcoL can be used by the lecturer based on the relevant field of study in the classroom. Using PBSEcoL can accelerate understanding of social science or other fields of study. Through PBSEcoL, students can construct new knowledge, research the projects' problems, make decisions related to the project and help and serve to solve environmental problems and mitigate disasters in their surroundings. The PBSEcoL is important to be implemented in learning because 1) it can connect education with society's needs, (2) it is able to develop an in-depth understanding with a learning process that refers to pedagogy through active learning, provide feedback to experts, students and the community, collaboration, and cognitive apprenticeships (lecturers and students can discuss generalizations, theories, principles, transfer of knowledge between theories and practice and analyze them), (3) PBSEcoL enriches multidisciplinary discussions. Environmental and disaster problems are handled by one discipline and this discipline must instead collaborate with various disciplines (Sumarmi et al. 2020).

Learning with Problem Based Service learning has risks, such as real problems that students have not mastered related to the environment and disasters and do not match the community's needs.

---

*Corresponding author: sumarmi.fis@um.ac.id

DOI 10.1201/9781003178163-1

The advantage of Problem Based Service learning is that students have a comprehensive and strong understanding of learning topics in the classroom that are closely related to the community's needs. Students can directly see the environmental problems that occur and mitigate disasters based on existing geographical conditions.

2 METHOD

The research is a quantitative study with a quasi-experimental research design. The subjects were students of Environmental Geography course in Geography programs and Social Science faculty in the State University of Malang. The research subjects were selected as two classes with homogeneous features: class A as the Experiment group and class B as the control group. Both classes have the same number of students, 31 people, and are taught by the same teacher. The research instrument used questionnaires, observation, and documentation. Environmental concern attitude data is compiled based on environmental concern indicators and is measured using a questionnaire with 20 questions. Observations are made to observe student and lecturer activities during the learning process and are carried out directly. Documentation was used to support the research, such as data and photos. The research was analyzed using the t-test (independent sample t-test) with SPSS for windows 21.00 to find the gain score (the difference between the pretest and posttest scores).

3 RESULT

The students' environmental concern attitude was obtained from the pre-test and post-test scores in the control and experimental groups to obtain the gain score. The result of environmental concern attitude was 13.11 for the control group and 23.43 for the experimental group. The result showed that the gain score in the experimental class using the PBSEcoL model was higher than the control class. Comparing the values between the pre-test, post-test, and gain scores of the environmental concern attitude of the control and the experimental group can be seen in the following table.

Table 1. The Average Pretest, Posttest, and Gain Score for the Control and Experimental Group.

Group	Pretest	Posttest	Gain Score
Control	62,83	75.53	13.11
Experimental	63,10	86,53	23,43

Table 1 showed an increase in the average pre-test and post-test scores in the control and experimental groups. Furthermore, the gain score in the experimental group was higher than the control group which was shown in the table was the increasing amount for the experimental group after treatment using the PBSEcoL model. This study supports the results that Ardianti (2017) and Kasi, Sumarmi and Astina (2018), stated in that the average value of environmental concern attitudes with the PBSEcoL model is higher than the average value using conventional models.

Students get personal, interpersonal, social and academic benefits in participating in Problem Based Service Learning (Kim & Lee 2018). Students' academic and leadership abilities have also improved. Through PBSEcoL learning, students have a high response to learning, apply concepts that have been learned in society, increase students' interest about social issues that occur, and build critical thinking skills and communication skills. Using PBSEcoL learning, students can see something more deeply to describe or explain the learning process and serving experience.

The implementation of PBSEcoL in the classroom consists of 4 stages: design to action, eco-action, reflection, and demonstration/celebration. (1) Design to Preparation is a preparatory step that explores and analyzes problems in the environment through direct observation, conducting interviews, and extracting information from various sources from books, printed media, and electronic media, and developing a suitable program. (2) Eco-Action is a real activity to implement environmental improvement programs. (3) Reflection is an activity to review the implementation, program implementation success and the obstacles in implementing the environmental problem improvement program. (4) Demonstration/celebration is a step to submit reports, articles and videos made for learning or community implementation and achievement (Sumarmi 2012; Sumarmi et al. 2020).

The learning has objectives to be achieved, so the assessment needs to be carried out based on the objectives and type of learning. Besides learning the topic in PBSEcoL, students also learn to serve immediately, so an authentic assessment is critical. Assessment can be obtained by conducting interviews, observing student group work practices and individual work, checking students' activities in a logbook, making product results and collecting data and articles presented in newspapers or journals.

J. Eyler and D.E. Giles Jr. (1999) stated that PBSEcoL provides positive benefits for the personal development of students, including helping personal development both personally and inter-personally, understanding and applying knowledge, developing critical thinking, changing ways of thinking and perspectives and forming a strong personal character as citizens to environmental problems. Also, PBSEcoL has a strong influence on character building (soft skills) such as caring, creative and critical thinking, leadership, building teamwork and communication skills. In the PBSEcoL method, students learn through service actions to solve environmental problems and serve the partner communities. Real situations and conditions in society and society are seen as real classrooms for learning through real experiences dealing with problems. It can also be said that the real situation and conditions in society are the "wisest teachers" that teach and develop intellectual-academic individuals.

Individual success is determined by well-scheduled activities to shape the attitude. This study seeks to discuss problem-based service learning-based learning strategies to respond to the problems previously discussed (Kolb 1984). Through PBSEcoL, there is a relationship between academic matters learned in school and activities to serve the community that can be realized step by step to increase environmental concern. Doing PBSEcoL in the community, students used their interest to solve social problems such as exploring and providing solutions to social problems (Muhaimin 2015). Students also identify environmental problems and solve environmental problems either individually or in groups or discuss possible disasters in their respective areas based on geographic conditions.

Students can implement PBSEcoL through the 'one man one tree' program around the campus, on the roadside, on the riverbank, in city parks and other places in areas with dry geographical conditions. Students must also remain responsible for maintaining these plants. The activity guides students to practice mindset shift about academics in the classroom and used it to solve environmental problems to increase the environmental concern (Sumarmi 2014). The changes can affect subsequent activities (Mamat et al. 2019). To study well in class and society, students need to have the right learning attitude. Students who are serious about learning will show qualities such as volunteering, joy, a love of learning, self-reflection, not being selfish and being honest.

4 CONCLUSION

Educational institutions have the responsibility to solve environmental problems and disasters that exist in Indonesia. It is necessary to increase student knowledge, skills, and environmental concern attitude to reduce vulnerability and maintain the existing ecosystem in Indonesia. This can only be established through geography education by applying the PBSEcoL model.

REFERENCES

Ardani, A., Utaya, S. and Budijanto, B. (2016) 'Pengaruh Model Pembelajaran Service-Learning terhadap Hasil Belajar Geografi SMA (The Effect of Service-Learning Learning Models on Geography Learning Outcomes in Senior High Schools)', *Jurnal Pendidikan: Teori, Penelitian, dan Pengembangan*, 1(11), pp. 2145–2151. Available at: https://doi.org/10.17977/jp.v1i11.7977.

Irfianti, M. D., Khanafiyah, S. and Astuti, B. (2016) 'Perkembangan Karakter Peduli Lingkungan Melalui Model Experiential Learning (Development of Environmental Concern through the Experiential Learning Model)', *UPEJ Unnes Physics Education Journal*, 5(3), pp. 72–79. Available at: https://doi.org/10.15294/upej.v5i3.13768.

Kasi, K., Sumarmi and Astina, K. (2018) 'Pengaruh model pembelajaran service learning terhadap sikap peduli lingkungan', *Jurnal Pendidikan Teori, Penelitian, dan Pengembangan*.

Kim, E. and Lee, Y.-J. (2018) 'Serve as you learn: Problem-based service-learning integrated into a product innovation and management class'.

Kolb, D. A. (1984) 'Experiential Learning: Experience as The Source of Learning and Development', *Prentice Hall, Inc.* doi: 10.1016/B978-0-7506-7223-8.50017-4.

Mamat, M. et al. (2019) 'Service-learning in Malaysia: Practice and implementation in four public universities', *International Journal of Civil Engineering and Technology*, 10(4), pp. 1682–1691.

Muhaimin (2015) 'Membangun Kecerdasan Ekologis Model Pendidikan untuk Meningkatkan Kompetensi Ekologis', 18(2), pp. 29–43. Available at: https://doi.org/10.7233/ijcf.2018.18.2.029.

Sumarmi (2012) *Model-Model Pembelajaran Geografi (Geography Learning Models). Yogjakarta: Aditya Media*. Yogyakarta: Aditya Media.

Sumarmi (2014) *Pengelolaan Lingkungan Berbasis Kearifan lokal (Environmental Management Based on Local Wisdom)*. Yogyakarta: Aditya Media.

Sumarmi et al. (2020) 'Problem-based service learning's effect on environmental concern and ability to write scientific papers', *International Journal of Instruction*. doi: 10.29333/iji.2020.13411a.

Development, Social Change and Environmental Sustainability – Sumarmi et al (Eds)
© 2021 Taylor & Francis Group, London, ISBN 978-1-032-01320-6

Community conservation in transition

Wolfram Dressler*
Melbourne University, Melbourne, Australia

ABSTRACT: This paper tries to explore more about the transition of community conservation in some areas around the world. There were some changes from the community conservation, which occurred from changing times and modernization itself. With the push of neoliberalism that is getting stronger, community conservation is changing. The empowerment of the indigenous people to save nature has some challenges to improve society's awareness about nature. Of course, this momentum needs a process to get expected results.

Keywords: community, conservation, transition

1 INTRODUCTION

When it emerged in the 1970s as a modern policy and practice – from the FAO to grassroots NGOs – community-based conservation rested on a seemingly intuitive assumption: because local people already use, rely on and manage natural resources, they are in the best position to conserve them (with external assistance as needed) (see FAO 1978). Over subsequent decades, the realization grew that top-down, centralized management can drive access restrictions at the expense of local knowledge and well-being (Agrawal & Gibson 1999). Policymakers and scientists found that centrally managed government systems had failed to curb deforestation and resource over-exploitation, and so moved to devolve initiatives to support a range of community-oriented conservation initiatives. In time, emphasis shifted to work with rather than 'on' local and indigenous peoples in the Global South. Much of this shift was based in figuring out how to best harness local and indigenous peoples' management abilities and knowledge to make forest conservation less disruptive to local livelihoods and more empowering to local people (Berkes 1989; Marcus 2001; Brosius et al. 2005). Various grassroots approaches to community conservation soon emerged to challenge previously centralized, state-controlled regimes of industrial forestry and governance regimes (Berkes 1989; Marcus 2001).

2 RESULT AND DISCUSSION

Such devolved approaches included everything from integrated conservation and development projects to community-based forest management, among others. In most cases, the programs and approaches varied in degree rather than kind: sharing a similar ethos of 'small is [not only] beautiful' (Schumacher 1973) but also collaborative, empowering, efficient and effective (Chambers 1983; Western & Wright 1994). Intuitively appealing, the community-based approach has maintained currency across disciplines and practices for decades (Dressler et al. 2010). In forestry, particularly, it has remained an enduring paradigm. While interpretations have varied, community forestry, or community conservation more generally, can be seen as an incremental social process of assisting

---

*Corresponding author: wolfram.dressler@unimelb.edu.au

DOI 10.1201/9781003178163-2

impoverished communities to set priorities and make decisions for developing forest resources in order to reduce livelihood vulnerability and improve forest conservation locally (Berkes 1989, 2004; Western & Wright 1994).

Several decades have now passed involving critical analysis of community conservation, with a range of social scientists drawing on case studies from the around the work to reconsider the relative potential and pitfall of such interventions across scale. In the last decade, a burgeoning literature has begun to examine how the institutional 'design' and 'packaging' of community conservation has been 'scaled up' as part of international governance regimes that are part of global climate change mitigation and biodiversity conservation efforts (Smith & Dressler 2019). Such investigations reveal how such local–global convergence may complicate community-based interventions. In the current, globalized era of neoliberal dominance, community conservation finds itself at the nexus of transnational currents bringing profound socio-ecological change (e.g., boom crop production), regional market integration (e.g., ASEAN (Association of Southeast Asian Nations)), burgeoning extractive industries (e.g., mining), and market-based environmental governance (e.g., REDD + (Reduced Emissions from Deforestation and Degradation)). Indeed, while the 1980–1990s saw greater emphasis on community conservation as a tool for achieving social well-being, poverty reduction and conservation with some broadly successful cases (e.g., Ikalahan Foundation (Balooni et al. 2008), the 2000s saw the idea of community conservation being scaled up as part of global policy arrangements and institutional frameworks. As Berkes (2007) noted, in an increasingly globalized world institutions have linked local processes (in particular, traditional knowledge, practices, and resources) to higher levels of social and political organization, spanning global scales.

3 CONCLUSION

In recent decades, community conservation ideals and procedures have been increasingly been incorporated into major international political–administrative frameworks aligned with neoliberal logic: with private sector support, community conservation would operate under market incentives to produce more 'value-added' commodities and engage in carbon offsetting and payments for ecosystem services schemes (Dressler et al. 2010). In the process, scholars have suggested that the discourse and practice of community conservation has become so entangled in market-oriented bureaucracies that organizational forms and relationships increasingly define procedures for local implementation, rather than the reverse (Lewis and Mosse, 2006). In being scaled up, some suggest that community conservation tends to be rolled out with predefined policy prescriptions that identify problems and solutions from dominant agency norms and beliefs (Dressler et al., 2010). As Li (2002) notes, these processes render otherwise complex situations into packaged, technical solutions that mismatch with the reality of local settings. What, then, does the future of community conservation hold?

REFERENCES

Agrawal, A. and Gibson, C. C. (1999) 'Enchantment and disenchantment: The role of community in natural resource conservation', *World Development*. doi: 10.1016/S0305-750X(98)00161-2.

Balooni, K., Pulhin, J. M. and Inoue, M. (2008) 'The effectiveness of decentralisation reforms in the Philippines's forestry sector', *Geoforum*. doi: 10.1016/j.geoforum.2008.07.003.

Berkes, F. (1989) 'Common property resources: ecology and community-based sustainable development', *Common property resources: ecology and community-based sustainable development*. doi: 10.1016/0921-8009(91)90040-l.

Berkes, F. (2004) 'Rethinking community-based conservation', *Conservation Biology*. doi: 10.1111/j.1523-1739.2004.00077.x.

Brosius, J. P., Tsing, A. L. and Zerner, C. (2005) *Communities and Conservation Histories and Politics of Community-Based Natural Resource Management*. AltaMira Press.

Chambers, R. (1983) *Rural development: putting the last first*. Harlow: Prentice Hall.

Dressler, W. et al. (2010) 'From hope to crisis and back again? A critical history of the global CBNRM narrative', *Environmental Conservation*. doi: 10.1017/S0376892910000044.

Food and Agriculture Organization of the United Nations Forestry Department (1978) *Forestry for Local Community Development*. Rome: Food & Agriculture Org.

Lewis, D. and Mosse, D. (2006) 'Encountering order and disjuncture: Contemporary anthropological perspectives on the organization of development', *Oxford Development Studies*. doi: 10.1080/13600810500495907.

Li, T. M. (2002) 'Engaging simplifications: Community-based resource management, market processes and state agendas in upland Southeast Asia', *World Development*. doi: 10.1016/S0305-750X(01)00103-6.

Marcus, R. R. (2001) 'Seeing the forest for the trees: Integrated conservation and development projects and local perceptions of conservations in Madagascar', *Human Ecology*. doi: 10.1023/A:1013189720278.

Schumacher, E. F. (1973) *Small Is Beautiful: A Study of Economics As If People Mattered*. Blond & Briggs.

Smith, W. and Dressler, W. (2019) 'Governing vulnerability: The biopolitics of conservation and climate in upland Southeast Asia', *Political Geography*. doi: 10.1016/j.polgeo.2019.04.004.

Western, D. and Wright, R. M. (1994) *Natural connections: perspectives in community-based conservation*. Island Press.

Development, Social Change and Environmental Sustainability – Sumarmi et al (Eds)
© 2021 Taylor & Francis Group, London, ISBN 978-1-032-01320-6

Sociology and geography of growing seaweed in the Philippines

Edo Andriesse*
Seoul National University, Seoul, Republic of Korea

ABSTRACT: The Philippines is a good example in the Asia and the Pacific of a country in which rural-urban migration has led to massive informal urban sectors and persistent urban poverty. Therefore, it also makes sense to continue exploring rural employment opportunities. This paper focuses on the impact of collective action dynamics on the livelihood resilience of Philippine's seaweed growing communities. Here we explain the successes and failures of collective action efforts among coastal communities in four Philippine provinces. The empirical insights are based on 41 semi-structured interviews (conducted in the Provinces of Guimaras, Palawan, Sorsogon, and Iloilo between 2016 and 2018) and 48 surveys in Iloilo (24 in 2015 and the same 24 seaweed farmers in December 2018). This contribution reveals the complexities of utilizing community support structures as a means of compensating for market and government failures. A gap continues to exist between collective action initiatives and household level capabilities.

Keywords: Seaweeds, Philippine, Farmers

1 INTRODUCTION

Coastal rural communities in Southeast Asia continue to be confronted with a wide range of vulnerabilities. Residents typically live near—and often on—the high tide line, making them more vulnerable to climate change, typhoons, the El Niño phenomenon, soil subsidence and increasing soil salinity. Many are farmers and fishers who find it difficult to sustain consistent levels of production from seafood (both capture and aquaculture) and agricultural crops (e.g. rice, vegetables). In addition, their livelihoods are profoundly influenced by resource management issues (overfishing, weak institutional arrangements) and market instability (price volatility, unscrupulous intermediaries, evolving product standards). As a result, millions of coastal households face persistent challenges in their attempts to escape poverty and achieve stable living standards with minimal risks of falling back (Ferrol-Schulte et al. 2013).

This article focuses on the impact of collective action dynamics on the livelihood resilience of Philippine's seaweed growing communities. Government agencies and civil society organizations generally have encouraged collective action. Yet, the strategies have not been able to facilitate the translation of economic growth into rural poverty reduction. The Philippine rural poverty incidence is still at 30%, with coconut farmers and fishers the worst off. This contribution explains the successes and failures of collective action efforts among fishers in four Philippine provinces where cultivating carrageenan seaweeds is one of the primary income generators, or used to be one. The following questions are addressed:

1. Under what circumstances do seaweed associations and cooperatives thrive?
2. Has collective action resulted in more resilient livelihoods and a more inclusive seaweed value chain?
3. What are the implications for local governance and rural employment?

---

*Corresponding author: edoandriesse@snu.ac.kr

2 TRADITIONAL PERFORMING ARTS AND THE HISTORY OF LUDRUK RUKUN FAMILI IN SUMENEP

The analysis of rural livelihoods has evolved from obtaining static livelihood snapshots towards adaptive livelihood strategies (de Haan & Zoomers 2005). It recognizes how rural communities continuously weigh their options, capabilities and vulnerabilities. Alternative rural employment initiatives are fostered through various support mechanisms which depend on the national institutional frameworks, the effectiveness of decentralization schemes, the quality of disaster risk reduction programs, the presence of vertical chain coordination and the trust farmers and fishers have in market participation and government and NGO intervention. There is no single blueprint for improving smallholders' insertion in global agribusiness value chains.

In his book, Unplanned Development, Rigg (2012) demonstrates that development in Southeast Asia has been a complex mosaic of (unexpected) international, regional (sub-national), and household events rather than the outcome of structured national planning. Non-forecasted events seem to have had a deeper and longer lasting impact on households' livelihood trajectories and national pathways of development compared to the detailed stipulations formulated in five-year national development plans, including capitalist systems in the region. The International Fund for Agricultural Development (2016) identified five potential benefits of collective action in rural areas: expanding access to markets and finance, enhancing natural resource access and management, improving access to infrastructure, widening access to information and knowledge and strengthening voice and power in policy processes.

In coastal areas as well as large lake environments, successful grassroots associations and cooperatives are able to tackle one or more issues such as facilitating access to micro-finance, mitigating overfishing, co-managing mangrove forests, promoting coastal eco-tourism, improving preparedness for typhoons and floods and selling agricultural and aqua-cultural products collectively (Stobutzki et al. 2006; Lashley & Warner 2015). However, the literature also identified complex dilemmas. The first dilemma is stakeholder competition (Ferrol-Schulte et al. 2013). Small-scale fishers, owners of large-scale fishing vessels, farmers who do not live near the shoreline and actors wishing to promote tourism have different interests with respect to coastal management and livelihood improvement efforts. A second dilemma is the intervening factor of local tensions. With respect to Vietnam, Van Hue and Scott (2008) argue that "coastal zones are areas of complexity, opportunity and conflict. They are naturally rich in resources but also fragile ecologies; they are narrow transition zones between land and ocean, and fresh and salt water, and are home to over half of Vietnam's people." Third is the possibility of collective action failure itself. The most disadvantaged groups are often "discouraged from participating in decision making" (Sick et al. 2014).

3 METHODS

Data for this study are primarily derived from 41 semi-structured surveys and 48 surveys in Iloilo with key informants and seaweed farmers/fishers in 10 municipalities across the provinces of Guimaras, Palawan, Sorsogon, and Iloilo. These provinces were chosen for their accessibility, variation in seaweed growing environments, promotion of seaweed by the Bureau of Fisheries and Natural Resources (BFAR) (2016) and diversity in developmental geographical settings. The insights obtained cover from 23 Barangays (lowest administrative level in the Philippines). Mindanao provinces are some of the top seaweed producers in the country, with the region comprising 62% of the national production. Palawan is the top producing province in the country. Its long and slender island geography has also made growing conditions more variable, depending on the Barangays' locations. Guimaras and Sorsogon are in the middle of national seaweed production rankings, with 2016 outputs of around 686MT and 374MT respectively (CountrySTAT Philippines 2017). They are increasingly struck by typhoons such as Typhoon Haiyan in 2013 and Typhoon Hagupit in 2014, making seaweed growing rather risky. Yet they receive extensive support in expanding seaweed production from multiple levels of government and international organizations because of the emphasis on livelihood diversification. Respondents were primarily composed of leaders from the fishing community, seaweed growers' associations and 24 seaweed growers whom we surveyed in both 2015 and 2018. The results from Iloilo provide a longitudinal dimension to this paper.

4 GENERAL INSTRUCTIONS

4.1 *Sorsogon*

In general, collective action efforts in all three provinces have indicated generally positive results. All four visited municipalities in Sorsogon have seaweed growers' associations; only in the Municipality of Pilar have associations ceased their activities. Interviews revealed that fraudulent market practices were widespread among growers and consolidators from 2000–2004, when seaweed prices were at their peak. Seaweeds naturally produce salt crystals during the drying process. When they have reached the required moisture content, they are packed in wicker-like baskets and sold in approximately 10kg bundles. Growers at the same time knew that their local intermediaries or consolidators only performed visual and aesthetic checks on the products as quality control. Growers saw it as an opportunity to maximize their income by adding table salt to the bundles, thus also increasing its weight.

Sorsogon also hosts successful collective action efforts in the neighbouring Barangays of Bagaycay, Gubat and Carayat, in Prieto Diaz. Both have long-standing seaweed grower associations whose successes can be attributed to several factors. Seaweed growers in Barangay Bagacay are primarily members of the local Rural Improvement Club (RIC), composed of women whose ages range from 18 to 81 years old. They described themselves as a "self-help association," which started in 1981 with swine growing to enhance the livelihoods of women in the Barangay. Eventually, the group diversified their income sources with vegetables and rice farming. They built their own store to sell the produce to other residents. Seaweed growing only started in 2012, two years after BFAR introduced the idea. As the farms grew, other members became interested.

When asked about their group's success, the interviewees cited several factors. First is their strict implementation and adherence to RIC bylaws. They do not collect monthly dues, but members in good standing can have access to group's capital to start their own livelihoods. Members who do not attend the regular meetings or do not pay back their loans are expelled. Second is that they have numerous fundraising initiatives. Members are asked to contribute PhP 10 (US$0.2) to the group fund per pig sold, while loans need to be repaid with interest. Third is recognizing group bonding and helping each other wherever necessary as key to member solidarity. Members are obligated to lend to those in need, attend meetings, or contribute PhP 1,000 (US$20.8) if a family member dies to cover funeral expenses. Similar factors are also present in the success of the seaweed growers' association in Barangay Carayat, Prieto Diaz. They have been growing seaweeds since 1995. Their farms, however, collapsed in 2002 after experiencing washouts from strong storms. Environmental conditions also deteriorated due to run-off from the mining operations on nearby Rapu-Rapu Island.

4.2 *Palawan*

Similar to Sorsogon, Palawan also experienced complete dissolution of collective action efforts in two Barangays. Seaweed growers' associations in Barangays Calawag and Bantulan in the municipality of Taytay have been completely disbanded. In both Barangays, these were the result of compounding environmental factors. Typhoon Queenie in 2014 had the largest impact, resulting in the complete washout of their farms. Recovery efforts were insufficient, with growers torn between immediate personal relief and farm recovery. The local government provided growers with seedlings and farm materials such as ropes, floaters, and plastic ties to help restart their farms. The number of seedlings, however, were insufficient for growers to earn a profit by the next harvest cycle.

They would have to start as a nursery where the seaweeds are grown and cut only to expand their available stocks. During this stage, they could only dry small quantities of seaweed for sale. Out of nine investigated associations, seven can be described as successes in the sense that they continued to be active for several years post-inception, with others even counting decades of operations. Four out of nine associations said that they are considering becoming a cooperative. It is a move that greatly expands their collective action efforts, where the association itself acts as a profit-making entity using the paid-up capital collected from members for other growth opportunities.

There is, however, some hesitation in following through with these plans. Association leaders find the process too cumbersome to comply with. Two interviewees said that the required documents could only be acquired and submitted in the Palawan capital of Puerto Princesa. For many coastal Barangays, this is a difficult and expensive journey to undertake. Many areas are underserved by or do not have regular public transportation available due to their geographic isolation and unpaved roads. Further, those with access to vehicles would have to cover the petrol costs for a return trip over considerable distances. Interviewees also complained about the difficulty meeting the capital requirements to establish a cooperative. The Cooperative Development Authority, the Philippine agency regulating cooperatives, requires at least PhP 15,000 (US$ 300) of paid-up capital for single-purpose cooperatives or those established to address one goal. What growers' associations have in mind, however, are multi-purpose cooperatives, entities that will fulfill various objectives. The required paid-up capital for multi-purpose cooperatives rises to at least PhP 100,000 (US$ 2000)(Cooperative Development Authority 2015), a huge sum that associations find impossible to meet. Two interviewees also mentioned the presence of the Northern Palawan Fisher Folks Cooperative (NPFC), a recently formed cooperative in the province. NPFC's area of operation covers the municipalities of Roxas, Taytay and El Nido. An interviewee on Green Island, Roxas, mentioned it is one of their active buyers.

4.3 *Guimaras*

Compared to Sorsogon and Palawan, seaweeds cultivation has not fared well on Guimaras after 2010. Between 2000 and 2010 many coastal communities diversified into seaweeds, but a range of natural and human-made factors led to a gradual decline after 2010. According to several key informants, there were more than 700 seaweeds growers on Guimaras in 2010; only between 200 and 250 remained at the time of the fieldwork in 2016. The following factors contributed to the decline: the 2009–2010 El Niño, declining profit margins as a result of a higher price for seaweed seedlings and a lower seaweed farm gate price, a failing collective action effort between 2010 and 2012, the 2013 super Typhoon that washed out many seaweeds, the collapse of a seaweed buying firm in 2014 and the 2015–2016 El Niño.

According to the Province of Guimaras (2015), seaweed farmers on Guimaras utilising a marine area of 1,000 sq. meters can generate an "additional net income of PhP7,470 (US$ 158) per cycle and they can do a maximum of five cycles in a year which means as much as PhP37,350 (US$ 795) annual supplemental money for the family". And based on a study for the Island Barangay Panobolon (part of Nueva Valencia Municipality), the Panobolon United Fisher Folks Association (PUFA) could successfully implement a new project as part of the World Bank funded 2014–2021 Philippine Rural Development Programme (PRDP) and generate an additional income of PhP 26987 (US$ 574) for participating households (Sea Knowledge Bank 2016). Nevertheless, these studies employ unrealistic assumptions. The calculations are based on five harvests per year yet, due to the factors described above, three harvests are more realistic and in line with the responses we obtained during the fieldwork. The fieldwork on Guimaras involved six Barangays: five in Sibunag Municipality and one in Nueva Valencia. In each of the four seaweed growing Barangays, there are active fishers and/or seaweed associations, but since many seaweed growers have stopped growing, they are less active than a few years ago. The most successful is Sabang Seaweed Growers Association with 300 members. During the fieldwork, around 100 members were actively engaged in seaweeds. In the future, this association hopes to diversify into seaweed chips, crackers, soap and potentially other products that can be manufactured in situ from seaweeds. In 2016, it was still waiting for PRDP funding. Seaweed successes before 2010 even led to the establishment of a cooperative in Sibunag Municipality in 2010. While it is too early to draw conclusions the first PRDP, implementation efforts in Guimaras Island paint a rather bleak picture.

4.4 *The difficulty to bring about alternative rural employment in Iloilo*

Iloilo Province is from a national perspective not a major seaweed producing region, yet BFAR has rolled out various programs in recent years to convince fisher folk to fish less and expand their livelihood sources. In Estancia and adjacent municipalities, typhoon Yolanda destroyed many fishing boats and washed away virtually all seaweeds in 2013. A first round of fieldwork early 2015 revealed how and to what extent environmental pressures were a cause of value chain vulnerabilities and disruptions. Not only do seaweed growers need to be constantly aware of the recurring typhoon threat and other environmental pressures, but they also occupy a marginal position within the value chain and do not have a stable income from selling dried seaweed. A second round of fieldwork late 2018 aimed at finding how the two local seaweed growing associations have evolved in recent years and how the seaweed growers have fared. This start of a longitudinal perspective has generated the following four observations:

- Out of 24 seaweed growers in 2015, only one is still engaged in seaweeds. The others have decided it was not possible to grow seaweeds anymore. Other typhoons such as Marce in 2016 and Ompong in 2018 washed away their seaweeds, and some had to stop growing because of a lack of capital to buy new seaweed seedlings or because they found the ocean water to be not clean enough. Some complained about chemical run-off from corn fields
- Associations have evolved. Compared to 2015 there is a new leadership, new members, and interestingly also some new beneficiaries of seaweed growing projects. The seaweeds growers of 2018 are not the same as the 2015. Those who stopped have stepped up fishing again. This result is quite problematic with respect to the perspectives of fostering inclusive value chains, reducing poverty and overfishing.
- Despite the challenges described above BFAR still appears to consider Estancia as a suitable site for seaweed. On the one hand it is true that seaweed growing households have at times enjoyed higher incomes. On the other hand, the multiple challenges coupled with the short-term nature of financial gains also gives rise to the question whether seeking alternative non-marine based livelihood opportunities would be more effective.
- As expected and as happened in other municipalities affected by Yolanda, there has been a large build-up of National Housing Authority housing communities who live within 40 meter of the shoreline, but many people prefer to stay near the beach and do not move to the new townhouses.

5 TOWARDS A TRIUMVIRATE OF CIVIL SOCIETY, STATE AND MARKET?

This article investigated to what extent community support structures and collective action, in particular associations and cooperatives, enabled seaweed growing communities in the Philippines to cope with environmental pressures, better navigate value chains and utilize value chain opportunities, and ultimately increase living standards. Our comparative analysis demonstrates that setting up associations and cooperatives does not guarantee success. There are mixed results. While a number of associations thrive in Sorsogon and Palawan, the situation in Guimaras and Iloilo has been more problematic, but also in the former two provinces there are cases of failure. The most successful association can be found in Barangay Bagacay in Gubat, Sorsogon. Strong community support and a diversified income structure has ensured longevity and effectiveness. On the other hand, there also have been cases where associations were dissolved either due to climate-related events, market failures or fraudulent practices.

Six factors appear to be important for thriving local collective action: (1) a substantial degree of financial literacy and planning capacities among the association leadership, (2) the absence of local tensions, (3) the presence of local social capital within the village, (4) the presence of non-marine livelihood options, (5) the inclusion of environmental threats in seaweed projects, and (6) opportunities to circumvent seaweed intermediaries and traders in order to gain higher prices.

Collective action can bring about more resilient livelihoods and a more inclusive seaweed value chains, but success is by no means guaranteed. In conclusion, this article reveals the complexities of utilizing community support structures as a means of compensating for market failures and government failures. A gap continues to exist between collective action initiatives and household level capabilities. Our empirical study offers two implications for state-civil society relations and processes of rural employment. First, initiating new livelihood projects through collective action, there is a need to focus more on path dependency and differentiated developmental-geographical settings. Still, admittedly, in situations in which local tensions continue to be disabling, it continues to be highly challenging to benefit from windows of opportunity to break out from locked-in vicious cycles and strengthen voices and power in policy processes. Second, large nationwide development interventions such as the World Bank-funded PRDP are only effective if the possibility of local failure is acknowledged. Seaweeds only thrive in clean ocean waters. It is increasingly recognized that markets, governments, and civil society can fail, but most development interventions do not build in the possibility of failure. Comprehensive investments need to be made for organizational development and capacity strengthening of seaweed growers associations. Only then can there be a triumvirate of civil society, state and market. Without strengthening associations, collective action efforts will continue to be in stasis, unable to successfully evolve towards higher forms of organizing, represent a larger constituency or influence the policy-making process. The challenge is thus to translate exogenous support mechanisms into endogenous processes of social capital formation.

REFERENCES

Bureau of Fisheries and Natural Resources (2016) *Comprehensive National Fisheries Industry Development Plan*. Quezon City: BFAR.

Cooperative Development Authority (2015) *Revised guidelines governing the registration of cooperatives*. Available at: http://cda.gov.ph/index.php/78-resources/issuances/memorandum-circulars-mcs/551-mc-2015-01-revised-guidelines-governing-the-registration-of- cooperatives.

CountrySTAT Philippines (2017) *CountrySTAT Philippines*. Available at: http://countrystat.psa.gov.ph.

Ferrol-Schulte, D. et al. (2013) 'Sustainable Livelihoods Approach in tropical coastal and marine social-ecological systems: A review', *Marine Policy*. doi: 10.1016/j.marpol.2013.03.007.

de Haan, L. and Zoomers, A. (2005) 'Exploring the frontier of livelihoods research', *Development and Change*. doi: 10.1111/j.0012-155X.2005.00401.x.

International Fund for Agricultural Development (2016) *Rural Development Report 2016. Fostering inclusive rural transformation*. Rome: International Fund for Agricultural Development.

Lashley, J. G. and Warner, K. (2015) 'Evidence of demand for microinsurance for coping and adaptation to weather extremes in the Caribbean', *Climatic Change*. doi: 10.1007/s10584-013-0922-1.

Province of Guimaras (2015) *Provincial commodity investment plan*.

Rigg, J. (2012) *Unplanned Development. Tracking Change in South-East Asia*. London and New York: Zed Books.

Sea Knowledge Bank (2016) *Panobolon Unified Fisher Folks Association's (PUFA) Seaweed Production and Marketing Enterprise*. Available at: http://seaknowledgebank.net/sites/default/files/icm_files/Panobolon Unified Fisherfolks Association's Seaweed Production and Marketing Enterprise_0.pdf.

Sick, D., Baviskar, B. and Attwood, D. (2014) *Rural cooperatives: A new millennium? In V. Desai & R. Potter*. 3rd edn. Abingdon: Routledge.

Stobutzki, I. C., Silvestre, G. T. and Garces, L. R. (2006) 'Key issues in coastal fisheries in South and Southeast Asia, outcomes of a regional initiative', *Fisheries Research*. doi: 10.1016/j.fishres.2006.02.002.

Van Hue, L. T. and Scott, S. (2008) 'Coastal livelihood transitions: Socio-Economic consequences of changing mangrove forest management and land allocation in a commune of Central Vietnam', in *Geographical Research*. doi: 10.1111/j.1745-5871.2007.00492.x.

Development, Social Change and Environmental Sustainability – Sumarmi et al (Eds)
© 2021 Taylor & Francis Group, London, ISBN 978-1-032-01320-6

History of the Ludruk Rukun Famili in Sumenep Madura Island, 1943–1997

Ronal Ridhoi*, Akbar Nugroho Adi Utama & Joko Sayono
Universitas Negeri Malang, Malang, Indonesia

ABSTRACT: Indonesia is a country with quite a lot of cultural wealth, from languages, daily habits, performing arts, and much more. One of the traditional performing arts in Indonesia is ludruk. This paper attempts to explain the history and the existence of the Ludruk Rukun Famili, in the small community in Madura. On the island of Madura, especially Sumenep, it turns out that there is a ludruk performance art like in Java, it's just that the performance model is a little different like most ludruk in Java. One of the well-known ludruk groups in Sumenep is the Rukun Family. This research uses qualitative descriptive approach and observation. Through this research, we found that in maintaining its existence in the world of folk performances, the Ludruk Rukun Famili carries out a lot of reforms. As science advances, people's tastes will change; this is the biggest factor that becomes a threat and a demand for the Ludruk Rukun Famili to keep innovating following the progress of the times.

1 INTRODUCTION

Madura Island, which is located in the northeastern part of the island of Java and is still part of the administrative area of East Java, has had a performance art known as ludruk (loddrok: Madurese pronunciation), but it is unique and different from the ludruk that developed in Java (Lisbijanto 2013; Rahman et al. 2019; Samidi 2019). It's just that the ludruk group originating from Madura is not as well-known as the ludruk groups in Java. The use of the Madurese language in every appearance of the ludruk group originating from the island of Madura causes not all regions in East Java to accept and understand Madurese ludruk (Wicaksono 2018; Samidi 2019; Wardhani 2019).

One of the ludruk groups originating from Madura is the Ludruk Rukun Famili group. This rukun family group has a long existence as a ludruk group. The market from this ludruk group apart from Madura Island is also found in several areas on the island of Java, especially areas that use the Madurese language such as Pasuruan, Probolinggo, Banyuwangi, Lumajang and Besuki. In order to compete with ludruk groups in Java, these rukun famili groups must also follow the development of performance models that occur in Java or even have to innovate on their own so that they continue to exist along with the progress of the times (Interview with Mas'odi).

During the ludruk journey, the model and technical performance of the show will also experience development. Advances in technology and science are supporting factors for the development of these traditional art performances. The technical performances of ludruk that also develop include stage performances (Juni et al. 2013; Hendriani 2014). The ludruk group that wants to continue to survive must also follow these developments so that the audience does not feel bored with the monotonous performance model. In addition to the above discussion points, this paper will introduce several traditional performing arts in Sumenep. In the past, traditional performing arts in Sumenep itself could be distinguished depending on where they were performed, namely the palace performance arts and folk performing arts (Naiborhu & Karina 2018; Suroso 2018).

---

*Corresponding author: ronal.ridhoi.fis@um.ac.id

DOI 10.1201/9781003178163-4

2 TRADITIONAL PERFORMING ARTS AND THE HISTORY OF LUDRUK RUKUN FAMILI IN SUMENEP

The condition of Sumenep, which was formerly a duchy, can support how the performing arts in Sumenep can develop. In the 17th to 18th centuries, the palaces in Madura were heavily influenced by the palaces of Central Java through various political and marital relationships (Bouvier 2002). The cooperation carried out by the court aristocrats at that time not only influenced the political and economic fields but also in terms of artistic taste. The initial purpose of performing arts within the palace was as a means of entertainment for the court nobles. Some of the traditional performing arts in Sumenep that first appeared in the palace environment are as follows (Interview with Imron).

One of the ludruk groups which exist and are quite well known in Sumenep to date is the Rukun Family group. This Rukun Famili can be said to be the oldest loddrok group in Sumenep Regency. The Rukun Famili group produced many well-known ludruk figures, such as H. Mas'odi and Suharun Keron as well as several other well-known ludruk actors in Sumenep. Even though in the current era there are many modern performing arts, this loddrok group can still exist today both in loddrok performances in Sumenep Regency and outside Madura. The beginning of the Sumenep loddrok art journey was started in 1943 when an art lovers association was founded by the name of Rukun Santoso in Pagar Batu Village, Saronggi District, Sumenep Regency. The initial formation of this association was coordinated by four brothers, namely H. Hairuddin alias Diporejo, Wiroguno, Yudho Prawiro, and Asmoro Sastro. This association later developed and became known as the Ludruk Rukun Famili Group (Interview with Arifin and Mas'odi; Moelyono & Al. 1985).

According to Mr H. Mas'udi, Rukun Sentosa at the beginning of its formation was still in the form of a simple theater performance known in the Saronggi District area as a mulahi. Mulahi art itself is similar to the East Javanese ludruk art, where the stories that are staged are mostly raised from the problems in society at that time or known as wan-tuwanan. Apart from this means of entertainment, this mulahi can indirectly ignite the fighting spirit of the people. This art developed around the end of the 40s and was only famous in the Saronggi District area, while in other areas at that time a similar art called ajhing was also developed (Azali 2016; Interview with Mas'odi). In 1945 the Rukun Sentosa association changed its name. This name change was triggered by Syamsul Gani, the oldest son in the family; the name Rukun Sentosa was changed to Rukun Famili which was then led by Mr Yudho Prawiro. This name change was carried out for the reason that the management of this art association was managed by four siblings in one family. By changing the name of Rukun Santoso to Rukun Famili, it is hoped that it can increase harmony, a sense of brotherhood and a sense of mutual care like a blood family of all members of the group (Interview with Rahmad; Zulkarnain 2018).

The story that was originally similar to the ludruk art in East Java, namely a simple drama theater, later turned into a Madurese loddrok story which is currently famous for being similar to the art of ketoprak. This change is inseparable from Mr Yudho, who is the former head of Tanjung Village and as a boat owner (sampan) carrying goods from Pagarbatu to several areas in East Java. This made it easier for Mr Yudho to get to know the folk performing arts in Java, the elements of reform that were found in Java and then applied in the Rukun Famili group. The core story of Rukun Famili similar to ketoprak (Interview with Mas'odi, Rahmad).

Around the mid-1950s, the Rukun Famili group began to use the same paid gedongan performance model as in Java for promotion to the public. Gedongan performances in Sumenep with gedongan in Surabaya are different, in Sumenep there is no closed theater theater like in Java. So to perform the show, the group usually uses bamboo booths (tabing bidik) as a dividing wall and a bamboo stage (kadduk) which is given a banana tree or a kates tree as a support for the stage (Wardhani 2019). This kind of performance system in Mojokerto is also known as the tobongan system. The ludruk group that uses a performance system like this usually stays in an area or place to hold performances for some time. This kind of performance is usually carried out when the group is not invited to perform so that to provide income to the members; this performance is carried out.

If the group considers that the audience in the area is decreasing, they will move to another place. In this way, the Rukun Famili can be increasingly famous by the public, and there will be more invitations to perform at weddings (Interview with Rahmad; Sayono et al. 2020).

In 1955, the Rukun Famili, which was still led by Mr Yudho Prawiro, had to split. This split led to two loddrok groups, namely Rukun Famili and Rukun Muda, led by Mr Wiroguno. This split was due to the fact that at that time Mr Yudho had finished serving as village head and moved to live in Tanjung Village with the move of Rukun Famili loddrok art. Mr Wiroguno, who also wanted to continue the art of loddrok, finally founded a new group to replace the Rukun Famili in Pagarbatu Village (Interview with Mas'odi; Sayono et al. 2020).

In 1963, the Rukun Famili had another split, namely the establishment of the Ludruk Seni Remaja which was led directly by Mr Asmoro Sastro. Unlike the Rukun Famili, the Seni Remaja group was also part of the Madura loddrok group, except that the members were children and young boys who lived in Pagarbatu. When the Rukun Famili was trying to improve new techniques to maintain its existence, this ludruk group had to meet new obstacles with the release of one of the professional players who had been famous for their performances on the stage, namely Mr Suharun Kerun who later founded the ludruk group Rukun Karya in 1977. The ludruk Rukun Karya performance model still has similarities with the Rukun Famili, namely the Madura loddrok model whose core story is similar to ketoprak (Hariadi; Sayono et al. 2020).

These problems and the increase in competitors did not make Mr Yudho Prawiro despair, the ludruk Rukun Famili group managed to survive and maintain its existence both in Sumenep and outside Madura Island. Until 1981 Mr Yudho Prawiro died due to an accident. To prevent the Ludruk Rukun Famili group disbanding and disappointing sympathizers and Rukun Famili fans who have spread both in Sumenep and outside Madura, this art was continued by his son, Mr H. Mas'odi, often nicknamed Yudho Prawiro II, who still maintains the existence of the Rukun Famili to date (Interview with Mas'odi and Rahmad).

3 PERFORMANCES OF LUDRUK RUKUN FAMILI

The innovations obtained by observing the folk arts that developed in Java were then modified and applied in the Rukun Famili performance. In the 1950s, during its performance, the Rukun Famili group began to replace the white cloth as the backdrop for the stage into paintings and displays. A display is a decoration that resembles a frame around the loddrok stage. Historically, displays used in the 1950s were made of kaddhuk (a kind of gunny sack) painted with dyes. The background painting for the performance or screen and display at that time was painted by a religious figure in Pagarbatu named K.H. Ahmad Zainal, because he is a kiai creating paintings in Islamic nuances such as mosques, date palms, and ka'bah (*Video of Rukun Famili's 68th Anniversary* 2013). Even though sometimes the stories with the settings used are not suitable, people are still happy and entertained. This was due to the absence of other entertainment options for the community at that time (Interview with Mas'odi).

After Mr Yudho Prawiro brought the Rukun Famili art loddrok to Tanjung Village in 1955, the performance model remains the same as in Pagarbatu Village, only nowadays he has begun to use a stage that is deliberately made slightly taller than the audience. This stage is made of bamboo and often called a sak-sak, which is supported by banana or papaya tree trunks. Meanwhile, for displays and colors that remain behind the stage, this model set has been used by the Rukun Famili group for a long time. The advantage of a stage set like this is to facilitate the interaction between players and the audience. All of the changes made by the Rukun Famili were almost entirely inspired by ludruk art in Java. Especially in the stage, there were many changes. In the 1960s, according to one of the senior members of the Rukun Famili, the stage turned into an on display. The stage model on the inside is still used today. The display that is used to be durable and strong is made of zinc (Sayono et al. 2020).

4 CONCLUSION

The description from the outset explains that the Ludruk Rukun Famili entourage performs a performance to entertain the public with simple instruments and visiting techniques. Along the way, it encountered many obstacles, both from within and outside the group, demanding that the Rukun Famili group carry out a new innovation to compete with other loddrok groups and other entertainment arts. The innovations applied in the Rukun Famili troupe are undeniably taken from the ludruk group on the island of Java. However, despite the many innovations made, public awareness of traditional arts such as the Rukun Famili is decreasing. Therefore, it is necessary to have special attention from the public and the government towards the subsequent existence of Sumenep loddrok art, so that the efforts of the group are not in vain.

REFERENCES

Azali, K. (2016) 'Ludruk: Masihkah Ritus Modernisasi?', *Lakon?: Jurnal Kajian Sastra dan Budaya*, 1(1), pp. 48–60. doi: 10.20473/lakon.v1i1.1916.

Bouvier, H. (2002) *Lebur! Seni Musik dan Pertunjukan dalam Masyarakat Madura*. Bogor: Grafika Mardi Yuana.

Hendriani, D. (2014) 'Eksistensi Kesenian Ludruk Sidoarjo Di Tengah Arus', *Avatara*.

Juni, O., Astawa, D. and Hakim, S. Al (2013) 'PERAN PEMERINTAH DALAM PEMBERDAYAAN KESENIAN LUDRUK PADA PAGUYUBAN ARMADA DI DESA REMBUN KECAMATAN DAMPIT KABUPATEN MALANG', *Journal of Chemical Information and Modeling*.

Lisbijanto, H. (2013) *Ludruk*. Yogyakarta: Graha Ilmu.

Moelyono and Al., E. (1985) *Mengenal Sekelumit Kebudayaan Orang Madura Di Sumenep*. Yogyakarta: Balai Kajian Sejarah dan Nilai Tradisional.

Naiborhu, T. and Karina, N. (2018) 'Ketoprak,Seni Pertunjukan Tradisional Jawa di Sumatera Utara: Pengembangan dan Keberlanjutannya', *Panggung*. doi: 10.26742/panggung.v28i4.714.

Rahman, T. et al. (2019) 'STRATEGI PELESTARIAN BUDAYA OJHUNG MADURA DI ERA GLOBAL', *PERFORMANCE: Jurnal Bisnis & Akuntansi*. doi: 10.24929/feb.v9i2.792.

Samidi, S. (2019) 'Identitas Budaya Masyarakat Kota: Teater Tradisi di Kota Surabaya Pada Awal Abad XX', *Indonesian Historical Studies*. doi: 10.14710/ihis.v3i1.5308.

Sayono, J., Ridhoi, R. and Prasetyawan, A. (2020) *DARI AJHING HINGGA KETOPRAK?: Perjalanan Historis Kesenian Ludruk di Sumenep Madura Sejak 1940-an*. Malang: Java.

Suroso, P. (2018) 'Tinjauan Bentuk dan Fungsi Musik pada Seni Pertunjukan Ketoprak Dor', *Gondang: Jurnal Seni dan Budaya*. doi: 10.24114/gondang.v2i2.11283.

Video of Rukun Famili's 68th Anniversary (2013).

Wardhani, J. K. (2019) 'Dramaturgi Ludruk Karya Budaya Mojokerto Jawa Timur Lakon Sarip Tambak Oso', *JURNAL SATWIKA*. doi: 10.22219/satwika.vol3.no1.27-42.

Wicaksono, P. M. (2018) 'Kesenian Ludruk RRI Surabaya Sebagai Media Propaganda Program Pemerintah Pada Dekade Akhir Pemerintahan Orde Baru (1989-1998)', *Avatara*.

Zulkarnain, I. (2018) *Sejarah Sumenep*. Sumenep: Dinas Kebudayaan Pariwisata Pemuda dan Olahraga Kab. Sumenep.

Others:

Video of Rukun Famili's 68th Anniversary. (2013)
Interview:
1. Interview with H. Mas'odi (77 y.o.) on 02 July 2020.
2. Interview with Abd. Rachmad (76 y.o) on 04 Juli 2020.
3. Interview with Arifin
4. Interview with Hariadi

Development, Social Change and Environmental Sustainability – Sumarmi et al (Eds)
© 2021 Taylor & Francis Group, London, ISBN 978-1-032-01320-6

Promoting moderatism, countering radicalism: Religious discourse of high school students in Malang

Ahmad Arif Widianto*, Joan Hesti Gita Purwasih, Nanda Harda Pratama Meiji & Rani Prita Prabawangi
Universitas Negeri Malang, Malang City, Indonesia

ABSTRACT: This article aims to map the religious discourse of high school (SMA) students in Malang. This mapping is important considering the strong contestation of religious ideology in educational institutions in recent years. The spread of radical ideology is massive and systematic, especially in students. This study explores the views of students and religious discourse circulating in the school environment with qualitative methods through in-depth interviews, observations and Focused Group Discussions (FGD) in 3 State Senior High Schools (SMAN). Students are aware of the infiltration of radicalism in schools through various modes and media. They are able to identify and classify religious views and discourses based on their respective rationalities and modalities. Although there are few students who agree with the vision and mission of radical understanding. However, in general, students with various religious identities counter radical ideology. Instead, they propagate religious moderation through actions and activities both intra- and extracurricular.

Keywords: Radicalism, Moderation, Religious Discourse of Students

1 INTRODUCTION

In recent years the discourse of ideology and religious behavior of students has strengthened in various countries (Woodward 2015). In Indonesia, the polemic of student religious discourse has led to discussions, studies and research (Arifianto 2019; Asrori 2016; Darraz 2013; Muchith 2016; Wijaya Mulya & Aditomo 2019). The strengthening of the discourse is inseparable from the spread of radicalism and acts of terrorism that penetrate educational institutions (Arifianto 2019; Fatgehipon & Bin-Tahir 2019; Wulansari & Hidayat 2018; Muchith 2016). The strengthening of radicalism in Indonesia has resulted in the deteriorating image and credibility of Indonesia as a friendly and polite country in the eyes of the international world. On the contrary, Indonesia is described as a country whose people are blinded by fanaticism and brutalism (Fealy 2004) Religious radicalism is not a new phenomenon in Indonesia, but the impacts that result from it are very counterproductive and destructive to social-political stability in Indonesia (Purwasih & Widianto 2020; Robingatun 2017).

Religious radicalism can be traced in historic tragedies through terrorist events that have harmed humanity in Indonesia. Although, radicalism does not always manifest in physical violence, radicalism can be transformed into terrorism (Ismail & Bonar 2012). Infiltration of religious radicalism in students becomes an emergency warning to immediately make prevention, treatment and recovery through a series of action interventions. One such effort is through the mapping of religious discourse in high school. During this time, radicalism can easily spread to schools because of the lack of understanding and awareness of the school related to the potential, form and patterns of infiltration so as to weaken the school's resilience system (Purwasih & Widianto 2020).

---

*Corresponding author: ahmad.arif.fis@um.ac.id

This article seeks to map the religious discourse of high school students in Malang, especially in 3 senior high schools. Historically, radical movements and terrorism have been linked to the Malang region which began in 1993 through the promotion of Hizb ut-Tahrir Indonesia in Brawijaya University and Malang State University (Yumitro et al. 2018). In the last few years in Malang it has been uncovered in the hideout of persons identified as terrorists. Such reality reinforces the indication of the spread of radicalism that threatens students in Malang. The purpose of this article is to give an overview of student religious discourse in the midst of the infiltration of radical understanding in senior high schools through various modes and media (Darraz 2013; Muchith 2016).

2 LITERATURE REVIEW

Strengthening radicalism according to Porta and Free is characterized by two things (Pranawati 2018). First, there is the strengthening of religious movements and ideologies that have scheduled social and political changes. Second is the strengthened pro-violence attitudes and actions in response to conflict and political contestation. One of the demands of the radical movement is to establish an Islamic State. In another version it is stated that the Islamic radical movement is limited to wanting the implementation of Islamic shari'ah (Jakarta charter). The demand means negating the legitimate state ideology, namely Pancasila. In fact, Pancasila itself according to the founders of the nation is sourced from religious principles and cultural moral values that are contextual and relevant to the socio-cultural style of Indonesian society (Beck & Irawan 2016; van Bruinessen 2002). The decline in the function of the Pancasila as an ideology according to Heywood can weaken state control over the socio-political practices of the community (Pranawati 2018).

The rise of radicalism in Indonesia is growing rapidly due to political pressure from the government regime and recolonization from the United States (Jati 2017). For young people, especially Muslims, radicalism is getting stronger because of (1) the phase of political transition (2) the transformation of the Islamic radical movement and (3) the high unemployment (Azca 2013). In this case, young people affected by religious radicalism are characterized as; (1) intolerant of differences; (2) finding it easy to radicalize other parties; (3) rigidly obedient to the leader; (4) trying to control campus political space (5) supporting violence by radicals; (6) being against the government which is considered secular and deviates from religion (Yusar 2016).

Religious moderation is the key to fighting radicalism and extremism (Ma'arif 2019; Suharto 2019) and at the same time is a way to care for harmony between religious communities (Kawagung 2019). A measure of moderation can be determined through the following indicators ("Buku Moderasi Beragama," n.d.). In line with these indicators, individual religious behavior that reflects moderation can be seen from the dimensions: (1) ideological (2) ritual (3) mystical (4) intellectual and (5) social (Fauzi 2007: 66–68). In the Indonesian context, Moderation is rooted in noble values and national consensus as set out in the 1945 Constitution, Pancasila and the motto of "Unity in Diversity." Thus, religious moderation is in line with the spirit of nationalism which upholds unity and mutual cooperation.

3 RESEARCH METHODOLOGY

This study uses qualitative methods in order to explore data and attain a deep understanding of social phenomena (Silverman 2013). This method emphasizes deeper description (thick description) which is one element of phenomenological research that looks at phenomena from the point of view of social actors and understanding of social processes rather than aspects of social statistics (Blaikie 2010). In qualitative research, the logic used is abstractive inductive, namely the flow of thinking from the specific to the general, namely conceptualization, categorization and description based on field data. The characteristics and procedures of qualitative research are very relevant to the design of this study, which is to map the model the structure of social cohesion in a multi-religious society. Of course, to be able to do this requires deep data mining and an understanding of social processes. This research was conducted on 200 students of 3 high schools in Malang through in-depth interviews, participatory observation and focus group discussion. Schools are chosen based on the level of heterogeneity of student composition in religion.

4 FINDING DAN DISCUSSION

Religious radicalism is pervasive among young Muslim students. Students are not only victims of religious radicalism but also as pioneers and agents of the dissemination of their teachings (van Bruinessen 2002). In the perspective of youth studies, students are subjects who are vulnerable to radicalism because they are still in the stage of transition and the search for identity. Young people are still unstable and do not yet have a mature personality, as well as an understanding of the outside world. In this unstable condition, young people experience a dilemma in the search for identity (Pranawati 2018). The flow of information and knowledge is taken for granted without careful thought (Azca 2013). The vulnerability and lack of understanding of young people facilitates the infiltration of notions that are contrary to the beliefs and ideology of the state.

Surprisingly, radicalism is now developing rapidly through various levels of educational institutions not only on campus but also in schools (Wulansari & Hidayat 2018; Prijanto et al. 2019). Even though the school is an institution that can shape the mindset and character of students. This is certainly a real threat to the life of the nation and state in the future. Various survey reports show that in the last 5 years radicalism has developed among high school students (adminppimuinjakarta n.d.). This is certainly very counterproductive to the survival and stability of the nation and state. Students who are supposed to be the next generation actually destroy the nobility of social cultural values in Indonesia. Schools as educational institutions and intellectual producers are not able to give birth to the nation's successors as expected. Radical groups in the future have the potential to transform into a terrorism movement, although not as a whole (Ismail & Bonar 2012).

The development of radicalism spread through various formal and informal public spaces and arenas (Azca 2013; Muchith 2016; Pranawati 2018). The entry of radical understanding into the school environment can come from the School Student Organization (Abdallah 2016; Darraz 2013; Yusar 2016), textbooks and LKS Radical Islamic subject matter, religious extracurricular activities, radical thinking teachers and school alumni who are radical incorporated in radical groups (Maulana 2017), until the education curriculum is radical. As a result of the inclusion of radical ideas, social life in schools becomes intolerant, exclusive, anti-diversity and colored by violence.

In this context, the results of previous research in high schools in Malang also show the growth of the seeds of radical thought (Purwasih & Widianto 2020). Although the percentage can still be tolerated, the stretching of its development and distribution is very worrying. For example, 24% of students in Malang stated that they strongly agreed with the statement "violence is sometimes needed to enforce religious rules." Meanwhile, the students that agree are 49% of the total. The hesitant answer is 26%, 1% disagrees, and 0% strongly disagrees (1 respondent). This number is only from one variable, not the whole. But interestingly, in the process of infiltration and recruitment of members of radical groups in SMA Malang there was a turmoil among students. Some informants stated that they had been targeted and ended up being members of radical groups even though they were not official (bai'at). However, in its development, they tried to go out and break relations with the group. According to the informant, radical teachings can cause followers to commit terrorism. Because radical teachings are deviant teachings in order to achieve a goal, but if the goal is not achieved then they will use violent methods such as terror in the name of a particular religion.

Radical teachings according to informants want to make changes in the social and political fields but use violent methods, such as wanting to replace the state ideology, namely Pancasila, with an ideology based on Islamic law. Because their desire was not heeded, they finally carried out terror everywhere, such as suicide bombings in Surabaya and Pasuruan some time ago in the name of jihad. Radicals have a political orientation not only to seize state power, but also carry the spirit of revivalism and religious understanding to respond to global conditions that are considered far from the ideal values of Islam.

In this research, Some informants consider the teachings of radicalism to teach jihad by violence according to the informant's remarks as walking in the path of Allah. But the informant in this research also stated that jihad at this time did not have to be by force but rather by competing in the field of knowledge. According to the informant, tolerance in religious life is important because we are Indonesian, even though we are different but still one. Even though they have different religious beliefs, they must help each other, as well as the two extracurriculars, namely SKI and BCF. Religious harmony can be seen from the help that is done by each organization, this is explained by the informant that if SKI or BCF will do an activity then they will help each other in funding. The fundraising they do is called shoping or in Islam is a kind of fundraising through a charity box during Friday prayers. The funds collected will be shared equally between SKI and BCF, the rest will be used for social services carried out by these two organizations. Forms of interfaith tolerance other than those described above are participation in inter-extra activities, for example SKI members hold activities in schools, BCF members also attend these activities, but when the activity takes place they perform their own worship based on their beliefs in a room or place provided.

5 CONCLUSION AND FURTHER RESEARCH

This research shows that high schools are also being targeted by the infiltration of radical ideas through various processes and media by exploiting the weaknesses of the schools' resilience systems. Students become victims as well as agents of the spread of radicalism from radical groups through various recruitment methods. Although some informants agreed with the goals set by radical groups, on the other hand the majority of students rejected the infiltration of radicalism in schools because they were considered not in accordance with teachings and beliefs. On the contrary, the students actually promote tolerance and moderation in religion through both intra and extra-curricular activities and activities such as celebrating collective and collaborative religious days, interfaith competitions, and scout activities. This reality shows that although students are susceptible to radicalism, in reality they are able to choose ideologies that are believed to be rational, moral and faith based.

REFERENCES

I., Wulansari, D. and Hidayat, N. (2018) 'Radicalism in indonesia and the reflective alternatives to reduce', *People: International Journal of Social Sciences*. doi: 10.20319/pijss.2018.33.15541564.

Abdallah (2016) 'Exclusivism and radicalism in schools: State policy and educational politics revisited', *Studia Islamika*. doi: 10.15408/sdi.v23i3.4425.

Arifianto, A. R. (2019) 'Islamic Campus Preaching Organizations in Indonesia: Promoters of Moderation or Radicalism?', *Asian Security*. doi: 10.1080/14799855.2018.1461086.

Asrori, A. (2016) 'Contemporary religious education model on the challenge of indonesian multiculturalism', *Journal of Indonesian Islam*. doi: 10.15642/JIIS.2016.10.2.261-284.

Azca, M. N. (2013) 'Yang muda, yang radikal: Refleksi sosiologis terhadap fenomena radikalisme kaum muda muslim di Indonesia pasca orde baru', *Maarif*.

Beck, D. M. C. and Irawan, I. (2016) 'Islam, pancasila and value systems of indonesian national education', *Jurnal Pendidikan Islam*. doi: 10.15575/jpi.v1i1.610.

Blaikie, N. (2010) 'Designing Social Research', in.

van Bruinessen, M. (2002) 'Genealogies of Islamic radicalism in post-Suharto Indonesia', *South East Asia Research*. doi: 10.5367/000000002101297035.

Darraz, M. A. (2013) 'Radikalisme dan lemahnya peran pendidikan kewargaan', *Dalam Menghalau Radikalisasi Kaum Muda: Gagasan Dan Aksi. Jakarta: Jurnal Institut Maarif*, 8, pp. 154–173.

Fatgehipon, A. H. and Bin-Tahir, S. Z. (2019) 'Building students state defending awareness in preventing the radicalism', *International Journal of Scientific and Technology Research*.

Fealy, G. (2004) 'Islamic radicalism in Indonesia: The faltering revival?', *Southeast Asian Affairs*, 2004(1), pp. 104–121.

Ismail, H. and Bonar, T. N. (2012) 'Dari Radikalisme Menuju Terorisme, Studi Relasi dan Transformasi Organisasi Islam Radikal di Jawa Tengah dan DI Yogyakarta', *Jakarta: Pustaka Media*.

Jati, W. R. (2017) 'Radikalisme politik kelas menengah muslim indonesia pasca reformasi', *MIQOT: Jurnal Ilmu-ilmu Keislaman*. doi: 10.30821/miqot.v41i1.309.

Ma'arif, S. (2019) 'Reinventing pesantren's moderation culture to build a democratic society in the post-reform Republic of Indonesia', *Pertanika Journal of Social Sciences and Humanities*.

Maulana, D. (2017) 'The exclusivism of religion teachers: Intolerance and radicalism in Indonesian public schools', *Studia Islamika*. doi: 10.15408/sdi.v24i2.5707.

Muchith, M. S. (2016) 'Radikalisme dalam dunia pendidikan', *ADDIN*. doi: 10.21043/addin.v10i1.1133.

Pranawati, H. L.; W. S.; C. S. B.; I. A.; M. N.; R. (2018) *Kaum Muda Muslim Milenial: Konservatisme, Hibridasi Identitas, Dan Tantangan Radikalisme*.

Prijanto, J. H., Padang, A. T. and Susanti, A. E. (2019) 'Indication of the Effect of Radicalism on Christian High School Students, Lippo Karawaci', in. doi: 10.2991/icskse-18.2019.4.

Purwasih, J. H. G. and Widianto, A. A. (2020) *School Resilience And Religious Radicalism In Senior High Schools, In: Emerging Trends In Psychology, Law, Communication Studies, Culture, Religion, And Literature In The Global Digital Revolution*. 1st Editio.

Robingatun, R. (2017) 'Radikalisme islam dan ancaman kebangsaan', *EMPIRISMA*. doi: 10.30762/empirisma.v26i1.684.

Silverman, D. (2013) *Doing qualitative research: A practical handbook*. Sage.

Suharto, T. (2019) 'Examining Moderate Understanding of Islam among Islamic Higher Education Students of State Islamic Institute Surakarta', *TEOSOFI: Jurnal Tasawuf dan Pemikiran Islam*.

Wijaya Mulya, T. and Aditomo, A. (2019) 'Researching religious tolerance education using discourse analysis: a case study from Indonesia', *British Journal of Religious Education*. doi: 10.1080/01416200.2018.1556602.

Woodward, K. (2015) 'Indonesian Schools: Shaping the Future of Islam and Democracy in a Democratic Muslim Country.', *Journal of International Education and Leadership*.

Yumitro, G., Kurniawati, D. and Saiman, S. (2018) 'Terrorism Issues and the Development of Transnational Islamic Movements in The Region of Malang'.

Yusar, Y. (2016) 'The Youth, The Sciences Students, and Religious Radicalism', *Al-Ulum*. doi: 10.30603/au.v16i2.154.

Development, Social Change and Environmental Sustainability – Sumarmi et al (Eds)
© 2021 Taylor & Francis Group, London, ISBN 978-1-032-01320-6

The female terrorism: Victimization in the striving for family

E. Malihah*, S. Nurbayani, P. Wulandari & Wilodati
Universitas Pendidikan Indonesia, Bandung City, Indonesia

ABSTRACT: There is something forgotten from the terrorism case involving family, particularly something which relates to women. The questions raised are how the women are perceived as part of the crime and how they are forgotten from the crime (terrorism) since, in fact, women are also the victim. This study uses a qualitative approach with a phenomenology design and is done through the technique of interview and observational study to the three religious groups and the three religious institutions (Pesantren) in the province of West Java, Indonesia. The researcher tries to expose the women's position in the terrorism case that involves the family. The result of this study reveals that there is a process of how women as wives act in the terrorism case. The religious literacy and the reinforcement of the religious groups becomes a crucial thing to do. The religious educational institution (Pesantren) can be the turning point in erasing radicalism from religion.

Keywords: Terrorism, The Women's strive, Terror act, Religious.

1 INTRODUCTION

Women are often forgotten in the issue of terrorism. Even when terrorism is executed by the group of people who have a family, the women and the children can potentially be the crime victims structurally. The second group, which is the women and the children, will be the group that is carried away by the criminalization based on the family's relationships. On the other side, these two groups are easily considered as criminals rather than a victims. It is based on the assumption of the "the terrorist family," which means that the label is for the whole family, whether the person in question is a father, mother or the children, no matter who is really the criminal.

The women have gone through the process to be the victims in terrorism. Declaration of Basic Principles of Justice for Victims of Crime and Abuse of Power, which is legitimated by the United Nations in the United Nations General Assembly Resolution No. 40/43, reveals that the victim is the person who is individually or as a group has suffered. This misery is like physical or mental injury, emotional injury, economic disadvantage, or human rights deprivation by act or omission. The victim's consideration will be viewed without seeing the criminal recognized, arrested, charged, sentenced, or without looking at the familial relationship between the criminal and the victim.

Therefore, in the status as a wife, women have actually experienced the victimization that is not realized by themselves. No wonder, since they only think that what they do is what they are supposed to do as the wife to their husband based on religious practice. But more than that, what really occurs is that the women have been a victim before the terrorism is executed. The women obtain "the terror education" forcedly because the marriage value attaches that in the religion which puts the husband as the leader, "Imam," and the representative of God. They have a responsibility to accompany, obey, and take care of the husband's name from all consequences. It would be shallow to perceive this as "the weakness in practicing religion." What is worthy of recognition is the essence of understanding and internalization in religious practices that the religion can often impose in social life and religious life.

---

*Corresponding author: ellyms@upi.edu

DOI 10.1201/9781003178163-6

In criminal cases, the group is often suspected as the criminals or the assumption is made that all the members of the group have a bad character, which is why the women and the children are often considered the same as the father in terms of their involvement with terrorism. They are a suspect community (Mythen et al. 2009) who are really harmed in terrorism. This harm can be moral or material. Every pressure and marginalization from society and negative stigma for what they wear as the religious symbol (burqa) becomes the symbol associating womens' positions in terrorism. There will be the opinion that not all women as the terrorist's wives are purely victims, and they can be perceived as the one who has full power for themselves so that they have freewill for what they are going to do or not. But, in terrorism that involves the family, there is actually a large structural process in being a women as the "criminal" involved.

Women have their own power, but the concept of this power will change over time with comprehending religious teachings and family structures that involve fear, pressure, and no protection until the attempt to protect themselves and the family. These can be the pull factor of the women's involvement in terrorism. The women's inability to protect themselves cannot be judged as the proof of surrender in their involvement as the terrorist, and it can be a long ordeal for the women themselves and the family as a whole.

2 PRELIMINARIES

2.1 *Jihad: in and for terrorism*

A false understanding of comprehending and interpreting the meaning of Jihad leads to negative impacts, such as possibly committing crime to harm themselves or others. Jihad and terrorism will be the unit that cannot be separated away. Some radical religious communities interpret the meaning of Jihad as they strive to defend Allah's religion. Otherwise, what really occurs is to have no relation between the religion and the decision to "Jihad" with terrorism. All religions are made unreasonable when used in the interests of crime (Asiyah et al. 2020).

Terrorism is not Islamic teaching. It is mentioned in the Quran on Surah Al-Maidah verse 32, which says strongly that Islam denies murder without justification, the killing of another innocent human is as same as killing all humans in the world. The radicalism is planted systematically and massively to the women who bring them to obedience based on false religious basics. The religion is made to be a strong legitimation of how women act and how they are treated. It will be a reason for the radical community to Jihad through terrorism.

2.2 *Women in terrorism*

The women's motivation in Indonesia to get involved in terrorism action is theologically rooted (Mulia 2019). Marriage bonding becomes one of the factors for women's presence in the terrorism world. The women's flexibility for the radical community is made as to the strength in executing the terror, whether they are the data collector of the victim candidate up to the women involved actively in executing the terror. The terrorism before only recognizes the men as the executor but now through the feminism approach, the women will be the actor even if, primarily, they are the victim. The women's disallowing in maintaining the family's values through their obedience to religion will be the weakness for them in terrorism which involves the family.

The women are always in a position as the victim when society has a radicalization process. The women and religion will be the centre of discrimination and exploitation of the fundamental groups of misogyny. The women's involvement in terrorism will be proof that the women become the target for the radical community who uses religion to justify controlling and attacking the women. Besides that, there are also cultural values that render women's domestication and involvement in terrorism. This domestication is the first political program because the women's domestication's social-political cost is easy and cheap.

3 METHOD

This study employed a qualitative approach to describe deeply and in more detail the women's involvement in terrorism which involves the family. The logical sequence of the inductive approach is utilized to generate a theory based on the observation that is performed during the research. The phenomenological design is used in this study to obtain a meaning that is contained in the women's involvement in terrorism. The approach, logic and study design are expected to cultivate the research aims comprehensively through deep identification of the subject's experience in this study on the phenomenon of terrorism which involves women.

This study is performed objectively by observing the experience of the subject study's behavior patterns as the social actor (Nindito 2013). As an attempt to comprehend the meaning of a phenomenon, the researcher develops a subjectivity meaning on the phenomenon observed (Mama 2002). It pushes the researcher to dive into the related values between women, religion, and the decision to take part in terrorism. The observational study, open-ended interview and reflecting session are performed in the study to some subjects of this study to balance the researcher and participant (McKinley Brayboy & Deyhle 2000).

The documentation study is obtained by examining secondary data that backs up the research and documenting every activity during the research. The literature study is utilized to strengthen the examination that is displayed in the analysis of the study in the future. Data validation is performed by sending the information of the study's result processed by the researcher to the expert on education, religion and gender to give a suggestion and reinforcement in developing the meaning and the researcher's credibility (Rodgers & Cowles 1993). The research process by using phenomenology design makes the researcher have to set aside their personal experience to understand various experiences of the subject in this study. It attempts to validate data and aims to avoid dualism of the informant's perception as the insider and the researcher as the outsider (Naples 1996).

4 RESULT AND DISCUSSION

4.1 *The women's victimization*

If it seems that the women execute terrorism, it is believed that they are also the victim. The women's role as the main actor of terrorism cannot be used to conclude that they are the criminal. Basically, the women's involvement in terrorism proves that the first person who becomes the victim of terrorism which involves the family is the women. The women become the victim of the husband's ideology as the Imam in the family. The women are also the victim from the access to the endless conflict, the victimization of religious indoctrination, the victimization of people's stigma and the victimization of media which is created by the elites who have an interest and utilize all of it to be the women's strength in striving and their dedication to the family.

Marriage becomes a promising facility in women's involvement in terrorism. The women's recruitment through marriage and the men's doctrine as the husband to the women as the wife becomes the radicalization process that is going on every day, easily and undercover behind the obedience of the husband and the religion. The massive indoctrination on the women is obtained from their husbands or the other women as wives from the men who are active in terrorism. They usually meet and gather in religious activity in groups to discuss the religion. The values of radicalism are planted from the group's meeting to the women, and the importance of the women defend the family (husband) and religion. The feeling of unity and relation to the group will strengthen the women in their involvement in terrorism.

Commonly, the women's role in the radical community is not fundamental and central. But on the other hand, the women's role will be recognized rapidly and respected if they can show their courage in sacrifice. The recognition of this role will be spirit for the women and one of the important keys in valuing the women's devotion to join the radical community. The radicalism is into the women and immediately the women without a doubt run their mission. The women in terrorism can be more militant than the men. It is because of the strong loyalty that the women have on the family and community. Some doctrines in radicalism can amaze the women and strengthen them in internalizing radical Islam. The meaning of life becomes one of the factors that are searched by the women in their loyalty to religion.

The women's totality in the family cannot be doubted. The women's roles allow the family to decide how they can live and survive (Wulandari et al. 2016; Malihah et al. 2018; Wilodati et al. 2019). The women with everything they have can be the strength in living the Jihad spirit and there is no exception with the women's stereotype as the one who cannot keep the secret, in reality, this role is utilized by the radical community as the companion and educator for the children as the radical fighter candidate (Sholukhah 2019). From this point of view, the women can trust and run the radical mission for themselves and the educator in planting the radical values in religion, convincing and approving of the terror.

Terrorism appears because humans are not empowered with the "civilization achievement" created by themselves. The modernization and globalization are able to erase the traditional living ways, norms, customs, and the institutions which are inherited hereditarily to every generation. The feeling of the "loss" of civilization leads some communities to alienation. These things will be the factors that fertilize the radical Islam communities who agree with the Jihad concept through terrorism. Not only that, but the women will also be the ones who live in those communities until becoming "the expert" in planting the radical religious values.

Religion becomes the protection place for the alienation groups in civilization. No exception with those who stick with the religious symbols which are worn, particularly, the women with Islamic wearing. No matter what they wear as the form of obedience to Islam, the women will get the negative stigma because they are labeled due to wearing "terrorist clothing." It becomes the turning point of how easy the women are in the radical community's recruitment, due to their willingness to be "obedient" and "same" in society.

The victimization on the women in terrorism involves based on the institution, actor, and the women as the victims in the system. The women as the terrorist's wives are related by the family relationship, which is husband-wife. The husbands play a big role in their wives' involvement in terrorism. The husband's domination of their wives is based on religion. The husband's domination that is played attaching to their wives generates the norm and value planted internalizing.

The internalization of values and norms in the terrorist's family becomes the concept that forms the women based on believing their understanding and making every attempt at what is "supposed" to be done as found in the guidance conveyed. The women believe that what they do is the right thing, believing what they are supposed to do as the women and the wife in "religious guidance." The values and norms are attached in the internalization process above the individual's identity of the women so that they can do what is requested without asking.

Basically, Islam appreciates women. Islam is the religion that does not differ between the men and the women which is that there is a fundamental value that underlies Islamic teaching such as peace, freedom and egalitarianism. It cannot be forgotten that the equality between men and women is reflected in the Quran. Therefore, it will be better if the women's theology issue in Islam starts to be discussed so that the women can be free from the structure and law injustice (Lubis 2009). This attempt has to be started from the women by the individual, group or religious educational institution so that the women can prove that they can put themselves as the carrier and spreader of love and not to be as the one who is easily swayed by conflicting interest or terrorism (Malihah et al. 2020).

4.2 *The gender analysis of the women's involvement and prevention attempt*

The feminism discourse perceives that women are the group that can be counted on if speaking about loyalty and obedience. Not only that, but the women are also the humans who can be trusted and obedient to everything related to religion. The feminism discourse is strengthened by half sociological perception, which reveals that women are the vulnerable groups. The simplicity of various media accesses is not comparable to the women's literacy that is perceived to be less. The women's acceptance of the news and religious teachings is no exception to the radicalism issue, which will be more accepted and followed by them by using their critical thinking.

Terrorism which involves the family as the terrorist, becomes one of the proofs about the men's hegemony which has created a universal phenomenon in human civilization's history in society, including in Indonesia. The men are in a superior position and the women are in the inferior. This belief is elaborated spontaneously on the men's and women's placement as how the women's place is in the domestic sphere while the husband's place is in the public sphere. The men's hegemony to the women obtains the legitimation from the social values which have been habituated, the religious values which are believed, the applicable laws and all of these have been customs and structures in life.

The women are contested in the discussion of actual issues about the position and the women's structure. Some researchers expose that the women may be involvement in terrorism because of depression, disappointment, mental illness, men's pressure in the name of religion, frustration with inequality of gender and also social injustice in society (Mulia 2019). Another factor is that women are perceived as human with minimum security. The women are going through the investigation process that is not too tight than the security officer's men. They are considered not dangerous so that the security officer is sometimes careless, and they succeed in executing the terror. It can be proven by the success of bombing in which the women execute the act by bringing their children to fool the security officer.

The development of the feminism movement persuades a big impact on the study of victimology. This concept's main assumption is that the women (as the terrorist's wife) are the first and real victims. The victimization that women experience is the impact of inequality in gender. Furthermore, the structural condition has a risk in the process of being a victim; as we have discussed before, the family relationship, husband-wife, becomes the structural condition of the women's presence in terrorism. The inequality of gender has taken its part in seeing the victimization that happens to the women as the terrorist's wife. The woman becomes a direct victim, enduring physical injury and material and immaterial loss. Also, the women become indirect victims, such as out of sympathy and support from society to the women who are really the victims of terrorism.

The relation inequality based on gender becomes a door for entering the doctrine of radical terrorism. The domination without limitation in the family relationship becomes something dangerous, not only for the husband-wife but also for their children. Therefore, one of the key points that needs to be attempted to cut the women's victimization chain is equality. The equality between the men and the women in all their differences. Equality becomes the together consciousness of the power of equality in developing the family based on religion. The together power in developing the family and open communication in the family based on religion makes it so the religious values and the internalization can exist as expected.

The scope of the terrorism prevention process consists of controlling, counterpropaganda, denial and alertness. Every scope requires structured steps, systematically and sustainability. Because terrorism prevention effectively depends on the eradication strategy (Goodwin 2006). The handling of terrorism effectively depends on the eradication strategy arranged by the government through the National Counter-Terrorism Agency (BNPT) and civil society.

Pesantren, as the religious educational institution, can be a door in planting the religious teachings necessary. This educational institution is considered to be able to deliver the concept of religion and obedience without being radical up to the point of preventing terrorism. Pesantren, through its value-norm of education and religious teaching that is structured and based on the educational value, is expected to be one of the three institutions which can control religious conflict.

This writing is made not to expose the women's involvement in terrorism covered by the primacy of Pesantren compared to other educational institutions. More than that, what is most important is the proficiency of religious literacy so that every information about religion, knowledge, and various demands in religion can be meant without sacrificing other people.

5 CONCLUSION

In the end, it will be our responsibility for how to be and take care of men and women as the humans who have religion and practice religious teachings. But it is not the reason to agree with everything that is believed, particularly, hurting other people. Religious education becomes crucial in the middle of globalization. Religious education supports religious literacy peacefully among religious people. The men and the women with every strength and weakness will be united in developing a family that obeys the religion and nation. This obedience will be basic in realizing the unity and togetherness in religion.

REFERENCES

Asiyah, U., Prasetyo, R. A. and Sudjak, S. (2020) 'Jihad perempuan dan terorisme', *Jurnal Sosiologi Agama*, 14(1), pp. 125–140.

Goodwin, J. (2006) 'How Not to Explain Terrorism – About Louise Richardson, What Terrorists Want: Understanding the Enemy, Containing the Threat (New York, Random House, 2006).', *European Journal of Sociology*. doi: 10.1017/s0003975606000269.

Lubis, A. (2009) 'Upaya Meningkatkan Partisipasi Masyarakat dalam Pembangunan', *Jurnal Tabularasa PPS UNIMED*.

Malihah, E. et al. (2018) 'Optimizing Social Capital of the Community of Suku Dayak Hindu Budha Bumi Segandhu Indramayu', in. doi: 10.5220/0007099304070411.

Malihah, E., Nurbayani, S. and Wulandari, P. (2020) 'Women in the Eye of Pesantren', *KnE Social Sciences*. doi: 10.18502/kss.v4i10.7387.

Mama, A. (2002) *Beyond the masks: Race, gender and subjectivity*. Routledge.

McKinley Brayboy, B. and Deyhle, D. (2000) 'Insider-outsider: Researchers in american indian communities', *Theory into Practice*. doi: 10.1207/s15430421tip3903_7.

Mulia, M. (2019) 'PEREMPUAN DALAM GERAKAN TERORISME DI INDONESIA', *AL-WARDAH*. doi: 10.46339/al-wardah.v12i1.136.

Mythen, G., Walklate, S. and Khan, F. (2009) '"I'm a Muslim, but I'm not a terrorist": Victimization, risky identities and the performance of safety', *British Journal of Criminology*. doi: 10.1093/bjc/azp032.

Naples, N. A. (1996) 'A feminist revisiting of the insider/outsider debate: The "outsider phenomenon" in rural Iowa', *Qualitative Sociology*. doi: 10.1007/BF02393249.

Nindito, S. (2013) 'Fenomenologi Alfred Schutz: Studi tentang Konstruksi Makna dan Realitas dalam Ilmu Sosial', *Jurnal ILMU KOMUNIKASI*. doi: 10.24002/jik.v2i1.254.

Rodgers, B. L. and Cowles, K. V. (1993) 'The qualitative research audit trail: A complex collection of documentation', *Research in Nursing & Health*. doi: 10.1002/nur.4770160309.

Sholukhah, R. (2019) 'PEREMPUAN DAN TERORISME: KETIDAKHADIRAN FENOMENA FEMALE SUICIDE TERRORISM (FST) DI INDONESIA TAHUN 2009-2015', *Journal of International Relations*.

Wilodati, W., Komariah, S. and Wulandari, P. (2019) 'From Women (A social movement for women in the family)', in *2nd International Conference on Educational Sciences (ICES 2018)*. Atlantis Press, pp. 79–82.

Wulandari, P., Hufad, A. and Nurbayani, S. (2016) 'The Status and Role of Women in the Community of Suku Dayak Hindu Budha Bumi Segandhu Indramayu', in *1st UPI International Conference on Sociology Education*. Atlantis Press, pp. 155–158.

Development, Social Change and Environmental Sustainability – Sumarmi et al (Eds)
© 2021 Taylor & Francis Group, London, ISBN 978-1-032-01320-6

Legal culture in cockfighting games in east Java communities, Indonesia

Sudirman, Rusdianto Umar*
Universitas Negeri Malang, Malang City, Indonesia

ABSTRACT: This article analyzes the legal culture of cockfighting lovers in East Java, Indonesia. Cockfighting in Indonesia is perceived as a tradition as well as an illegal economic activity. If it is tradition, it will engender a legal culture, but as an illegal economic activity, it must be prohibited. This study investigates if the East Java society, especially cockfighting lovers, have the same view. This requires further analysis. This research is quantitative research with descriptive analysis. Data was collected by surveying 400 respondents. The results showed that the perception of cockfighting lovers in East Java considered that cockfighting is a hobby and not a tradition or a forbidden economic activity. The hobby of cockfighting breeds disobedience to the law, even though it is forbidden for them to do cockfighting. Therefore, it can be assumed that the hobby gave birth to its legal culture.

Keywords: legal culture, cockfighting, east Java, community.

1 INTRODUCTION

Cockfighting's existence in Indonesian society is a cultural phenomenon of the Indonesian people. Geertz research in Bali, Indonesia, reveals that cockfighting is inherent in the daily lives of Balinese and Javanese people (Geertz 2000). A different opinion about cockfighting in Indonesia was put forward by Lindquist (Lindquist 2007), who stated that cockfighting is not a community tradition but is seen as a forbidden economic act. Cockfighting is a means of gambling to obtain a source of income illegally. Reviewed from a legal perspective, these two opinions have their own consequences for the legal views of the cockfighting phenomenon. Geertz's view is that cockfighting is a cultural phenomenon, which contains a set of upheld social values, making it inherent in the daily life of Indonesian people. The value of the cockfighting tradition, in view of legal sociology, will engender legal culture. This means that in the society's traditional values, the legal values that are realized and inherent in these traditional values will also be stored as part of the values upheld collectively. If the public realizes that cockfighting is a tradition, then automatically the legal awareness of the community will also see cockfighting as not a forbidden act. This is because the legal culture of society is in line with the culture of the community itself (Friedman 1969, 2009; Syamsudin & SH 2011). The community will not have a legal culture against a state law that is contrary to the culture of society (Nelken 2004; Polak & Nelken 2016) and will not obey the legal provisions governing cockfighting. Instead, they will still do cockfighting even if secretly. Therefore, to create legal awareness (Merry 2010; Wang & Chen 2019) for the community, the law must be in line with the legal culture of society. Cockfighting must be empowered because it saves tourism potential (Sudirman 2019).

Conversely, if based on Lindquist's opinion which states that cockfighting is an illegal economic activity, then the legal consequence of the phenomenon of illegal economic activity is to prohibit it.

---

*Corresponding author: sudirman.fis@um.ac.id

DOI 10.1201/9781003178163-7

The law must clearly and definitively outlaw any prohibited economic activity. Thus, cockfighting must be restrained. Lindquist's view is in line with the state view of cockfighting. Cockfighting is seen as illegal and violates the law by categorizing it as gambling. This is based on the provisions of article 303 KUHP, article 542, article 542 designation, and article 303 of the Indonesian Criminal Code. The State view of cockfighting legitimizes the view that cockfighting is an illegal economic motive. This illegal concept has resulted in the crackdown of cockfighting by law enforcement officials in Indonesia, arresting the perpetrators and subjecting them to criminal sanctions.

Based on the two opinions above, this study analyzes the correctness of the opinion expressed by Geertz and Lindquist that cockfighting is a tradition and/or cockfighting is a forbidden economic act. Cockfighting lovers in East Java have to reveal their perception of cockfighting. If cockfighting lovers in East Java regard cockfighting as a tradition, it is in line with Geertz's opinion, and they will have the awareness that cockfighting is not illegal. However, if cockfighting lovers in East Java consider cockfighting to be the main occupation that generates economic income through gambling activities, then it is in line with Lindquist's opinion and cockfighting must be prohibited. This research took place in the province of East Java, Indonesia.

2 METHOD

This study uses a quantitative research approach (Neuman 2011; Sugiyono 2008) with the type being survey research. The procedure of this research was broadly carried out by formulating operational definitions, formulating questions, collecting data and analyzing data. The population in this study was specifically the cockfighting lovers. However, because there was no definite data about cockfighting lovers, the population used was the entire adult and married population (17+) population of East Java. Based on population data from the Central Statistic Body of East Java, there were 31,011,960 people assigned to the population at the same time and the slovin formula determined that the research sample was 400 respondents who had joined cockfighting. The sampling technique used was multi-stage random sampling. The sampling process was carried out and stratified from the Provincial-District-Village-level. The province which was the research location in East Java consists of 38 districts. The main instrument of this research was a questionnaire. The type of question used was a closed question, where the respondent chose between the alternative answers given. The data obtained was analyzed using descriptive analysis.

3 RESULTS AND DISCUSSION

The results of the study describe the responses descriptively regarding main occupation background, perceptions of cockfighting, and how much cockfighting was started.

3.1 *Main work background*

The main occupational background of the respondent of the study is presented in Table 1:

Based on Table 1, it is known that their main job is not actually cockfighters. Respondents stated that the main job of cockfighters is only around 6.5%. This indicates that cockfighting is not an economic activity for the majority of respondents. The main occupation of the most respondents is as farmers or farm laborers (by 34.5%), then entrepreneurs (29.3%), private employees (15.8%), government employees (2.5%) and breeders or fishermen (11.5%). This data shows that cockfighting is not merely an act of economic motive. This data provides a rebuttal that the cockfighting phenomenon is a social phenomenon with an economic motive, namely the illegal economy. In fact, the perpetrators of cockfighting in East Java do not work as cockfighters. Thus, cockfighting is not a job that can generate economic benefits.

Table 1. Main work.

	Frequency	Percent	Valid Percent	Cumulative Percent
Farmers/farm laborers	138	34,5	34,5	34,5
Government employees	10	2,5	2,5	37,0
Private employees	63	15,8	15,8	52,8
Entrepreneur	117	29,3	29,3	82,0
Breeders/fishermen	46	11,5	11,5	93,5
Cockfighters	26	6,5	6,5	100,0
Total	400	100,0	100,0	

Table 2. Perceptions of cockfighting.

	Frequency	Percent	Valid Percent	Cumulative Percent
Hobbies/Fun/Entertainment	345	86,3	86,3	86,3
Profession	23	5,8	5,8	92,0
Culture/Tradition	32	8,0	8,0	100,0
Total	400	100,0	100,0	

3.2 *Perceptions of cockfighting*

The respondents' perceptions of cockfighting are shown in Table 2

Table 2 confirms that cockfighting is not the main job for cockfighting lovers. This means that cockfighting lovers do not have the perception that doing cockfighting will benefit them economically. 86.3% of the respondents perceive cockfighting as a hobby or pleasure or entertainment. Respondents consider cockfighting as a hobby that brings entertainment for themselves, not as a job because only 5.6% perceive it as a profession. This data is in line with data on their main job, which only 6.5% mentioned cockfighting as their main job (see Table 1). These two data clearly show that cockfighting is understood not as a social phenomenon with economic motives but rather as a hobby or pleasure. Data Table 2 also shows that respondents who have a perception of cockfighting as a culture or tradition are only 8%. This data can be used as a reference that cockfighting in East Java is not perceived as a tradition. This is related to Geertz's statement which states that cockfighting is tied to tradition. This means that this data can be used as a basis for criticizing the statement that cockfighting is related to community traditions. The fact that most respondents consider cockfighting as a hobby or entertainment will also form the basis for the assumption that hobbies or pleasures will affect legal compliance and disobedience.

3.3 *The beginning of loving cockfighting*

The respondents' driving factors to first tried cockfighting are presented in Table 3

Base on Table 3, it is known that the driving factors of people joining cockfighting are more due to the influence of friends or other people (by 37.8%) and also because of experiment and then love (36.5%). This data also shows the fact that respondents do not like cockfighting at first for the sake of earning a living. This means cockfighting is not a social phenomenon with an economic motive. Respondents who initially liked cockfighting because it was meant to earn a living (work) is only 4.3%. Thus, this is in line with the respondents' data on their main job and perception of cockfighting. The respondents who stated that they liked cockfighting in the first place because of the community's tradition also only represented 16%. This data also strengthens the perception

Table 3. The driving factors of respondents' love for cockfighting.

	Frequency	Percent	Valid Percent	Cumulative Percent
Influence of friends/other people	151	37,8	37,8	37,8
Offspring (parents like cockfighting)	22	5,5	5,5	43,3
Experiment and then love	146	36,5	36,5	79,8
Make a living from cockfighting	17	4,3	4,3	84,0
Community traditions	64	16,0	16,0	100,0
Total	400	100,0	100,0	

of respondents who say cockfighting as a tradition is only 8% (see Table 2). These two data sets also form the basis of the argument that cockfighting is a tradition, especially for the people of East Java who are the research subjects. Based on the results of research conducted in East Java, it is known that the people who love cockfighting in East Java do not consider cockfighting as a tradition. This means that there is no actualized cultural value when cockfighting lovers engage in cockfighting. The motive for the traditional values that make up cockfighting as conveyed by Geertz is less relevant. People who love cockfighting in East Java prefer cockfighting as a hobby or pleasure or entertainment (see Table 2).

It is in contrast with Lindquist's view, which states that cockfighting is based on illegal economic motives. Judging from the background of the main occupation of the cockfighting lovers community in East Java, it is known that those who stated that the main job of cockfighters is only around 6.5%. This indicates that cockfighting is not an economic activity for the majority of respondents. The main occupation of most respondents is farmers or farm laborers (by 34.5%), followed by entrepreneurs (29.3%), private employees (15.8%), government employees (2.5%), and breeders or fishermen (11.5%), as presented in Table 1. This data confirms that cockfighting is not merely an act of economic motive. This data provides a rebuttal that the cockfighting phenomenon is a social phenomenon with an illegal economic motive. In fact, the majority of cockfighters in East Java do not work as cockfighters. Thus, cockfighting is not merely a job that generates economic benefits.

As a consequence, cockfighting in East Java is neither a tradition nor an economic activity. Cockfighting, for the people of East Java, is a fun and entertaining activity. So, some cockfighting lovers in East Java engage in cockfighting with stakes, while some others engage in this activity because of the urge to get pleasure and entertainment. The existence of cockfighting in the life of the people of East Java is a hobby, even though the state law prohibits it with criminal threats. This means that cockfighting lovers in East Java prioritize the encouragement of a hobby rather than an urge to obey the law. It can be indicated that hobbies also contain legal culture. The law will be obeyed more if it empowers hobbies instead of prohibiting hobbies.

4 CONCLUSION

In the case of cockfighting in East Java, it is known that cockfighting is not a tradition but an entertainment or pleasure or hobby. Cockfighting lovers in East Java do cockfighting, with bets or without bets, for entertainment and pleasure. Cockfighting is considered by the state as an illegal activity, so it is prohibited. The perpetrators are chased, raided and arrested by the police. However, cockfighting lovers in East Java continue to do cockfighting, despite the repressive police action. This is done to channel the hobby of cockfighting. Thus, a state law prohibiting people's hobbies will only result in disobedience. This means that disobedience to the law is not only because the law conflicts with the legal culture of society, but also because it is conflicting with hobbies.

REFERENCES

Friedman, L. M. (1969) 'Legal Culture and Social Development', *Law & Society Review*. doi: 10.2307/3052760.

Friedman, L. M. (2009) 'Sistem Hukum Perspektif Ilmu Sosial', *Bandung: Nusa Media*.

Geertz, C. (2000) 'Deep Play: Notes on the Balinese Cockfight', in *Culture and Politics*. doi: 10.1007/978-1-349-62397-6_10.

Lindquist, J. (2007) 'Deep Pockets: Notes on the Indonesian cockfight in a globalizing world', *SPAFA Journal (Old series 1991-2013)*, 17(3).

Merry, S. E. (2010) 'What Is Legal Culture-An Anthropological Perspective', *J. Comp. L.*, 5, p. 40.

Nelken, D. (2004) 'Using the concept of legal culture', *Austl. J. Leg. Phil.*, 29, p. 1.

Neuman, W. L. (2011) *Social Research Methods: Qualitative and Quantitative Approaches*, Pearson Education.

Polak, P. and Nelken, D. (2016) 'Polish prosecutors, political corruption, and legal culture', in *Central and Eastern Europe After Transition: Towards a New Socio-legal Semantics*. doi: 10.4324/9781315571119-15.

Sudirman, S. (2019) 'POTENSI DESA WISATA SABUNG AYAM NON JUDI DI KELURAHAN NGLE-GOK, KEC. NGLEGOK, KAB. BLITAR (Strategi Kontruktif Mengatasi Judi Sabung Ayam Berbasis Wisata)', *Jurnal Praksis dan Dedikasi Sosial*. doi: 10.17977/um032v2i2p82-89.

Sugiyono (2008) *Metode penelitian pendidikan:(pendekatan kuantitatif, kualitatif dan R & D)*. Alfabeta.

Syamsudin, M. and SH, M. H. (2011) *Konstruksi Baru Budaya Hukum Hakim Berbasis Hukum Progressif*. Kencana.

Wang, Z. J. and Chen, J. (2019) 'Legal Culture and Historical Development of Law', in *Dispute Resolution in the People's Republic of China*. Brill Nijhoff, pp. 15–48.

Development, Social Change and Environmental Sustainability – Sumarmi et al (Eds)
© 2021 Taylor & Francis Group, London, ISBN 978-1-032-01320-6

"Sumberawan water site": History, sustainable preservation and use as a learning source

Wahyu Djoko Sulistyo* & Maharani Arya Dewanti
Universitas Negeri Malang, Malang City, Indonesia

ABSTRACT: Malang is one of regions with historical traces (sites) in the form of water sources. One of them is *'Petirthaan Sumberawan'*. The existence of *Petirthaan Sumberawan* listed in ancient manuscripts shows that the water site has an important position to the community since a long time ago. Various development and preservation efforts have been made by supporting communities. Some of them are irrigation, daily water needs, rituals, religious tourism and historical tourism. This article reveals the sustainable existence of *"Petirthaan Sumberawan"* in Malang by tracing its history, conducting a review to describe the efforts made by the community and various interested parties for its preservation, and analyzing the potential of *Petirthaan Sumberawan* as a source of historical learning for students.

Keywords: *Sumberawan*, water site, history, sustainability

1 INTRODUCTION

In any country, history always gets its own attention for its role as a reminder of national identity and advocates of a sense of love for the country. The Indonesian government pays attention, among others, to history. It can be seen from the stipulation of Republic of Indonesia's Law Number 11 the 2010 concerning culture clearly providing clarity in the maintenance of sites in Indonesia. In this law, there are definitions and rules and penalties related to the site. A form of cultural heritage contained in Malang is a water site in the form of *petirthaan*. In Hindu-Buddhist religion, water means holy water which can make the people holy. This holy water is usually also referred to as *Tirtha Nirmala* or *Tirtha Amerta* believed to have such benefits as cleansing sins. Gods also drink water, so they have eternal life (Herwindo 2015; Kinney et al. 2003).

Centuries ago, people used water sites to fulfill their daily needs, including for religious ritual purposes. Because it is an important part of life, water sites are often mentioned in ancient manuscripts. The water sites mentioned in the ancient *Nagarakertagama* manuscripts include, for example, *Polaman, Watu Gede Kendedes, Sumbernagan* and *Kasuranggan* or *Sumberawan* water sources (Poerbatjaraka 1924). In its development, *petirthaan*, which was originally a water site from the Hindu-Buddhist era, is still often used today. For example, the source is an ancient source of water that is relatively functional until today (Ari et al. 2013; Buwono et al. 2017; Titisari & Wulandari 2018).

The optimization of water site utilization presently is only limited to the utilization of water. The utilization of water sites cross-times is less maximized in the learning in schools. In fact, if it is used as a source of historical learning, water sites can support information visualization and strengthen the meaning and appreciation of supporting events. The utilization of local historical potentials is a source of historical learning and history learning material (Sulistyo et al. 2020; Sulistyo & Kurniawan 2020). Based on this, this study analyzes water source sites. The importance

---

*Corresponding author: wahyu.djoko.fis@um.ac.id

34   DOI 10.1201/9781003178163-8

of this research is to provide new insights into the use of local historical sites viewed from various aspects, including the sustainable use and the efforts to preserve the site. That is why this research is different. This study discusses what has been done by the community and various interested parties to preserve it and analyzes the potential of *Petirthaan Sumberawan* as a source of historical learning, specifically for students

2 METHOD

This research proposes the idea of utilizing water sites as a source of learning. The idea emerged based on the potential of Malang as an area with many historical relics, in this case in the form of water sites, but less optimized in learning activities. This study is a historical research, the one conducted to reveal the past (Kuntowijoyo 2003). In this method, the researcher can understand and explain the past situation with heuristics (data collection), verification (criticism) and interpretation (interpretation) on writing (historiography) stages. In addition to seeing conserving efforts, a qualitative approach is carried out through observing and interviewing the members of community and site managers (Bernard 2013; Creswell 2009; Ragin 2014). Data was obtained by searching literature and to support the completeness of information, field observations were carried out on *Petirthaan Yai Beji Sari, Petatu Watu Gede Kendedes, Patirtaan Sumbernagan, Polaman* and *Petirtaan Sumberawan*. This study focused its examination on *Petirthaan Sumberawan*.

3 RESULT AND DISCUSSION

3.1 *Distribution of water sites in Singosari-Lawang Region*

The water sites spread from Singosari to Lawang areas, both of which have been used optimally and those traditionally used by the local community are as follows:

Table 1. Water site data in the Singosari-Lawang area.

Water Site	Location	Preservation
Patirtaan Watugede	Gondorejo Krajan, Tamanharjo, Singosari, Malang, East Java	Daily water source needs of surrounding community, tourism, cultural preservation
Sumberawan	Bodean Krajan, Toyomarto, Kec. Singosari, Malang, East Java	Irrigation, community's daily water source, managed by PDAM, water and religious tourism, cultural preservation
Sumbernagan & sumberbiru	Pesanggrahan, Candirenggo, Singosari, Malang	Spiritual tourism, utilized by surrounding community for their daily needs
Sumber Polaman	Polaman, Kalirejo, Kec. Lawang, Malang, East Java	Managed by PDAM, irrigation source for surrounding communities and water tourism

3.2 *Historical study and conservation of Sumberawan water sites efforts*

Human settlements in a region for a long time will certainly create a culture. Culture can represent human life aspects of its proponents. One of the Hindu-Buddhist human cultures is especially in the form of sacred buildings and the remnants of religious rituals which can be examined in petirthaan Malang until today. Tirtha derives from Kawi language (ancient Javanese) meaning water (Purwanto 2017). Whereas in Sanskrit, *patirthaan* means bath or river, sanctification or speck of water, *toya* or holy water, purifying with water (Macdonell 2004) (Monier-Williams 2001). In Hinduism, water as a source of life holds an important position and is often used in sacred ceremonies. Almost every

Hindu religious ceremony always includes the role of water. *"Tirtha (air sutji* or holy water) is also a tool to cleanse souls" (Dharma 1968). Water is symbolized as a blessing from God as well as a purifier of body and soul. In Hinduism, water is a symbol of god Vishnu. As water preserves life, Lord Vishnu is the preserver of the world (Dekker & Panjarikan 1972). Therefore, water that is manifested into the water sites of the Hindu Buddhist period is found in Malang.

Another water site examined specifically in this study is *Sumberawan*. In the 35th verse of Pu Prapanca's *Nagarakertagama* poem, it is told that in 1359, the Maharaja Putra Dewa Rajasanagara Hayam Wuruk took a trip and stopped in several places including Kedung Biru, Kasurangganan (Taman Bidadari) and Bureng (Poerbatjaraka 1924). Experts predict that is what is meant by *Kasuranggaan* is *Sumberawan* (Widodo 2006).The *Sumberawan* spring is at the foot of Mount Arjuno. This water source is in the form of a small lake with clear water and abundant water discharge and is in a swampy area. In the belief held by this water source, it functions as *patirthan*, which of course also deals with *amerta* water. Conservation of *Sumberawan* water sources is closely related to the belief in *amerta* water believed to be holy water that must be preserved.

3.3 *Potential water sites as historical learning resources*

The utilization of water sites as learning resources will support information visualization. There are three stages of learning schemes based on the use of sites in learning history, including orientation, exploration and evaluation stages (Morton et al. 1997). The stages are described in the following scheme:

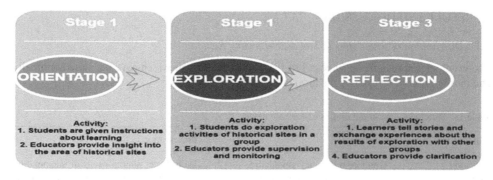

Figure 1. Schematic of learning activities from learning resources.

3.3.1 *Stage 1: orientation*
In the orientation phase, educators provided an introduction to the material in the form of objects constituting the source of learning. Learning orientation is important to provide clear direction and instruction, so that learning can run well (Alfieri et al. 2011). At this stage, students were given an explanation concerning the existence of Hindu Buddhist kingdom represented by the findings of water sites in the Malang area. Among the existing water sites, educators and students made an agreement on the location to be visited, namely *Petirthaan Sumberawan*. Furthermore, educators provided knowledge about *Petirthaan Sumberawan*

3.3.2 *Step 2: exploration*
After the previous stage, educators and students left for the location. Arriving at the location, it was better for educators to assign students to write new knowledge they have obtained at the *Petirthaan Sumberawan* location. Furthermore, educators guided and provided flexibility for students to explore the water sites visited. With this, the students can see and even touch historical traces so that it can facilitate the appreciation of historical stories. Students will pay more attention to this site because they already have basic knowledge by learning in class in the previous stage. The

approach used in this learning activity is the adoption of outdoor learning (Bilton 2010; Fägerstam 2012). This activity gives students the freedom to explore the field in a structured manner with a variety of targeted knowledge to be acquired (Burriss & Burriss 2011).

3.3.3 *Step 3: reflection*

In the final stage, educators facilitated the students to exchange information about their learning experiences at the water site. Educators are also assigned to confirm or clarify the information students convey. In addition to conveying historical information and the community and various stakeholders' efforts to preserve the water site, the students are also required to take the educational value that can be taken from this exploration of water site (Coulson & Harvey 2013; Coulson & Harvey 2013; Sulistyo 2019). Educational value that can be taken in petirthaan exploration activities is a source of learning. Hindu-Buddhist water sites provide a great learning for anyone wanting to study them. Tirtha (holy water) functions as a tool to cleanse body and soul, so that Tirtha can be said to be a component in harmonizing human relations with their Lord. By interpreting each of the signs conveyed by the ancestors through inanimate objects, the humans in the present will learn art, technology, thought flow and social relations of the ancestors. In addition, humans must also be wiser in positioning themselves on their relationship to God – whatever their religion – because through these relics, there are messages and perhaps warnings that God wants to convey to His people. When students understand and are able to interpret the learning, a historical awareness and love will emerge to preserve it.

4 CONCLUSIONS

The research focuses on one water site, *Petirthaan Sumberawan*. *Petirthaan Sumberawan* is pervaded by certain myths that continue today. The myth then becomes a form of guarding the sustainability of site. In addition to myth, the measures to conserve the water source sites at this time are governed straightforwardly in cultural preservation law and through other utilizing efforts. *Petirthaan Sumberawan* is now used for fulfilling daily water needs, irrigation, religious rituals, religious tourism studies and historical tourism purposes. As a manifestation of human worship to nature and ancestors, historical relics need to be preserved and interpreted. In the context of historical meaning in learning activities, the use of historical heritage as a source of learning needs to be optimized. The utilization of water sites as a source of history learning can be packaged in three stages of learning activity scheme: orientation, exploration and evaluation. This phase emphasizes on student learning activities by visiting locations, allowing *Petirthaan Sumberawan* to be a historical learning tour for students while also making the students the preserver and perfecter of site. The Utilization of *Sumberawan* water site as a source of learning in relevant historical learning will provide more values in the appreciation and ease of visualizing information for students, so that the learning will run more effectively.

REFERENCES

Alfieri, L. et al. (2011) 'Does Discovery-Based Instruction Enhance Learning?', *Journal of Educational Psychology*. doi: 10.1037/a0021017.

Ari, I. R. D. et al. (2013) 'Community Participation on Water Management; Case Singosari District, Malang Regency, Indonesia', *Procedia Environmental Sciences*. doi: 10.1016/j.proenv.2013.02.098.

Bernard, R. H. (2013) *Social Research Methods; Qualitative and Quantitave Approaches*. Second Edi. Sage Publications.

Bilton, H. (2010) *Outdoor learning in the early years: Management and innovation*. Third Edit. Routledge.

Burriss, K. and Burriss, L. (2011) 'Outdoor play and learning: Policy and practice.', *International Journal of Education Policy and Leadership*, 6(8), pp. 1–12.

Buwono, N. R., Muda, G. O. and Arsad, S. (2017) 'Pengelolaan Mata Air Sumberawan Berbasis Masyarakat di Desa Toyomarto Kecamatan Singosari Kabupaten Malang [The Management Of Sumberawan Wellspring

Based On The Community in the Toyomarto Village Singosari District Malang Regency]', *Jurnal Ilmiah Perikanan dan Kelautan*, 9(1), pp. 25–36.

Coulson, D. and Harvey, M. (2013) 'Scaffolding student reflection for experience-based learning: A framework', *Teaching in Higher Education*. doi: 10.1080/13562517.2012.752726.

Creswell, J. W. (2009) *RESEARCH DESIGN Qualitative, Quantitative, and Mixed Methods Approaches*, *SAGE Publications*. doi: 10.2307/1523157.

Dekker, N. and Panjarikan, K. S. (1972) *Pokok-Pokok Agama Hindu*. Malang: Lembaga Pembina Pendidikan Agama (LEPPA) IKIP Malang.

Dharma, P. H. (1968) *Upadeca tentang adjaran-adjaran agama Hindu*. Parisada Hindu Dharma.

Fägerstam, E. (2012) *Space and place: perspectives on outdoor teaching and learning, Linköping Studies in Behavioral Science*.

Herwindo, R. P. (2015) 'Kajian Arsitektur Percandian Petirtaan di Jawa (identifikasi)', *Research Report-Engineering Science*, 1.

Kinney, A. R., Klokke, M. J. and Kieven, L. (2003) *Worshiping Siva and Buddha: The Temple Art of East Java*. University of Hawaii Press.

Kuntowijoyo (2003) *Metode Sejarah*. Tiara Wacana.

Macdonell, A. A. (2004) *A practical Sanskrit dictionary with transliteration, accentuation, and etymological analysis throughout*. Motilal Banarsidass Publ.

Monier-Williams, M. (2001) *English Sanskrit dictionary*. Asian Educational Services.

Poerbatjaraka, R. (1924) *Negarakertagama*. Bijdr. TLV, Deel LXXX.

Purwanto, H. (2017) 'FUNGSI PATIRTHAN DI KABUPATEN GIANYAR, BALI', *Siddhayatra*. doi: 10.24832/siddhayatra.v22i1.60.

Ragin, C. C. (2014) *The comparative method: Moving beyond qualitative and quantitative strategies*. Univ of California Press.

Sulistyo, W. D. (2019) 'MENGGUGAH SENSITIVITAS SOSIAL MAHASISWA MELALUI IMPLEMENTASI PRAKSIS SOSIAL', *Jurnal Sosiologi Pendidikan Humanis*. doi: 10.17977/um021v4i1p38-46.

Sulistyo, W. D. et al. (2020) 'Learning experience from learning sources: Exploiting geographic and historical potential of guerrilla sites in Wonokarto Pacitan as a source of historical learning', in *IOP Conference Series: Earth and Environmental Science*. doi: 10.1088/1755-1315/485/1/012109.

Sulistyo, W. and Kurniawan, B. (2020) 'The Development of 'JEGER' Application Using Android Platform as History Learning Media and Model', *International Journal of Emerging Technologies in Learning (iJET)*, 15(7), pp. 110–122.

Titisari, E. Y. and Wulandari, L. D. (2018) 'Water Resource as Axis-Mundi: an Effort to Preserve Water Resource Sustainability', in *IOP Conference Series: Earth and Environmental Science*. IOP Publishing, p. 12005.

Widodo, D. I. (2006) 'Malang tempo doeloe. Djilid doea', Malang: Bayumedia Publishing.

Development, Social Change and Environmental Sustainability – Sumarmi et al (Eds)
© 2021 Taylor & Francis Group, London, ISBN 978-1-032-01320-6

Coping strategy based on socio-agriculture approach in Landslide Prone Area in the Gede Catchment, Malang Regency

Nurul Muddarisna, Heni Masruroh* & Eny Dyah Yuniwati
Agriculture Faculty, Wisnuwardhana University of Malang, Indonesia

Aulia Rahman Oktaviansyah
Wisnuwardhana University of Malang, Indonesia

ABSTRACT: The aim of this paper is to elaborate the copy strategy using socio-agriculture by the community for living harmony in a high potential landslide area. The method was carried out by field survey and deep interview regarding the community's coping strategy using socio agriculture and the agriculture system. A field survey was done using a grounded research technique. Based on the data shows that the community of Gede Catchment has a coping strategy for living harmony using socio-agriculture. The community has local indigenous value to mitigate the impact of landslide disaster. They have a high tolerance for each other not only when disaster occurs but in daily activities. The community uses the former landslide to plant vegetable crops. The community has a coping strategy for arrangement their environment between permanent tress and vegetables crops in the each single topography as control landslide. It is this coping strategy to mitigate the landslide disaster because with high tolerance and arrangement the spatial arrangement of plants and topography can decrease the chance of a landslide disaster.

Keywords: agriculture, disaster, community

1 INTRODUCTION

Based on the data types of Disaster which occurred in Indonesia, the number of landslide disasters is the second-ranked after a forest fire disaster. In the year 2019, there were 1.483 landslide disaster occurrences (BNPB 2020). A landslide is the process of soil movements with a sloping direction from its original position and separated from a stable mass due to the influence of gravity. Mostly landslides will occur in the mountainous and hilly areas with thick soil. Landslide events usually occur during the peak of wet season and in the hilly areas (Igwe 2015). Geomorphology is the one of factors that affects landslide occurrence. But sometimes, landslides can occurr by accelerating community activities who manage their environment improperly (Skilodimou et al. 2018; Barnard et al. 2001; Zhang et al. 2012). Sometimes, the community manages their environment and neglects the soil characteristic. This will increase the landslide potential (Muddarisna et al. 2019).

Landslide disasters are the most common disaster types in Indonesia. The potential of landslides will be higher when the communities don't conserve their environment and the communities are rising. Generally, landslides will occur in the rough geomorphology. To prevent landslides, the communities has to consider the soil characteristic to determine the type of mitigation which will reduce the landslide risk disaster chances. Improper mitigation which had been done by the communities without paying attention to soil characteristics will increase the landslide potential. Generally, the communities will use woody plants to reduce landslides. Even though in the thick

---

*Corresponding author: henimasruroh11@gmail.com

DOI 10.1201/9781003178163-9

soil conditions, woody plants are not proper for decreasing landslide potential. The woody plant will increase the soil mass, Thus the land-slide potential will increase also. Landslide conservation without considering the soil condition will trigger a landslide. Sometimes to reduce the risk of landslides, optimizing the local wisdom of the community in the social aspects and ways of the community in managing their environment, including managing their agricultural systems can be performed. This is called community coping capacity and is an effort to reduce the risk of landslides.

The impact of landslide disaster is varied between each landslide prone area (Tjah-jono et al. 2018; Setyono et al. 2005). It depends on the condition of environmental vulnerability and the coping capacity of communities to manage their environment and their local knowledge. If the risk element has a low vulnerability value, and the community has good coping capacity, the disaster risk can be minimized. The coping capacity is regarding the social aspect and managing the agriculture system. The social aspect is regarding gender, age, occupation and also some other local wisdom related to communities social relation ships which had been applied in an area when disasters occur. For instance, there are regular local meetings to discuss landslide disaster risks or there is a community in an area which focuses on reducing the landslide disaster risk. How to manage agricultural land in areas prone to landslides is also important and can be considered an effort to reduce landslide risk. Most of the landslides occur in agricultural areas with various types of crops. If the plantation and managing agricultural land is not appropriate with soil conditions, it can trigger landslides. On the other hand, if managing agricultural land and the plantation is proper with the land, it can be an effort to reduce the potential of landslides. Both of them can be coping strategies for the community in landslide prone areas.

Humans or society in the context of a disaster are the object as well as the subject of the disaster itself. They not only deal with the pre-disaster threat, but also take the risk of losing lives due to the disaster, and still have to face the post-disaster conditions. Therefore, there needs to be an effort to improve the ability or capacity of the society in facing disaster. The coping capacity, which is focusing on the social-agriculture aspect, is still rare (Rieux, Karen, Jaquet, Stephanie, Derron, Henri, Jaboyedoff 2012; Bohle & Adhikari 1998; Gurung 1989). The research objective of this research is to elaborate the coping strategies of society based on the socio-agriculture aspect in the Gede Catchment.

Gede Catchment is the upper part of Bromo Mountain. It is located in the Malang Regency, East Java province. Mostly, the land use of this area is agriculture with several crop plantations in every single topography. The subsurface material is dominated by deposition of Bromo Volcano material i.e andesitic, basalt, tephra, alluvium, young material Bromo Volcano, and limestone.

2 METHOD

The data used in this research is DEMNAS data for making the landslide susceptibility map. It is created by a geomorphometric approach which several steps: 1) DEM download processing; 2) DEM processing analysis; 3) Landslide susceptibility map processing using thematic map analysis; 4) field check; 5) re-interpretation; and 6) layout land-slide susceptibility map. DEM analysis data was done by Integrated and Water Information System Software (ILWIS).

The field survey was done for accuracy of landslide susceptibility maps, observation and a deep interview with society regarding the socio-agriculture system which applies in this research area. The field survey and observation is including the condition of social aspects when the disaster occurs and the kind of the plantation which planted in this area as an effort to control and mitigation landslides. The social aspect is also including observation the community behaviour in their environment including planting and harvesting their agriculture. The field survey is also completed with the purposive in-depth interview of community.

The result of this research is focused on elaborating the formula of socio-agriculture systems in the community as a coping strategy as control and landslide mitigation. The scientific explanation based on the real conditions. We found the several fact that socio-agriculture which had been applying in the research area has a positive impact as a coping strategy.

3 RESULTS AND DISCUSSION

3.1 *Landslide susceptibility analysis*

A landslide is a natural disaster which has a characterization that includes its physio-graphic characteristics. Landslide susceptibility can be analyzed based on several factors. The landslide inventory can be collected by field surveys and analyzing remote sensing data. Landslide susceptibility mapping is producing in this research based on the analysis of remote sensing data and field survey as an accuracy check. The landslide disasters are influenced by several factors causing a landslide, i.e. elevation, slope, topographic position index, curvature, plan curvature, and profile curvature. Each factor can cause soil material movement.

Based on the landslide susceptibility mapping shows that this area has a high potential of landslide around 52.9%, middle potential landslide 30.5% and low potential landslide around 16.6%. The landslide has become an environmental problem in this area. There were several landslides which had occurred, and they damaged the agricultural land, roads and settlements. The typology of a landslide in this area is a rotational landslide and is translational. Each typology landslide has its own characteristics. Both active and inactive landslides are used for agricultural crop cultivation.

Based on the landslide susceptibility mapping, this area consists of a stable zone such as the landslide area and an unstable zone. The stable zone is in the peak interfluves and foot slope. Both of them have a low slope, thus, there is no energy to move the soil material. Whereas, for the unstable zone, it started from the upper slope and went until the lower slope. The topographic position of the slope is started from peak interfluves until the channel was bad. Soil material starts to move in the topographic position of the upper slope. The geomorphological processes found on the upper slope as an indicator of the movement of soil material is the presence of cracks (soil cracks) and erosion. Both geomorphological processes can initiate the movement of soil material, so that it can initiate material movements (Samodra 2014). The topographic position of the slope that has no force to move the material, namely alluvial and colluvial plains. The topography of the Gede Catchment is largely unstable because of slope cutting for road and river

3.2 *Socio-agriculture as a coping strategy for landslide susceptibility*

Capacity is elaborated as a combination of all strengths existing in a community, society and organization that may reduce the impact of disaster risk. Capacity as mitigation of disaster risk can be structural and non-structural capacity. Mostly, several areas which have disaster risks use structural mitigation as a coping strategy. Non-structural mitigation is still rarely done by the community. The capacity is not only for reducing the disaster risk, but it is also to develop a safety culture, to make the community aware, to self-protect and a supporting effort to protect others and society in general.

For the social aspect, the pattern of life and livelihoods of the Gede Catchment communities is harmonious interaction with nature and with each other's communities. The existence of community interaction is to supply all the needs in their daily life. Interaction among people in the Gede Catchment has used a kinship system. The interaction of communities with nature is part of the community's livelihood pattern to survive.

A family system and a culture of mutual assistance emerged because the people of the Gede Catchment lived in areas prone to landslides. The settlement pattern of the Gede Catchment community can be identified based on the interpretation of the Spot 5 imagery. The results of the interpretation of the Spot 5 imagery of the Gede Catchment settlement show that the settlement pattern of the Gede Catchment community is elongated and clustered. The dispersed settlement pattern is located on the outrigger of the Catchment and follows the road network pattern. The clustered settlement pattern is located on the slopes of the foothills. The clustered settlement pattern is an indicator that the Gede Catchment community uses a family system with a culture of helping out.

The spatial distribution of settlements is close to each other (cluster family system). The communities of Gede Catchment are aware that the Gede Catchment area is an area prone to landslides. Public awareness regarding disasters as evidenced by the existence of relief activities, humanitarian activities and routine activities of the Gede Catchment community. Through these activities, kinship between communities, disaster training, disaster information and other activities related to disaster response can be improved, especially for landslides. Activities have been routinely carried out in the Gede Catchment to teach each other community to be responsive to signs of landslides, actions taken when landslides and actions were taken after landslides occur (Interview at Downstream Gede Catchment Community 2020).

For aspect agriculture, it emphasizes how people manage their agricultural environment. The aspect of agriculture in this area is an important factor that must be considered be-cause most of the land use in this area is agricultural land with seasonal vegetable crops. Planting types of plants that are not suitable for soil conditions can lead to movement of soil material. Efforts to reduce the risk of landslides by planting woody plants in this area are not proper because this area has thick soil. Managing the agricultural system regarding the type of plantation is necessary to reduce the landslide disaster risk because mostly the land use is agricultural.

The communities have a coping strategy regarding agriculture to reduce landslide disaster risk. The communities had been planting their agriculture with mixed crop plantation in each single of topography. Mixed crop plantation can be one of the solutions in environmental management (Zuazo & Pleguezuelo 2008). This happens because plants are one of the factors that have an influence on soil conditions. This includes influencing the infiltration process, run off and soil mass load. The communities of Gede Catchment practiced the mixed garden for economic income and one of the ways for landslide conservation, particularly vegetative conservation. They assume that a mixed garden is the solution that provides economic and environmental benefits. Gede Catchment's society had been an awareness of living in the study area that has a high potential of landslide. The community is more selective for determining the types of vegetation in each unit morphology and in considering land cultivation and uncultivated land. Both of them have the potential to influence of occurrence of a landslide. The inclination of the slope will be changed if the landslide occurs. It will affect soil erosion, run off and infiltration.

The land utilization in the Gede Catchment shows spatial arrangement based on the physical characteristics in the study area. The spatial arrangement includes the type of vegetation, unit morphology and landslide site. The types of vegetation such as bamboo, clove and other woody plants have been planted in the peak interfluves. The mixed garden such combining of coffee plantation with the holticulture plants such as carrots, apples and potatoes was applied in the upper slope until lower slope. The foot slope was used for seasonal vegetation.

The spatial arrangement also applied in the landslide site. There are differences between spatial arrangements in active landslides and inactive landslides. For the active landslides the type of vegetation is just grown naturally without human planting. It will differ with the inactive landslide. Mostly, the society planted several local agroforestry plantations in the spatial arrangement of the landslide site. At the crown area, the society planted woody plantation such cloves and bamboo. The communities have assumed that these plants could conserve the soil movement.

The socio-agriculture which had been applying in the Gede Catchment as a coping strategy is indicative about how the community attitude is regarding landslide mitigation. In the Gede Catchmentm a family system with a cultural of mutual assistance emerged. The community management system of the Gede Catchment is shown by the location of the settlements between families that are close to each other. The communities of Gede Catchment are aware that the Gede Catchment area is an area prone to landslide. There were several activities which had been applied by the Gede Catchment community to decrease the risk of landslide potential. The activities is tend to public awareness regarding disaster through the existence of relief activities and routine activities i.e. weekly street cleaning and routine check activities to identify land condition which has the potential of landslides. In addition, the community also has the monthly routine agenda for disaster training, an early warning system as disaster information and other things related to disaster response especially for landslides. These activities improve the capacity of communities regarding decreasing the risk potential of landslides. These activies teach each other to be responsive to signs of landslides.

4 CONCLUSSION

The study area is the mountainous area which has a high potential of landslide. For reducing the landslide disaster risk, the communities of Gede Catchment had been applying the socio-agricultural aspect. The social aspect is tended about the harmony interaction with nature and with each other and with the lives and livelihoods of the Gede Catchment communities. They applied the family system in their daily activities including when the disaster occurs. Whereas, for the agriculture, they applied very appropriate conservation efforts in their agricultural systems with the crop plantation in each unit morphology for reducing the soil movement. The socio-agricultural aspect had been applying in this study area as a coping strategy for reducing landslide disaster risk.

REFERENCES

Alkhasawneh, M., Umi, K., Lea, T., Nor, A., dan Mohammad, S. (2013). Determination of Important Topographic Factors for Landslide Mapping Analysis Uisng MLP Network. *The Scientific World Journal*, 1–12.

Blaga, L. (2012). Aspect Regarding The Significance of the Curavture Types and Values in the Studies of Geomorfometry Assited By GIS. Seria Geografie, 327–337.

Barnard, P.L. et al., 2001. Natural and human-induced landsliding in the Garhwal Himalaya of Northern India. *Geomorphology*, 40(1–2), pp. 21–35.

BNPB, 2020. *Data Bencana*, Available at: https://bnpb.cloud/dibi/laporan5 (Accessed, August 26th, 2020).

Bohle, H.-G. & Adhikari, J., 1998. Rural livelihoods at risk how Nepalese farmers cope with food insecurity. *Mountain Research and Development*, pp. 321–332.

Gallant, J.C., dan Wilson, J.P. (2000). Primary Topographic Attribut: Terrain Analysis Principles and Application. New York.

Hengl, T., Gruber, S., dan Shresta, D. P. (2003). Geomorphometry in Ilwis: Concept, Software, applications. Development in Soil Science. Elsevier, 497–525.

Igwe, O., 2015. The geotechnical characteristics of landslides on the sedimentary and metamorphic terrains of South-East Nigeria, West Africa. *Geoenvironmental Disasters*, 2(1), pp. 1–14.

Olaya, V. (2009). Basic Land Surface Parameters. Application Developments in Soil Science, 141–169.

Reneau, S. L., dan Dietrich, W. E. (1987). The Importance of Hollows in Debris Flow Studies; Examples from Marin Country, California. Engineering Geology, 165–180.

Rieux, Karen, Jaquet, Stephanie, Derron, Henri, Jaboyedoff, M., 2012. A case study of coping strategies and landslides in two villages of Central-Eastern Nepal. *Applied Geography*, 32(2), pp. 680–690.

S.M, G. (1989). Human Perception of Mountains Hazard in the Kakani Kathmandu Area: Experience from The Middel Mountains of Nepal. Mountains Researcg and Development, 353–364.

Samodra, G., 2014. DEVELOPMENT OF RISK ANALYSIS TECHNIQUE AND ITS APPLICATION TO GEO-DISASTER MANAGEMENT IN INDONESIA.

Skilodimou, H.D. et al., 2018. Physical and anthropogenic factors related to landslide activity in the northern Peloponnese, Greece. *Land*, 7(3).

Shary, J. A., Sharaya, L. S., dan Mitusov. (2002). Fundamental Quantitative Methods of Land Surface Analysis. Geoderma, 1–32.

Tjahjono, Heri., Suripin., Kismartini. (2018). Community Capacity in the Face of Landslide Hazard Southern of Semarang City. ICENIS (pp. 1–7). Web of Science.

Zhang, Fanyu., Chen, Wenwu., Liang, Shaouyun., Chen, R., 2012. Human-induced landslide on a high cut slope: a case of repeated failures due to multi-excavation. *Journal of Rock Mechanics and Geotechnical Engineering*, 4(4), pp. 367–374.

Zuazo, V.H.D. & Pleguezuelo, C.R.R., 2008. Soil-erosion and runoff prevention by plant covers. A review. *Agronomy for Sustainable Development*, 28(1), pp. 65–86.

Development, Social Change and Environmental Sustainability – Sumarmi et al (Eds)
© 2021 Taylor & Francis Group, London, ISBN 978-1-032-01320-6

Utilization of new media as a promotion facility in entrepreneurship development for students at SMAN 1 Torjun

Elya Kurniawati*, Joan Hesti Gita Purwasih, Prawinda Putri Anzari & Deny Wahyu Apriadi
Universitas Negeri Malang, Malang, Indonesia

ABSTRACT: Entrepreneurship is one of the parameters determining the high level of progress of a country. The Indonesian government is committed to improving the quality of its human resource productivity, creativity, innovation and effectiveness by implementing the educational curriculum. This article reports on a training method that aims to increase the knowledge and interest of SMAN 1 Torjun students regarding entrepreneurship. SMAN 1 Torjun is a school for implementing Entrepreneurship Government Assistance in 2019. In preparing students to have adequate capabilities, mentoring is carried out through lectures, demonstrations, questions and answers, discussions, and assignments. The mentoring process carried out for students of SMAN 1 Torjun was able to increase students' knowledge and skills regarding entrepreneurship and technology, as evidenced by students' ability to process local potential into new businesses. Information technology and "new media" awareness training for students of SMAN 1 Torjun also increases students' enthusiasm for entrepreneurship.

Keywords: entrepreneurship development, high school, new media

1 INTRODUCTION

The government has made efforts to improve human resources' quality to be more creative and productive (Kominfo 2017). Education is an effective way to give birth to a qualified national generation to realize a nation's progress (Permendikbud 2016). The world of education is expected to play an active role in preparing educated human resources to face various challenges. The low level of creative spirit and independence in students is the main problem in our country, so entrepreneurial education is an alternative solution. Law Number 20 of 2003 concerning the National Education System states that the purpose of education is to prepare Indonesian people to have the ability to live as individuals and citizens who are productive, creative, innovative and effective and able to contribute to the life of society, nation, state and world civilization.

Entrepreneurship education promotes applying principles and methodologies for students' formation of life skills through an integrated curriculum in schools. Presidential Instruction No. 4 of 1995 states about the national movement to promote and cultivate entrepreneurship, mandating all Indonesian people to develop entrepreneurial programs. At the primary and secondary education levels, the Ministry of Education and Culture has described it through strategic steps in the implementation of the 2013 Curriculum. The 2013 Curriculum objectives will be more achieved when students have entrepreneurial spirit and skills, and they will become productive, creative and innovative citizens based on character values nation and able to contribute to social life. Curriculum design 2013 implements 21st-century skills or termed 4C (Critical Thinking, Creativity, Collaboration and Communication).

---

*Corresponding author: elya.kurniawati.fis@um.ac.id

Entrepreneurship is a spirit, behavior and ability to seize positive opportunities to generate benefits for oneself or provide better service to customers/society and create and provide useful products and work efficiently (Siagian et al. 1995). Entrepreneurs can bring change, face challenges and produce innovations. This is because entrepreneurship is a very dynamic process. The process of creating a new product/service requires a lot of time and effort. Physical, financial, and social risks are very vulnerable to accompany the entrepreneurial process (Hisrich 2001).

The effectiveness of business management also depends on the readiness of technology and digital infrastructure (Misnawati & Yusriadi 2018). Technological advances have had many positive impacts on entrepreneurship, such as the ease of communication and access to information and the expansion of business networks (Kurniawati & Setiawan 2019). This has spurred the emergence of social media. The public's response to the presence of social media is excellent. There are almost no students who do not own and use social media in their daily lives. The development of science and technology can also stimulate the growth of students' entrepreneurial spirit.

The emergence of social media can be an effective solution to entrepreneurs' problems in adopting technology to run their businesses. Social networking sites are becoming an effective means of promotion. Also, media use can reduce costs and make the promotion process run efficiently (Kurniawati et al. 2019). The social media often used are Instagram, Facebook and Marketplaces such as Lazada, Shopee, Bukalapak, etc. The development of existing science and technology should also be able to provide its stimulus to students. Social media and technology are emerging as effective sales, marketing and communication tools for businesses globally (Veldeman et al. 2015).

Since 2016, the Directorate of Senior High School Development has strengthened entrepreneurship programs by providing grants to several schools spread across 34 provinces. Then in 2018, the Directorate of High School Guidance conducted evaluation and supervision at the school. The supervision results at the schools implementing entrepreneurship programs and recipients of entrepreneurship program assistance funds carried out in 2018 showed that 97.14% of students had shown their creativity by using local cultural wisdom. Only 2.86% of students should be given guidance in increasing creativity. This shows the great potential of entrepreneurship programs in schools to develop the entrepreneurial spirit of students. These problems are quite diverse, starting from schools that are not ready to run the program; the local potential is not optimal, too product oriented. Based on the supervision results, the implementation of entrepreneurship programs needs to be optimized and made improvements, both in determining beneficiaries and implementing entrepreneurship programs.

SMAN 1 Torjun is a school for the implementation of Entrepreneurship Government Assistance in 2019, requiring that it be implemented optimally to impact the school positively later. One technique is to build cooperation and collaboration with the association, business, community, government and media ecosystem. Furthermore, entrepreneurship education programs introduce entrepreneurial thinking patterns and business planning. In preparing students to go in that direction, we assist students of SMAN 1 Torjun. This assistance is carried out to obtain it (1) Increase the knowledge and interest of students of SMAN 1 Torjun regarding entrepreneurship; (2) Increase the knowledge and skills of students of SMAN 1 Torjun regarding technology and "new media" as a means of entrepreneurship support.

2 METHOD

The training method is an effective way to increase students' knowledge and skills of SMAN 1 Torjun. These activities are expected to solve various problems faced by SMAN 1 Torjun in developing entrepreneurship programs in schools. This service activity is carried out in 2 (two) activity stages, namely:

2.1 *Training entrepreneurship, which is applied through the methods:*

– Lecture: conducted to deliver materials about entrepreneurship and local potential in Torjun, Sampang Regency.
– Question and answer: conducted to answer or resolve problems faced by participants related to entrepreneurship material, entrepreneurial motivation and local potential of Torjun, Sampang Regency
– Discussion: through this discussion forum, students are expected to gain reinforcement and confidence related to entrepreneurship, entrepreneurial motivation and local potential of Tojun, Sampang Regency.

2.2 *Information technology and "new media" awareness training for students of SMAN 1 Torjun, which is applied through the method:*

– Demonstration: conducted to convey material about its importance in information technology and "new media" to support entrepreneurship for students of SMAN 1 Torjun.
– Question and answer: conducted to answer or solve the problems faced by the participants related to information technology and "new media" as a means of supporting entrepreneurship for students of SMAN 1 Torjun
– Assignment: through this assignment, students are expected to gain increased knowledge and skills of information technology and "new media" to support entrepreneurship for students of SMAN 1 Torjun

The series of activities were carried out simultaneously to optimize Torjun's potential and students' entrepreneurial abilities.

3   RESULTS AND DISCUSSION

SMAN 1 Torjun is one of the secondary schools located in Sampang Madura Regency. Since 2018, SMAN 1 Torjun has been a school for implementing Entrepreneurship Government Assistance. Government assistance is provided to provide stimulus to students in carrying out entrepreneurship programs. The year 2018 shows that as many as 97.14% of students have demonstrated their creativity by using local cultural wisdom. This indicates that the level of student interest in entrepreneurship is very high. The problem is not ready to run the program, not optimal local potential, too product oriented. Through this assistance, we assist schools in solving these problems.

3.1 *Uneducated and lack of motivation regarding entrepreneurship*

Based on the results of supervision conducted by the Directorate of Senior High School Development, it was found that high school students' creativity was very high. It indicated by student's high comprehension when solving business problems. Also, students can create original ideas based on those problems. This student creativity is a significant asset for the school to carry out the next stage's optimization process. This ability will be more optimal in line with the increase in knowledge and entrepreneurial motivation in students. This is the basis for holding training to increase entrepreneurial expertise and inspiration for students of SMAN 1 Torjun. This transformation process requires students' attitudes, motivation and interest to become entrepreneurs. Sensitivity is the main requirement that entrepreneurs must-have. This ability enables them to identify opportunities, exploit businesses, and create new businesses and job opportunities. The growing interest in student entrepreneurship is expected to change their mindset to create jobs through their businesses after graduation, in which the average Indonesian people are assumed to become employees after graduating.

The first step in raising student sensitivity can be done through the identification of existing local potentials. Some of the local prospects owned by the Torjun area are people's salt, tobacco, sugar cane, coconut, tubers and various other tourism and cultural prospects. This sensitivity will increase students' awareness and knowledge of local potentials that can be used as business opportunities. Some of the products that students can produce from developing sensitivity. Students can process salt water with 97% NaCl levels as a nutrient to prevent acne on the skin. Also, there are student preparations such as papaya shredded, bidaran soap, boba drinks, plastic waste bags, etc. Developing an entrepreneurial spirit in students is not an easy thing. Students and parents still consider the importance of entrepreneurship. Ideally, in developing entrepreneurship, people can transform and have an entrepreneurial mentality and spirit who also have high sensitivity in doing business.

Entrepreneurship is essential for economic growth in any country. Today, entrepreneurship is recognized as one of the most effective economic development strategies that promote economic growth and sustainable competitiveness while facing increasing internationalization (Schaper & Volery 2004). Entrepreneurs can be described as individuals who set up and manage businesses for the primary purpose of profit and growth. Entrepreneur students typically use academic skills as steppingstones to starting their own business. Usually, he is a young entrepreneur who adopts innovative behavior and takes advantage of unorthodox management practices to achieve a strategic advantage over his competitors (Bailetti 2011).

3.2 Figure captions lacking in knowledge and skills of students regarding technology and "new media" as a means of supporting entrepreneurship

Sufficient knowledge of one's entrepreneurship will not automatically give birth to an entrepreneur (Nursito & Nugroho 2013). Other things can support entrepreneurship management's effectiveness, namely regarding the readiness of technology and digital infrastructure in entrepreneurship (Misnawati & Yusriadi 2018). Technological progress is 1 (one) of 8 (eight) driving factors for entrepreneurial progress (Nordiana 2014). Many positive impacts are obtained through the use of technology in entrepreneurship, such as the ease of communicating and accessing information and expanding business networks (Kurniawati and Setiawan 2019). The public's response to the presence of social media is excellent. Therefore, social media's emergence can be an effective solution to entrepreneurs' problems in adopting technology to run their businesses (Kurniawati & Ananda 2019). Social networking sites are becoming effective means of promotion. Besides, media use can reduce costs and efficiently run the promotion process (Kurniawati et al. 2019).

The development of the world of technology also requires the use of "new media" as an alternative means of enriching creativity and as a promotional tool for products produced by students of SMAN 1 Torjun. Smartphones are the most effective tools for running digital technology. Mobile phones have been conceptualized as a technology of connectivity, security and emancipation that allows users to interact with colleagues and relations abroad without time and space (Ling 2004). Students should use the ease of this technology in developing their business. Technology can assist students in obtaining information to improve the quality of their products. On the other hand, technology is also able to help market the products/services produced. Unfortunately, so far, students still use technology and other facilities as personal means, not support for existing businesses. Therefore, students' knowledge and skills must be improved through information technology awareness training and "new media" for students of SMAN 1 Torjun.

Entrepreneurship run by students is inseparable from the new era of the digital economy at the global and national scope. The information and communication sector has grown by more than 9% in the last two years, the growth of e-commerce in Indonesia has been the most dominant (Bappenas 2018). The development of the world of technology also demands the use of "new media" as an alternative means of promotion. Various forms of communication and business are carried out through digital media, such as Facebook, WhatsApp, Instagram, Marketplace and other social media. Technology and "new media" are the driving factors for advancing entrepreneurship (Nordiana 2014). Social networking sites are becoming an effective means of promotion.

Social media and technology are emerging as effective sales, marketing and communication tools for businesses globally (Veldeman et al. 2015). Research has revealed that social media allows companies to communicate economically and immediately with consumers. This supports organizations in building databases that can generate competitive businesses (Kurniawati et al. 2020). Such databases can further translate into increased sales, thereby enhancing SME growth and neutralization of geographic barriers (Jagongo & Kinyua 2013). According to previous research, young entrepreneurs have excellent innovational power and entrepreneurial skills to produce successful commercial start-ups (Fueglistaller et al. 2009). Therefore, it can be felt that the adoption and use of innovative technologies such as social media by young entrepreneurs for business purposes can lead to successful enterprises, which in turn have the potential to significantly contribute to the economic development of fast-growing countries, such as Malaysia (Nawi et al. 2017). The training on supporting skills for entrepreneurial success given to students is expected to be a good stimulus. Additional knowledge and skills about the importance of technology and "new media" can improve the entrepreneurial progress of students of SMAN 1 Torjun.

4 CONCLUSION

Entrepreneurship is the foundation of a country's progress. The National Education System is one of the systems used to prepare Indonesians to have the ability to live as individuals and citizens who are productive, creative, innovative, effective and able to contribute to the life of society, nation, state and world civilization. The high level of student creativity is the main capital in the entrepreneurial development of students of SMAN 1 Torjun. Unfortunately, students of SMAN 1 Torjun about entrepreneurship and students' knowledge and skills regarding technology and "new media" as supporting entrepreneurship are still very low. Through training to increase entrepreneurial knowledge and motivation for students of SMAN 1 Torjun, it was seen that students' entrepreneurial knowledge and motivation could grow. This is proven by the ability of students to identify local potentials and process them into new businesses. Information technology and "new media" awareness training for students of SMAN 1 Torjun also had a good impact.

REFERENCES

Bailetti, T. (2011) 'Fostering Student Entrepreneurship and University Spinoff Companies', *Technology Innovation Management Review*, 1(1), pp. 7–12. doi: 10.22215/timreview/485.

Bappenas (2018) 'Population and social policy in the disrupted world. National Planning and Development Agency'.

Fueglistaller, U. *et al.* (2009) 'An international comparison of entrepreneurship among students', *International report of the Global University Entrepreneurial Spirit Students' Survey project (GUESSS 2008).*, (Guesss), p. 52.

Hisrich, R. (2001) *Entrepreneurship*.

Jagongo, A. and Kinyua, C. (2013) 'The Social Media and Entrepreneurship Growth (A New Business Communication Paradigm among SMEs in Nairobi)', *International Journal of Humanities and Social Science*, 3(10), pp. 213–227.

Kominfo (2017) 'Peluang Besar Jadi Pengusaha di Era Digital'.

Kurniawati, E. and Ananda, K. S. (2019) 'The decision taken by the SME kopi malam jumat (friday night coffee) towards improving their culture by adopting e-commerce as a vehicle towards internationalisation', *African Journal of Hospitality, Tourism and Leisure*, 2019(Special Issue), pp. 1–11.

Kurniawati, E., Chrissendy, M. and Saputra, D. (2019) 'BEHAVIORAL FACTOR INFLUENCING INDONE-SIAN MICRO, SMALL AND MEDIUM (MS ME ' S) OWNERS DECISIO N-MAKING IN ADOPTING E-COMMERCE', 7(1), pp. 92–105.

Kurniawati, E. and Setiawan, A. (2019) 'The Role of Indonesian Micro, Small, and Medium Enterprises Owners in Choosing e-Commerce Strategy in the Global Market', 320(Icskse 2018), pp. 191–194. doi: 10.2991/icskse-18.2019.37.

Kurniawati, E., Al Siddiq, I. H. and Idris (2020) 'E-commerce opportunities in the 4.0 era innovative entrepreneurship management development', *Polish Journal of Management Studies*, 21(1), pp. 199–210. doi: 10.17512/pjms.2020.21.1.15.

Ling, R. (2004) *The mobile connection: The cell phone's impact on society.*

Misnawati, M. and Yusriadi, Y. (2018) 'EFEKTIFITAS PENGELOLAAN KEWIRAUSAHAAN BERBA-SIS KOGNITIF PERSONAL MELALUI PENGGUNAAN INFRASTRUKTUR DIGITAL (MEDIA SOSIAL)', *Jurnal Mitra Manajemen*, 2(3).

Nawi, N. che *et al.* (2017) 'Acceptance and usage of social media as a platform among student entrepreneurs', *Journal of Small Business and Enterprise Development.*

Nordiana, E. (2014) 'Peran jejaring Sosial Sebagai Media Peningkat Minat Berwirausaha Mahasiswa untuk Berbisnis Online (Studi Pada Mahasiswa Jurusan Ilmu Ekonomi Universitas)', *Jurnal ilmiah*, p. 12.

Nursito, S. and Nugroho, A. J. S. (2013) 'Analisis Pengaruh Interaksi Pengetahuan Kewirausahaan dan Efikasi Diri Terhadap Intensi Wirausaha'.

Permendikbud (2016) 'National Education System'.

Schaper, M. and Volery, T. (2004) *Entrepreneurship and Small Business: A Pacific Rim Perspective.*

Siagian, Salim and Asfahani (1995) 'Indonesian Entrepreneurship with the Spirit 17.8.45'.

Veldeman, C., Van Praet, E. and Mechant, P. (2015) 'Social Media Adoption in Business-to-Business: IT and Industrial Companies Compared', *International Journal of Business Communication.*

Development, Social Change and Environmental Sustainability – Sumarmi et al (Eds)
© 2021 Taylor & Francis Group, London, ISBN 978-1-032-01320-6

Plague in Malang 1910–1916

Slamet Sujud Purnawan Jati*, Arif Subekti, Wahyu Djoko Sulistyo & Moch Nurfahrul Lukmanul Khakim
Jurusan Sejarah, Fakultas Ilmu Sosial, Universitas Negeri Malang

ABSTRACT: This article aims to reconstruct the history of the spread of the bubonic plague in Malang in the early twentieth century, as well as its reflection on the spread of the current pandemic. Medical and mitigation measures were taken by the Dutch East Indies colonial government in dealing with bubonic plague in Malang. Likewise, medical policies and treatment are implemented by the government of the Republic of Indonesia, especially local governments in dealing with pandemics. There are some patterns that emerge and recur in the attitude of the government and society in responding to the two outbreaks. Presumably, these patterns can be taken into consideration for policy holders and the affected community in general in dealing with disease outbreaks.

Keywords: Plague, Malang, Pandemic

1 INTRODUCTION

The first bubonic plague was reported in the Dutch East Indies (now Indonesia) in 1905. Two workers as coolies were reported to have contracted the disease at the Port of Bandar Deli, North Sumatra. However, the colonial government did not care about the report because the victims were only 2 coolies, so it was considered a wind. 6 years later, reports of the bubonic plague have resurfaced in Indonesia, this time reportedly in Malang, East Java. This outbreak is predicted to occur in Malang due to the presence of imported rice from Burma as a solution to crop failure and food shortages in Java (Luwis 2008).

The discovery of the death toll was first reported at the beginning of the rainy season 1910. Throughout this season, there have been many casualties without any known cause of illness. However, it was not until the end of March 1911 that a doctor sent a patient's blood sample from Malang to a medical laboratory in Weltevreden, Batavia. The caused is that the bacteria that causes bubonic plague in the blood sample.

Meanwhile the colonial government always argued that there was no bubonic plague in Malang, only malaria. The discovery of the bubonic plague in Malang did not necessarily lead the Dutch East Indies colonial government to believe it. They always argue because they believe Burmese rats are different from local rats. But in fact, Burmese rats were able to adapt to the local environment of Malang, so that bubonic plague could spread. Why did PES spread earlier in Malang than in Surabaya? Malang at the time ago had some cold climates. This temperature makes the rat fleas stronger and easier to spread.

The continued denial by the Dutch colonial government had caused fatal problems. Pes was only recognized in Indonesia on March 27, 1911. On the other hand, this case had entered Malang at the end of 1910. From such a short time, the government of Dutch colonial reported 2,000 cases of bubonic plague victims in 1911. This number is somewhat dubious because the media actually reveals that the bubonic plague has claimed 300 victims per day. So there are government efforts to

---

*Corresponding author: slamet.sujud.fis@um.ac.id

50   DOI 10.1201/9781003178163-11

reduce the number of victims. As a result of underestimating the arrival of the bubonic plague case in Malang, the colonial government gasped when they saw the record of bubonic plague victims reaching around 2,000 throughout 1911. Then it continued to grow and reached its peak of up to 15,000 people in 1914. And in 1916, the number of residents who died from bubonic plague nearly reached 250,000 people. Even until 1919, there were still reports of victims of bubonic plague. It was only after 1920 that there were no more victims in the Indies.

2 RESULT AND DISCUSSION

The disease that was caused by the Yersinia pestis bacteria (named after its founder Alexander Yersin, a French bacterial expert), is malignant because it easily spreads and attacks the vital body parts. Until the 19th century, people were familiar with 3 types of bubonic plague, the lymphatic system or bubonic plague. Those with bubonic plague will experience swelling around the lymph nodes in the victim's neck, armpits, or groin. The shape can be as big as an egg to an apple. The second is bubonic plague or septicemic plague. Those who catch bubonic plague will show symptoms of fever, diarrhea, muscle aches, and some blackened body parts. The third is bubonic plague in the lungs as pneumonic bubonic plague. Apart from the symptoms mentioned above, those who were attacked by bubonic plague also experienced coughs and shortness of breath (Firdausi 2020). Of the three types of bubonic plague, the most dangerous and deadly is the pneumonic bubonic plague which can be transmitted between humans.

The bad images incident occur when Malang is hit by the bubonic plague. That images of Malang which is nicknamed "Paris of The East" together its beautiful natural potential that was turned into a tense area. Since the first time it caused casualties in November 1910 until the end of 1919. Human outbreaks by a disease and then outbreaks were widely influenced by various things, namely poor immunity, interactions with the sufferer, genetic factors, environmental geography, biogeography, and others. Therefore, efforts to deal with bubonic plague patients are related to the factors that cause the spread and persistence of this disease. Firstly, the open economic traffic factor in East Java. The expansion of the railroad network and roads makes it easier for a resident of Turen (Malang) to arrive in Surabaya in a few hours. This condition causes a seasonal worker to come to Surabaya to return to his village, not realizing that he has brought the bubonic plague. The initial areas under attack were the port and the area around the train station. In Malang City, the areas of Chinatown and Jodipan Village, which incidentally are areas not far from the station, are the first areas to have this disease.

Secondly, the other factors are climates and environmental geography. Malang has a cool and cold climate. It is located about 440-460 meters above sea level and the temperature reaches 14-16 degrees Celsius. This climate causes this disease to survive longer than other areas with hotter air. Thirdly, the bad factor is housing. Most of the houses in rural areas at that time were made of gedek or woven bamboo walls which were made in layers. The point is to protect the occupants from the cold. This house is comfortable for the occupants, but also comfortable for the rats. These rodents also like to nest in roof ridges made of whole bamboo sticks.

It is clear that bubonic plague is a vicious plague that must be tackled quickly. However, efforts to control the bubonic plague in Malang had stalled due to several things. Apart from being a health disaster, the bubonic plague also had an impact on the socio-economic sector of life. What is immediately apparent, of course, is the problem of discrimination which manifests in racism. European doctors are reluctant to go out in the field to treat patients. Apart from reasons of difficult access from the city, the unwillingness of European doctors is due to class disparities and racial sentiments that make white doctors reluctant to touch their native patients. Many European doctors who worked for government agencies refused to be sent to the Malang area (Balfas 1957). As it is known, that time was a time full of racism. The politics of division of society based on skin color and origins plagued the Dutch elite as well as other European people who were looking for fortune, supported by the colonial government. Let alone approaching plague-carrying rats or native people with bubonic plague, these Europeans didn't want to be close to native people on a daily basis.

Apart from racial sentiments, they do not want to interfere because the pay is small compared to treating their fellow Europeans. Of the 20 doctors who were urged to tackle this epidemic, only 11 people reported, including Raden Koesman, a Javanese who without hesitation stopped his studies, when he saw that his homeland needed his strength (Poeze 2014).

The discrimination that appears striking is the difference in treatment of European and indigenous patients which is very unequal. Europeans with bubonic plague are generally rushed to the hospital for free, get free nutritious food, and have regular daily checkups by European doctors. Meanwhile, people who live with the bubonic plague patient of Europe must undergo isolation for 2 weeks. They live it with very decent facilities, in the form of a strong and strong observation barracks.

This condition was very different from what was accepted by the colonized. If one resident is proven to have suffered from bubonic plague, then one village is immediately evacuated to the observation barracks. They already have to suffer from bubonic plague and are ostracized by society. The barracks for the natives are made of planks, roofed with leaves, and there are bamboo poles. Many residents refused to be moved to the barracks. Most indigenous people considered the excesses of implementing colonial government policies to be far more frightening and miserable than the bubonic plague itself (Safitry 2020). The treatment of bubonic plague to natives was not because the colonial government cared about the health of its colonies, but simply because they did not want to catch the disease.

Based on that condition, health workers ranging from mantri, European nurses, to Javanese doctors were sent to the villages to check on the indigenous population. Dr. Tjipto Mangoenkoesoemo, for one, did not remain silent and volunteered to participate in eradicating PES in Malang. As soon as his offer was approved by the colonial government, he left for Malang. It is from this stage of life that great stories about Dr. Tjipto emerge. Dr. Tjipto Mangoenkoesoemo later became known as a figure in the national movement. As usual in medical protocol, doctors who go to the villages must wear masks, gloves and other equipment to prevent the transmission of bubonic plague. But not with Dr. Tjipto who works almost without personal protective equipment or PPE (Reksodihardjo 2012).

The panic and fear caused by bubonic plague also diminishes social solidarity between residents. Dr. Tjipto saw for himself how a bubonic sufferer was ostracized by his neighbor. The sufferer is neglected because people are afraid of getting infected if he cares for him. The man finally slept under a Cambodian tree and it was there that he breathed his last. Also one more moment that is very famous. While in a village, Dr. Tjipto heard the crying of a baby from a hut that was almost burnt. It seems that the baby girl has been orphaned because her parents died in the bubonic plague. It was adopted by the baby girl to become Dr. Tjipto's son and was given the name Pesjati. This child was then raised and educated by Dr. Tjipto and his wife (Reksodihardjo 2012). The name Pesjati is a reminder of the terrible plague that hit Malang at that time.

REFERENCES

Balfas, M.D., 1957. *Dr. Tjipto Mangoenkoesoemo: Demokrat Sejati*, Djakarta-Amsterdam: Djambatan.

Firdausi, F., 2020. *Wabah-wabah di Hindia Belanda Akibat Impor Beras Tak Diawasi, Wabah Pes Merundung Hindia Belanda. (Online)*, Available at: https://tirto.id/eFYg.

Luwis, S., 2008. *Pemberantasan Penyakit Pes di Malang. Skripsi tidak diterbitkan*, Depok: FIB-UI.

Poeze, H.A., 2014. *Di Negeri Penjajah: Orang Indonesia di Negeri Belanda 1600-1950*, Jakarta-Amsterdam: KPG & KITLV.

Reksodihardjo, S., 2012. *Biografi dr Cipto Mangunkusumo*, Jakarta: Kemendiknas.

Safitry, M., 2020. Kisah Karantina Akibat Pandemi Pes di Paris of The East pada 1910 (Online). Available at: https://www.republika.co.id/berita/299194385.

Vogel, W. Th. de. 1912. Extract from The Report to The Government on The Plague Epidemic in The Subresidency of Malang (Isle of Java), November 1910 till August 1911. Dalam *Mededeelingen den Burgelijken Geneeskundigen*. Batavia: Javasche Boekhandel & Drukkerij.

Development, Social Change and Environmental Sustainability – Sumarmi et al (Eds)
© 2021 Taylor & Francis Group, London, ISBN 978-1-032-01320-6

The problems of COVID-19 waste management in East Java

A. Tanjung*, A. Kodir, I.K. Astina, M.Y. Affandi & M.G. Rosyendra
Universitas Negeri Malang, Malang City, Indonesia

ABSTRACT: The increase in the number of positive COVID-19 patients in Indonesia shows that the Indonesian government has not been fully prepared to face this outbreak. As a consequence, there has been an increase in COVID-19 medical waste. This study aims to explain how the management of COVID-19 medical waste has been handled properly or not. In addition, this study aims to explain whether the government has prepared special efforts to overcome this problem. This research was conducted in the East Java region. This study used qualitative research methods. The data collection process was carried out through semi-structured interviews with several relevant stakeholders. The results of this study indicate that medical waste management in East Java, especially in Surabaya, has not been optimally realized. This is due to the availability of infrastructure, funding, strict licensing, and the low human resource capacity for medical waste management.

Keywords: COVID-19, Medical Waste, Management, East Java.

1   INTRODUCTION

The increase in the number of COVID-19 patients in East Java ranks 2nd in Indonesia. This shows that the East Java provincial government is not yet fully prepared to face this outbreak. To date, there are 37,839 positive patients treated in all hospitals in East Java (Task Force for the Acceleration of Handling COVID-19, 2020). As a consequence, there is an increase in the amount of medical waste COVID-19. The waste produced by COVID-19 is a class of infectious waste that can transmit disease if special handling is not done (Yu *et al.* 2020).

It is easy to spread COVID-19 through medical devices that have been used to treat COVID-19 patients. The use of single-use PPE (Personal Protective Equipment) to treat COVID 19 patients and maintain the safety of health workers is considered able to increase the amount of medical waste produced (Saadat et al. 2020). So, it can be assumed that a logical comparison of the amount of PPE waste produced is directly proportional to the amount of PPE needed to handle one COVID-19 patient until they are cured.

PPE and B3/medical waste management has not been carried out optimally. This is evidenced by the occurrence of several cases related to waste disposal, one of which was at the Surabaya Acne Babat public cemetery by health officials on June 27, 2020 (Davina 2020). This careless disposal of PPE waste shows the weakness of supervision regarding medical waste management. A study shows that COVID-19 can survive on plastic and metal objects for 2–3 days (Peng et al. 2020). This condition raises concerns in the surrounding community regarding the transmission of COVID-19.

The impact of medical waste can affect the environment. Improper disposal of B3/medical waste poses serious risks to public health and the environment (Ilyas et al. 2020). In addition, according to Ghayebzadeh (in Kargar et al. 2020) B3/medical COVID-19 waste is dominated by plastic base materials and can threaten the environment if disposed of without further management. However, given the limited infrastructure, funding, and low awareness, the increase in the generation of PPE and B3/medical waste needs to be prioritized and requires special attention and handling.

---

*Corresponding author: ardyanto.tanjung.fis@um.ac.id

DOI 10.1201/9781003178163-12

2 METHODS

This research used qualitative research methods. The data collection process was carried out in several stages, namely determining the study area, interview, discussion forum, observation and literature study. The interview process was carried out in-depth and semi-structured to several relevant stakeholders. Interviews were conducted in person and by telephone, given the limited access to some areas. Meanwhile, a focused discussion process was carried out with several local communities who took the initiative to make efforts to handle COVID-19 waste. Some of the informants who will be interviewed include the East Java Province COVID-19 Task Force Team, the East Java Provincial Health Office, the East Java Provincial Environmental Service, East Java WALHI, the ITB Environmental Engineering Alumni Association (IATL ITB), Bappenas, PT. Medifast Services and Indonesian Hospital Association (PERSI).

The data analysis instrument is adapted to qualitative methods where the meaning of findings or facts about complex phenomena on the relationships and patterns and configurations between factors. Investigations and evidence of COVID-19 medical waste treatment consisted of the availability of a sanitation unit responsible for Health Care Waste Management (HCWM), HCWM design, HCWM guidelines, waste separation practices, and HCWM technology used by the surveyed hospitals. This fact is a predetermined estimate of the need for health services and the population.

3 RESULTS AND DISCUSSION

Based on data from the Ministry of Health, the number of COVID-19 patients experiencing a graph of increase every day was recorded as of August 31 as being 37,839 in East Java (Task Force for the Acceleration of Handling COVID-19 2020). Based on the data above, there are around 100 hospitals that are used as a reference for handling COVID-19 patients, which can produce a large amount of medical waste along with the increasing trend in the number of COVID-19 patients. As recorded in the 2019 East Java Province Medical Hazardous Waste Inventory and Management Study, the total number of B3/Medical waste piles from 38 Hospitals in Regencies and Cities in East Java were 15,745.94 Kg/day and 5,747.27 Tons/day (Dinas Lingkungan Hidup JawaTimur 2020).

The pile of B3/Medical waste that has accumulated indicates the need for action in good waste management. Management of medical waste from health facilities prior to the pandemic is regulated in the Minister of Environment and Forestry Regulation 56/2015 Procedures and Technical Requirements for Management of Hazardous and Toxic Waste from Health Service Facilities (Bappenas dan Ikatan Alumni Teknik Lingkungan 2020). The regulation describes the stages of waste management starting from reduction and sorting, container and storage, transportation, processing, burial and landfilling. In 2018 the Directorate for Performance Assessment of Hazardous and Non-B3 Waste Management of the Ministry of Environment and Forestry also issued a roadmap related to waste management from health facilities from 2019 to 2028. This is also regulated in Permenkes 7/2019 concerning Home Environmental Health Sick.

In the flow of health facilities medical waste management, this becomes a concern for the environment because B3/medical waste is not handled properly. This can lead to new problems such as the emergence of diseases and environmental damage caused by pollution, so there is a need for serious handling of B3/Medical waste (Saadat et al. 2020). Referring to the Circular of the Minister of Environment for 2020 SE.2 / MENLHK / PLB.3 / 3/2020, the tools used for handling B3/Medical waste are incinerators and autoclaves. However, it does not mean that the incinerator and autoclave tools listed in the Ministerial Regulation can be used just like that, but there are strict regulations in the use of these tools. This is what causes not all hospitals/health care facilities in East Java to have an incinerator due to licensing constraints.

Based on the results of interviews with the Environmental Agency of East Java Province in East Java, the number of hospitals is around 133 units, but only 26 hospitals have medical waste treatment equipment with a thermal method (incinerator) with an operating license. This is a gap when all hospitals can produce waste which is increasing in quantity during the COVID-19 pandemic. However, the amount of utilization of medical waste processing equipment is still insufficient (Bappenas dan Ikatan Alumni Teknik Lingkungan 2020). The city of Surabaya was designated by the Ministry of Health as the Black Zone because it is the largest contributor to positive COVID-19 patients in East Java (Sunuantari & Zarkasi 2020). In the data recapitulation of medical waste generation in East Java in 2019 by DLH, Surabaya City holds the first position with the highest number of medical waste generation with a total of 2,060, 92 tons/year from a total of 5,747.27 tons/year (Dinas Lingkungan Hidup Provinsi Jawa Timur, 2020). Seeing the amount of medical waste produced and the number of hospitals that have licensed incinerators cross, this is an opportunity for third parties to cooperate. However, third parties cooperating with hospitals that do not have a responsibility to manage waste must be in accordance with regulations from the Government, the Ministry of Health, the Environmental Service, and related agencies.

Based on the results of interviews with the Indonesian Hospital Association (PERSI) and the Environmental Service of East Java Province, it was stated that the procurement of medical waste processing equipment had obstacles, including the procurement cost factor, the human resource factor and managing equipment operation permits. In terms of cost factors when referring to PP. No. 101 of 2014 concerning Hazardous Waste Management, the construction of an incinerator tool must be in accordance with the standards, with a chimney height of at least 14m from the ground. Operating costs of the incinerator, equipment maintenance costs and medical waste management costs are often large. The human resource factor in question is the inadequate knowledge of medical waste managers in understanding the good management standards that have been set by the relevant agencies. Finally, related to licensing, in carrying out permits/licensing extensions to operate the incinerator tool, it takes a long time and the criteria that must be met by the agency (hospital) are strict as stated in the legal basis for infectious waste management.

4 CONCLUSION

In summary, COVID-19 cases and victims who die from the pandemic in East Java continue to increase every day. The Indonesian government and the regions were not responsive enough to respond to the COVID-19 pandemic until it was finally declared a national disaster. The increase in the amount of B3/medical COVID-19 waste is a new problem during this pandemic. Medical waste management in East Java, especially in Surabaya, has not been implemented optimally. This is due to the availability of infrastructure, funding, strict licensing and the low human resource capacity for medical waste management. Therefore, special attention is needed regarding the management of B3/medical COVID-19 waste.

REFERENCES

Bappenas dan Ikatan Alumni Teknik Lingkungan, I. T. B. (IATL I. (2020) *Pengelolaan Limbah B3 Medis dan Sampah Rumah Tangga Penanganan COVID-19.*

Davina, D. (2020) 'Limbah APD Berserakan Di Pemakaman, Pemkot Surabaya: Bukan Milik Petugas Makam', *Kompas TV*. Available at: https://www.kompas.tv/article/90444/limbah-apd-berserakan-di-pemakaman-pemkot-surabaya-bukan-milik-petugas-makam.

Dinas Lingkungan Hidup Provinsi Jawa Timu (2020) 'Pengelolaan Limbah B3 Medis Pada Masa Pandemi COVID-19'.

Ilyas, S., Srivastava, R. R. and Kim, H. (2020) 'Disinfection technology and strategies for COVID-19 hospital and bio-medical waste management', *Science of the Total Environment*, 749, p. 141652. doi: 10.1016/j.scitotenv.2020.141652.

Kargar, S., Pourmehdi, M. and Paydar, M. M. (2020) 'Reverse logistics network design for medical waste management in the epidemic outbreak of the novel coronavirus (COVID-19)', *Science of the Total Environment*, 746, p. 141183. doi: 10.1016/j.scitotenv.2020.141183.

Peng, J. *et al.* (2020) 'Medical waste management practice during the 2019–2020 novel coronavirus pandemic: Experience in a general hospital', *American Journal of Infection Control*, 48(8), pp. 918–921. doi: 10.1016/j.ajic.2020.05.035.

Saadat, S., Rawtani, D. and Hussain, C. M. (2020) 'Environmental perspective of COVID-19', *Science of the Total Environment*. Elsevier B.V., p. 138870. doi: 10.1016/j.scitotenv.2020.138870.

Sunuantari, M. and Zarkasi, I. R. (2020) 'Tata kelola black zone COVID-19 berbasis komunitas'.

Yu, H. *et al.* (2020) 'Reverse Logistics Network Design for Effective Management of Medical Waste in Epidemic Outbreaks: Insights from the Coronavirus Disease 2019 (COVID-19) Outbreak in Wuhan (China)', *International Journal of Environmental Research and Public Health*, 17(5), p. 1770. doi: 10.3390/ijerph17051770.

Development, Social Change and Environmental Sustainability – Sumarmi et al (Eds)
© 2021 Taylor & Francis Group, London, ISBN 978-1-032-01320-6

The dynamics of community response to the development of the New Capital (IKN) of Indonesia

A. Kodir*, N. Hadi, I.K. Astina, D. Taryana, N. Ratnawati & Idris
Universitas Negeri Malang, Malang, Indonesia

ABSTRACT: This research focuses on mapping the responses of the actors involved in the development plan for the New Capital (IKN) of Indonesia in East Kalimantan. The research method used is descriptive-qualitative with the main data source through in-depth interviews with several key informers and supporting informants. The results showed that there were three forms of response dynamics to the development of IKN in East Kalimantan. 1) Those who accept the construction of the IKN, this group are optimistic that the existence of the IKN will bring about socio-economic changes in the community for the better. 2) Most of the parties who reject the IKN development consist of indigenous peoples and several NGOs in East Kalimantan. The reasons for rejection were the concern about the land of indigenous peoples in the construction site. 3) Moderate or middle-class parties: this party views the IKN development from two sides.

Keywords: Capital, Development, Dynamics, Indonesia, Response.

1 INTRODUCTION

DKI Jakarta Province, which is currently the State Capital (IKN) of the Republic of Indonesia, has a role as the center of government and the center of the economy. This dual function of authority has caused this area to continue to experience an increase in population. These conditions have not been matched by environmental capabilities and urban planning (Yahya 2018). There are still many problems that have not been resolved, such as floods (Pratiwi & Rahajoeningroem 2020), urban heat islands (Hamdani 2020) air pollution (Gavrila & Rusdi 2020), and river water pollution (Rachmawati et al. 2020).

DKI Jakarta has potential hazards related to the sea and climate change, because the city is located in a coastal area where interactions between land and sea land are occurring. In addition, the burden of buildings and infrastructure above the city of Jakarta causes land subsidence (Ramadhanis et al. 2017). As a result, areas that are located close to the sea will be easily affected by flooding. This problem will get worse if there is an increase in sea level. The complexity of the problems in Jakarta caused the government of the Republic of Indonesia to decide to move one of the functions owned by DKI Jakarta, namely as the center of state government (Hasibuan & Aisa 2020).

It is hoped that the relocation of the National Capital City (IKN) can mobilize residents from Jakarta, so that problems in this city are more easily resolved. Right on Monday, 26 August 2019, the elected President of the Republic of Indonesia (2019–2024) Ir. Joko Widodo officially announced through a press conference that the new location for the IKN was in East Kalimantan Province, to be precise in parts of North Penajam Paser Regency (PPU) and partly in Kutai Kartanegara Regency (Nugroho 2020). After announcing the location of the IKN move, the government began holding competitions related to the IKN city planning design, determining the advisory board, foreign consultants, recruiting special employees to handle the IKN move, and looking for investors.

---

*Corresponding author: abdul.kodir.fis@um.ac.id

DOI 10.1201/9781003178163-13

The government claims that East Borneo is a location which from a geological point of view is very likely to be used as a place for the construction of a new capital city, because it is not included in the red route of Mount Merapi so there is minimal risk of disaster. In addition, according to a written statement by the Head of BMKG Dwikorita Karnawati that although there is a fault structure and has a record of earthquake activity, in general Borneo Island is still relatively safer than other regions or islands in Indonesia (Kurniadi 2019). Apart from that, economic factors are also a strong reason for the gov-ernment to move the State Capital to East Borneo.

So far, the City of Jakarta still dominates the economic cycle in Indonesia (Toun 2018). Business activities centered on the island of Java, especially in DKI Jakarta, have hampered the growth of new economic centers outside Java. The movement of the capital is expected to increase economic equality in Indonesia and the gap between the islands of Java and outside Java. In several studies, it is stated that relocating the capital city will be able to increase the economy by 0.1 0.2% due to the encouragement of new investment (Hasibuan & Aisa 2020).

The plan to relocate the National Capital has generated a variety of responses from various circles, from the government, Non-Government Organizations (NGOs), local communities, to indigenous peoples in the East Kalimantan region, especially in the location of the construction of the State Capital, namely in Penajam. Paser Utara (PPU) and Kutai Kartanegara. This paper will discuss the dynamics of the response from these parties.

2 METHODS

This research uses qualitative methods which are carried out in two stages. First, conducting interviews with several relevant stakeholders, such as: community leaders, village heads, village officials, customary communities, and several nongovernment organizations (NGOs) who are con-cerned with environmental issues. Second, through focus group discussions with local communities. This research was conducted in Penajam Paser Utara (PPU) and Kutai Kartanegara Municipality. The process of determining information using purposive sampling technique. There are several requirements in choosing a participants, namely residents in both locations, both indigenous and nonindigenous, village and subdistrict officials, private parties who own companies around the location, NGOs engaged in the environmental sector.

3 RESULT AND DISCUSSION

Dynamics of Community Response to the Development of the State Capital (IKN) in East Kalimantan in a Political Ecology Approach

Political ecology sees environmental change as not neutral and in a vacuum but a form of "envi-ronmental politics" that involves interested actors at the local, regional and global levels (Bryant & Bailey 1997). This is where we will see how the power of the political economy can influence environmental change. Raymond L Bryant and Sinead Bailey in their book entitled Third World Political Ecology emphasize that there are several actors involved in ecological political issues, including the state, companies or business groups, Environmental Non-Governmental Organiza-tions (NGO), and society (Herdiansyah 2018; Kodir 2019). The four actors have different interests in relation to the case of the development of the State Capital in East Kalimantan, thus giving rise to different perceptions regarding whether or not it is necessary to move the capital city. This has resulted in various pro and contra opinions in response to the IKN development plan.

These pros and cons can be said to be reasonable considering the relocation of the National Capital City (IKN) requires a lot of consideration from various parties to measure the effectiveness of governance in the new capital. Based on the research results, the perception formed in the public is still dominated by negative sentiments. The threat of environmental degradation that has the potential to arise due to development is the reason for refusing to move the IKN (Salsabila & Nurwati 2020). In addition, there are also issues of interest from certain groups behind the development of the IKN in East Kalimantan (Ilmawan, no date). However, there are also groups who agree with the IKN development. The strong reason behind this is the belief that IKN can create socioeconomic changes for the better, especially for the people of East Kalimantan.

3.1 Community groups who are pro against the development of the state capital (IKN) in East Kalimantan

Most of the communities who agree with the development of the IKN in East Kalimantan are those who feel benefited from this project, ranging from local communities themselves, NGOs, investors, to political leaders (Mardhiyah 2020). There are several reasons behind this group agreeing with the development of the IKN in East Kalimantan, among others: first, the land in the area that will be the location for relocating the capital city is in great demand by investors and businesspeople. This is beneficial for local communities who own a large area of land in the area. Land prices experienced a significant increase after East Kalimantan was designated as the location for the new IKN, where per hectare reached a price of 1 billion. In addition, the development of the capital city also requires a large amount of funds. Of course, this is beneficial for investors who will invest in the project.

Second, based on the findings of the East Kalimantan Indonesian Forum for the Environment, there are a number of names from the political elite who support the existence of the IKN (Hutasoit 2019), because they have the potential to benefit from the megaproject. These politicians have extractive industry concessions, namely mining, coal, palm oil, timber, coalfired power plants and giantscale hydropower plants, as well as property entrepreneurs (Nahak 2019). The IKN project is used as a means of whitening the company's sins for environmental destruction due to their activities. This condition is called by Doris Capistrano and Carol J. Pierce Colfer (2006) as elite capture, or the ability of those who have power and wealth to take advantage of new opportunities and increase their power/authority and wealth.

Third, East Kalimantan is considered to be an island that is relatively safe from earthquakes (technical and volcanic) because it is not crossed by faults in the earth's crust and does not have a series of active volcanoes (Kurniadi 2019), so it deserves to be recommended as a candidate for the capital city. Fourth, the proIKN movement groups think that spatially Jakarta is too densely populated, as the center of government, tourism, industry, poor spatial planning, and there are many contradictory land uses. In contrast to the island of Kalimantan, which has quite extensive land availability (Pandit 2019), so that it can compile an ideal capital city layout.

Fifth, the proIKN movement groups also reasoned that by moving the local women it would shift the epicenter of national development from Java to outside Java. This is considered as a strategy for equitable development. So far, economic development has been centered on the island of Java, especially in Jakarta, while people in Kalimantan are still living in limitations. People living in the border area of Kalimantan Malaysia actually have easier access to their basic needs from this neighboring country than from Indonesia, because of the further distance to cities in Indonesia and difficult access to them. The island of Kalimantan is also an area located in the middle of Indonesia, so the proIKN movement groups believe that economic equality will be more easily realized.

3.2 Community groups who counter the development of the national capital city (IKN) in East Kalimantan

Various rejection reactions have also colored the plan to build the State Capital (IKN) in East Kalimantan. In general, the actors who oppose the existence of the IKN development are indigenous peoples, local communities, and NGOs engaged in the environmental sector in East Kalimantan, such as the Indonesian Forum for the Environment (Walhi), Jarangan Mining Advocacy (Jatam) East Kalimantan, Working Group (Pokja 30), Coastal and Fishermen Working Groups, and the Balikpapan Bay Care Forum (FPTB).

The main issue that concerns the contra group is the land problem in Sepaku District, North Penajam Paser Regency (PPU), the location where the capital will be built (Safra & Zuliarso 2020). There are still several villages and subdistricts whose land management systems use customary law or an inheritance system so that they do not have legality over the land, one of which is in Pemaluan village. For people in this village, land is something sacred, as stated by Abiodun Alao (2007) that land is one of the natural resources that must be preserved for future generations. However, this subdistrict is located in Ring 1 of the IKN or the area closest to the development site, causing anxiety for indigenous peoples if their land is taken over by the state without clear compensation because there is no legality.

The community's rejection of the IKN development is not only because of their respect for the environment, but more on their dependence on the environment in which they live. The same thing was said by Raymond L. Bryant that the life of rural communities has a very strong attachment to the environment in which they live. If there are policies that disturb the stability of their place of life, the grassroots actors will defend their environment (ROBBINS 2005).

Another problem that causes people to reject the presence of IKN in East Kalimantan is that the government does not involve them in planning the IKN (Sujana 2019), so that people feel marginalized from their own place of life. This marginalization is perceived by the community as a form of injustice, so that those who feel pressured take up resistance. So far the community has made efforts to meet between traditional institutions in Penajam Paser Utara (PPU) to discuss these issues. However, the customary institutions that attended this meeting were only formal institutions made by the regional government located in the PPU Regency, while the traditional leaders in rural areas were not involved. Even though it is the customary head who better understands the complexity of the problems in their customary territory.

Another reason that causes rejection is that the construction of the IKN will only duplicate the existing problems in Jakarta to East Kalimantan. Based on several studies conducted by NGOs in East Kalimantan, it was found that behind the IKN project there were the oligarchs' dirty business. These findings state that the IKN development is only a mega (sharing) project after the 2019 presidential election. This can be seen from the political supporters of the elected president in 2019–2024, who have a background in coal business in East Kalimantan. The need for coal energy for the needs of the IKN itself is estimated at 1.5 GW (Nugroho 2020), this of course will be a reason to build an even bigger Coal Power Plant industry in East Kalimantan. This industry will certainly have a negative impact on the environment on the island of Kalimantan, as well as the environmental problems currently facing Jakarta.

4 CONCLUSION

The plan to relocate the State Capital from Jakarta to East Kalimantan still requires a more in-depth and comprehensive scientific study so as not to produce rash decisions that will result in the stability of the administration of the state. In general, it can be concluded that the public response to IKN development is still dominated by negative sentiment. This can be seen from the rejection of several parties who do not support the presence of IKN in East Kalimantan. There are various reasons behind this rejection, including: 1) there is no clear protection of the ownership of land belonging to indigenous peoples around the development site, so this project only gives people a sense of worry if their land is taken over by them. 2) The IKN development plan has not involved the local community in making policies. 3) There is an assumption that moving the capital city is the same as moving problems in the old capital to East Kalimantan. Despite the objections, some people also agree with the development of the State Capital in East Kalimantan. The most common reason is the desire for socioeconomic changes for the better for the people of East Kalimantan after the island officially becomes the capital. Besides the pros and cons of the IKN development, there are also those who respond to the IKN neutrally.

REFERENCES

Bryant, R. L. and Bailey, S. (1997) *Third world political ecology*. Psychology Press.

Gavrila, N. and Rusdi, F. (2020) 'Analisis Framing Detik. com dan Kompas. com Terhadap Pemberitaan Kualitas Udara Jakarta Terburuk di Dunia', *Koneksi*, 3(2), pp. 366–371.

Hamdani, R. S. (2020) 'Proyek Lintas Batas Administrasi: Analisis Partisipasi Publik dalam Proses Perencanaan Ibu Kota Negara Republik Indonesia', *Journal of Regional and Rural Development Planning (Jurnal Perencanaan Pembangunan Wilayah Dan Perdesaan)*, 4(1), pp. 43–62.

Hasibuan, R. R. A. and Aisa, S. (2020) 'DAMPAK DAN RESIKO PERPINDAHAN IBU KOTA TERHADAP EKONOMI DI INDONESIA', *AT-TAWASSUTH: Jurnal Ekonomi Islam*, 5(1), pp. 183–203.

Herdiansyah, H. (2018) 'Pengelolaan Konflik Sumber Daya Alam Terbarukan di Perbatasan dalam Pendekatan Ekologi Politik', *Jurnal Hubungan Internasional*, 7(2), pp. 144–151.

Hutasoit, W. L. (2019) 'Analisa Pemindahan Ibukota Negara', *Dedikasi*, 39(2), pp. 108–128.

Ilmawan, M. I. (no date) 'Analisis Isi Pemberitaan Pemindahan Ibu Kota Negara Republik Indonesia di Portal Berita Online Detik. com dan Republika. co. id'. Fakultas Ilmu Dakwah dan Ilmu Komunikasi Universitas Islam Negeri Syarif ….

Kodir, A. (2019) 'Political Ecology of a Spring', *Journal of asian sociology*, 48(2), pp. 179–198.

Kurniadi, A. (2019) 'Pemilihan Ibukota Negara Republik Indonesia Baru Berdasarkan Tingkat Kebencanaan', *Jurnal Manajemen Bencana (JMB)*, 5(2).

Mardhiyah, T. A. (2020) 'WACANA PEMINDAHAN IBU KOTA DI MEDIA SOSIAL (Analisis Wacana Kritis Model Teun A. Van Dijk Pada Youtube Kumparan) SKRIPSI'. IAIN.

Nahak, S. (2019) 'Implikasi Hukum Pertanahan Terhadap Pemindahan Ibu Kota Negara Republik Indonesia Dari Jakarta Ke Kalimantan Timur', *Ganaya: Jurnal Ilmu Sosial Dan Humaniora*, 2(2–2), pp. 31–40.

Nugroho, H. (2020) 'Pemindahan Ibu Kota Baru Negara Kesatuan Republik Indonesia ke Kalimantan Timur: Strategi Pemenuhan Kebutuhan dan Konsumsi Energi', *Bappenas Working Papers*, 3(1), pp. 33–41.

Pandit, I. G. S. (2019) 'Dampak Pengelolaan Lingkungan Hidup Bagi Kalimantan Timur Sebagai Ibu Kota Negara Serta Penyelesaian Sengketa Hukumnya', *Ganaya: Jurnal Ilmu Sosial Dan Humaniora*, 2(2–2), pp. 15–21.

Pratiwi, V. and Rahajoeningroem, T. (2020) 'Perencanaan Prasarana Dan Sarana Sistem Pengendalian Banjir Kota Administrasi Jakarta Pusat', *Indonesian Community Service and Empowerment (IComSE)*, 1(1), pp. 36–44.

Rachmawati, I. pramudita, Riani, E. and Riyadi, A. (2020) 'Status Mutu Air Dan Beban Pencemar Sungai Krukut, Dki Jakarta', *Jurnal Pengelolaan Sumberdaya Alam dan Lingkungan (Journal of Natural Resources and Environmental Management)*, 10(2), pp. 220–233. doi: 10.29244/jpsl.10.2.220-233.

Ramadhanis, Z., Prasetyo, Y. and Yuwono, B. D. (2017) 'Analisis korelasi spasial dampak penurunan muka tanah terhadap banjir di jakarta utara', *Jurnal Geodesi Undip*, 6(3), pp. 77–86.

ROBBINS, P. (2005) 'Political Ecology Oxford: Blackwell Publishing, 2004, 242 p. ISBN 1 40510265 9', *Doc. Anàl. Geogr*, 45, p. 181.

Safra, I. A. and Zuliarso, E. (2020) 'ANALISA SENTIMEN PERSEPSI MASYARAKAT TERHADAP PEMINDAHAN IBUKOTA BARU DI KALIMANTAN TIMUR PADA MEDIA SOSIAL TWITTER'.

Salsabila, A. H. and Nurwati, N. (2020) 'DEFORESTASI DAN MIGRASI PENDUDUK KE IBU KOTA BARU KALIMANTAN TIMUR: PERAN SINERGIS PEMERINTAH DAN MASYARAKAT', *Prosiding Penelitian dan Pengabdian kepada Masyarakat*, 7(1), pp. 27–39.

Sujana, I. N. (2019) 'Penguatan Hak Penguasaan Tanah Adat Masyarakat Hukum Adat di Kalimantan Timur sebagai Rencana Ibu Kota Negara', *Ganaya: Jurnal Ilmu Sosial Dan Humaniora*, 2(2–2), pp. 49–57.

Toun, N. R. (2018) 'Analisis Kesiapan Pemerintah Provinsi Kalimantan Tengah dalam Wacana Pemindahan Ibu Kota Negara Republik Indonesia ke Kota Palangkaraya', *Jurnal Academia Praja*, 1(01), pp. 129–148.

Yahya, M. (2018) 'Pemindahan Ibu Kota Negara Maju dan Sejahtera', *Jurnal Studi Agama dan Masyarakat*, 14(1), pp. 21–30.

Development, Social Change and Environmental Sustainability – Sumarmi et al (Eds)
© 2021 Taylor & Francis Group, London, ISBN 978-1-032-01320-6

Geo-ecological interaction: Community based forest management in Karanganyar, Indonesia

Alan Sigit Fibrianto* & Ananda Dwitha Yuniar
Departmen of Sociology, Faculty of Social Sciences, Universitas Negeri Malang, Indonesia

Ifan Deffinika
Department of Geography, Faculty of Social Sciences, Universitas Negeri Malang, Indonesia

Aulia Azzardina
Department of Accounting, Faculty of Economics, Universitas Negeri Malang, Indonesia

Dina Afrianty
La Trobe University, Melbourne, Australia

ABSTRACT: This study aimed to describe the social life of forest village communities and their participation in LMDH attachments. This research used a geo-ecological approach with a case study qualitative method to describe the relationship between the local com-munity with LMDH, located in Tambak Hamlet, Berjo Village, Ngargoyoso District, Ka-ranganyar Regency. This study uses primary and secondary data. Preliminary data was collected through in-depth interviews, while secondary data was obtained from village monographs. The results show that the management and utilization of forest resources are still thick with local wisdom, such as traditions and rituals. Social and economic character-istics are closely related to geographical conditions. Irrigated agriculture is the dominant activity in the agricultural sector. The use of agricultural land is very suitable for the suita-bility of the ground there. The embededdness between LMDH and the people of Tambak Hamlet, Berjo Village, is at the level of the programs established by LMDH following the characteristics of natural processing and daily community activities.

Keywords: ecology, forest, management

1 INTRODUCTION

National and regional development cannot be separated from village development activi-ties, in its implementation there is nothing that is not feeling the development or can be called "No-one left behind" (CNBC Indonesia 2020; Deswimar 2014; Rahayu 2017; Némethová 2020; Payne 2018; Saberifar & Mishrab 2020; Afifuddin 2010; Akbar et al. 2019; Mardhiah 2017; Bappenas 2020; Hermayana 2019; Khairuddin 2000; Siswijono 2008; ICCTF 2020). Community-driven develop-ment is the development of the concept of people-centered development. The existence of this concept is a reaction to the existing development concepts in economic growth. This concept is a form of social plan-ning to carry out planned social changes, namely, change the community's atti-tudes and social behavior so that they can become empowered and able to carry out development in their environment (Sitorus 2017; Haryanto 2012; Zaenudin et al. 2014; Birgantoro & Nurrochmat 2007; Arifandy & Sihaloho 2015; Theresia et al. 2014; Siagian 2005; Adisasmita 2006; Marbun 1983). Adimihardja and Hikmat (2003) state that a product must come from the community itself,

---

*Corresponding author: alan.sigit.fis@um.ac.id

including a village's development (Sumbi & Firdausi 2016). One type of development carried out by the government in rural areas is establishing the Forest Village Community Institution, or in Indonesia, it is called 'Lembaga Masyarakat Desa Hutan/ LMDH'. LMDH was formed to increase a sense of concern for the forest by not cutting forests carelessly. The establishment of the LMDH in Berjo Village is sharing roles, shar-ing space and time, and sharing results. By involving village communities in forest man-agement, planning, implementation, monitoring, and evaluation will give them deep mean-ing. The mission or activity carried out by LMDH in Tambak Hamlet, Berjo Village, Ngar-goyoso District, Karanganyar Regency is to optimize forest use by managing forests as fruit plantations, the potential for educational tourism, and citronella oil refining. Howev-er, the obstacles faced are the people of Tambak Hamlet, Berjo Village, Ngargoyoso Dis-trict, Karanganyar Regency, most of whom do not know and understand the function of LMDH itself. Therefore, this research's title is "Geo-ecological Interaction: Community Based Forest Management in Karangan-yar, Indonesia." Based on the background of the problem above, the formulation of the situation in this study is how the community's life and the closeness between LMDH and the community in Tambak Hamlet, Berjo Village, Ngargoyoso District, Karanganyar Regency?

2 METHODS

This research used a geo-ecological approach with a case study qualitative method to de-scribe the relationship between the local community with LMDH, located in Tambak Ham-let, Berjo Village, Ngargoyoso District, Karanganyar Regency. This study uses primary and secondary data. Preliminary data was collected through in-depth interviews, while second-ary data was obtained from village monographs (Salim 2006; Miles & Huberman 1992; Moleong 2007).

3 RESULTS AND DISCUSSION

Berjo Village is one of the villages located in Ngargoyoso District, Karanganyar Regency. The town with an area of 1,623,865 hectares is located on the lower slopes of Mount Lawu. When viewed based on the topography, this village is at an altitude of ±800 masl and has a tropical climate with an average temperature of ±22°C–32°C. Girimulyo Vil-lage borders the northern part of Berjo Village; in the east, it is bordered by Mount Lawu forest, the west is bordered by Puntukrejo Village, and to the south, it is bordered by Ta-wangmangu District. The total population in Berjo Village is 5,551 people or 16% of the total population in the Ngargoyoso District. The community of productive age in this vil-lage is 3,741 people. The majority of the population in Berjo Village have a livelihood as farmers and farm laborers. As many as 85% of the total population in this village work as farmers and farm laborers. The second-largest livelihood after farmers is construction or industrial workers, which is 6%, and traders occupy the third position with a total of 4% of the population. The large number of residents who work as farmers and farm laborers is closely related to the geographical conditions of Tambak Hamlet, Berjo Village, Ngar-goyoso District, Karanganyar Regency as one of the villages with high soil fertility poten-tial. It can be seen in Figure 2 that 84 Ha or 5% of the land in this village is rice fields, 92 Ha or 6% of the total area of Berjo Village is a built-up area (settlement), 191 Ha or 12% of the total land area is used as Plantation land, 1,236 Ha or 76% of the whole earth is forest, and 20.87 Ha is another land use. The potential for high soil fertility is utilized by carrying out economic activities in the agricultural sector. Data from BPS (2019) states that around 57% of the land area in Ngargoyoso District is used for rice fields. Berjo is one of the villages that use its land to dominate simple irrigated rice field farming activities. As for the community's economic activities, which in this case, are farmers, apply a subsist-ence economy as their survival strategy. The purpose of a subsistence economy is an agri-cultural financial system by consuming its agricultural products as a fulfillment of daily needs. Berjo Village, Ngargoyoso District, Karanganyar Regency is a village where most of its territory is a forest under Mount Lawu. The existence of natural resources in the form of woods with an area of 1,236 hectares or

76% of the total area of Berjo Village is managed by the surrounding community so that they can be utilized optimally. In terms of forest management, there are three main parties, namely Tamah Hutan Raya, the Indone-sian State Forest Company (Perhutani), and the Forest Village Community Institution (LDMH) (Setiyawan 2019).

The field findings show that the people of Berjo Village have an economic pattern as veg-etable farmers. In contrast, the primary source of income is then supported by several side economic activities and a form of investment in the form of livestock. The vegetable farming community pattern that has existed for a long time is not necessarily the only sec-tor that is highlighted by the people of Tambak Hamlet; there are several parts of life that link the community to their economic system. Several sectors of people's life are indirectly related to their economic system. Thoughts on the economy have many variations of con-cepts; the concept of embeddedness, coined by Marc Granovetter, sees the financial sys-tem as closely related to various external things, such as values and norms, networks where These social relations build the economic system in it. Granovetter's study sees that the economic system will not be separated from the various social relations around it (Granovetter 1985; Swedberg 2003; Blikololong 2012; Chalid 2011; Haryanto 2011). Like in Tambak Hamlet, their economic activities as garden farmers are not only about planting in the fields and producing crops at a particular time, but several things affect the progress of their economic cycle, their welfare, the wealth they have, how to manage their wealth. And others. Some of the dimensions used to study the financial organization of Tambak Hamlet include the leading economy, path dependency, investment, ownership, valuation, and trust. Each of these things has a relationship with the people's lives, using Granovetter's frame of mind to explain that these things have a relationship or attachment to people's lives, so the economic organization there will continue to run and survive. The extension of financial organizations to society will cause a slice or intersection, which causes the two things to have part of one another.

4 CONCLUSION

The embeddedness between the community and the LMDH is at the program level estab-lished by the LMDH because these programs have natural processing characteristics, espe-cially village forests, by the community's daily activities, so it does not require long ad-justments to realize LMDH programs. Analysis of the life of the people of Tambak Ham-let, among others: (a) The community economy; (b) Community investment; (c) Commu-nity ownership; (d) Valuation in society; (e) People's beliefs; and (f) Leadership in the community

REFERENCES

Adisasmita, R., 2006. *Pembangunan pedesaan dan perkotaan*, Graha Ilmu.

Afifuddin, 2010. *Pengantar Administrasi Pembangunan*, Bandung: Alfabeta.

Akbar, G.G., Hermawan, Y. & Karlina, A.L., 2019. Analisis Perencanaan Pembangunan Desa Di Desa Sukamaju Kecamatan Cilawu Kabupaten Garut. *Jurnal Pembangunan dan Kebijakan Publik*, 10(2), pp. 1–8.

Arifandy, M.I. & Sihaloho, M., 2015. Efektivitas pengelolaan hutan bersama masyarakat sebagai resolusi konflik sumber daya hutan. *Sodality: Jurnal Sosiologi Pedesaan, Agustus*.

Bappenas, 2020. "Apa Itu SDGs." Available at: http://sdgsindonesia.or.id/.

Birgantoro, B.A. & Nurrochmat, D.R., 2007. Pemanfaatan Sumberdaya Hutan oleh Masyarakat di KPH Banyuwangi Utara. *Jurnal Manajemen Hutan Tropika*, 13(3), pp. 172–181.

Blikololong, J.B., 2012. Evolusi Konsep Embeddedness dalam Sosiologi Ekonomi (Sebuah Review). *UG Jurnal*, 6(12), pp. 23–29.

Chalid, P., 2011. *Sosiologi Ekonomi*, Jakarta: Universitas Terbuka.

CNBC, I., "No One Left Behind Untuk Kesejahteraan Masyarakat." Available at: https://www.cnbcindonesia. com/market/20200713134319-19-172238/no-one- left-behind-untuk -kesejahteraan-masyarakat.

Devi Deswimar, A., 2014. PERAN PROGRAM PEMBERDAYAAN MASYARAKAT DESA DALAM PEMBANGUNAN PEDESAAN. *Jurnal EL-RIYASAH*, 5(1), p. 41.

Granovetter, M., 1985. Economic action and social structure: The problem of embeddedness. *American journal of sociology*, 91(3), pp. 481–510.

Haryanto, S., 2011. Sosiologi ekonomi. *Yogyakarta: Ar-Ruzz Media*.

Haryanto, T.D., 2012. Pengelolaan Sumberdaya Hutan Bersama Masyarakat Dalam Sistem Agroforestry. *Wacana Hukum*, 10(1), pp. 17–30.

Hermayana, 2019. "Peran Milenial Menyongsong SDGs (Sustainable Development Goals)." *Kompasiana*.

ICCTF, 2020. "Tentang SDGs."

Khairuddin, 2000. *Pembangunan Masyarakat*, Yogyakarta: Liberty.

Marbun, B.., 1983. *Proses Pembangunan Desa*, Jakarta: Erlangga.

Mardhiah, N., 2017. IDENTIFIKASI TUJUAN DAN SASARAN PEMBANGUNAN DESA KABUPATEN ACEH BARAT. *Jurnal Public Policy*.

Miles, M.B. dan H.A.M., 1992. *Analisa Data Kualitatif*, Jakarta: UI Press.

Moleong, L., 2007. *Metodologi Penelitian Kualitatif*, Bandung: PT Remaja Rosdakarya.

Némethová, J., 2020. Comparison of implementation of rural development programmes focussing on diversification in Slovakia in the years 2007-2013 and 2014-2020. *Folia Geographica*, 62(1), pp. 35–51.

Payne, M.I., 2018. Slovak Roma Village of Origin and Educational Outcomes: A Critical Evaluation. *Folia Geographica*, 60(1), pp. 31–49.

Rahayu, D., 2017. Strategi Pengelolaan Dana Desa untuk Meningkatkan Kesejahteraan Masyarakat Desa Kalikayen Kabupaten Semarang. *Economics Development Analysis Journal*, 6(2), pp. 107–116.

Saberifar, R. & Mishrab, P.K., 2020. Analysis of National Development Using Labour Market Model: A Case Study of Khaf. *Folia Geographica*, 1(62), pp. 5–20.

Salim, A., 2006. Teori & Paradigma Penelitian Sosial. *Yogyakarta: Tiara Wacana*, p. 6.

Setiyawan, K.B., 2019. "Modal Sosial dalam Pengelolaan Hutan Rayat: Studi Kasus di Desa Berjo Ngargoyoso Karanganyar Jawa Tengah." *Jurnal Sosial Ekonomi Pertanian*, 15(2), pp. 156–63.

Siagian, S.P., 2005. Organisasi Kepemimpinan dan Perilaku Administrasi, Cetakan Pertama, PT. *Gunung Agung, Jakarta*.

Siswijono, Bambang, dan Wisadirana, D., 2008. *Sosiologi Pedesaan dan Perkotaan*, Malang: Agritek YPN.

Sitorus, Y.L.M., 2017. Community Driven Development In Traditional Communities In Papua. *Journal of Regional and City Planning*, 28(1), pp. 16–31.

Sumbi, K. & Firdausi, F., 2016. Analisis Pembangunan Berbasis Masyarakat dalam Pengembangan Sumber Daya Masyarakat. *Jisip: Jurnal Ilmu Sosial dan Ilmu Politik*, 5(2).

Swedberg, R., 2003. *Principles of Economic Sociology*, United Kingdom: Princeton University Press.

Theresia, A. et al., 2014. *Pembangunan berbasis masyarakat: acuan bagi praktisi, akademisi, dan pemerhati pengembangan masyarakat*, Penerbit Alfabeta.

Zaenudin, Dundin, Anang Hidayat, and T.L., 2014. *"Pengelolaan Hutan Berbasis Masyarakat,"* Polict Brief 02 LIPI.

Development, Social Change and Environmental Sustainability – Sumarmi et al (Eds)
© 2021 Taylor & Francis Group, London, ISBN 978-1-032-01320-6

The development of application for child care services in facilitating distance learning

Rezka Arina Rahma*, M. Ishaq & Sucipto
Department of Nonformal Education, Malang City, Universitas Negeri Malang

Yessi Affriyenni
Faculty of Mathematics and Natural Sciences, Malang City, Universitas Negeri Malang

ABSTRACT: Child Care (Taman Penitipan Anak/TPA) is a form of nonformal Early Childhood Education (PAUD) services that are continuously growing in line with the needs of today's society. During this Covid-19 pandemic, TPA continues to provide learning services but remotely. Therefore, TPA services need to be extended to reach children's activities at home through distance learning. TPA Melati Dharma Wanita Persatuan is one of the nonformal education. The objectives of this study have developed an application for child care services in Covid-19 pandemic era. This research is used to research and development methods (R & D) with 4-D Models. The results showed that the application for child care services is very feasible. The application for child care services received a very good category (88%) from parents/guardians of students as user regarding convenience, suitability, and usefulness of the application. The service model provided at TPA Melati Dharma Wanita Persatuan UM included care services, educational services, health services, and infrastructure services. The services provided by TPA Melati Dharma Wanita Persatuan UM can be accessed through the application so that students still get care services during the Covid-19 pandemic.

Keywords: *Application, Child care Service, Covid-19 Pandemic Era*

1   INTRODUCTION

Children in early childhood are the group of children who are in a unique process of growth and development. They have a specific growth and development pattern that is in proportion to the level of growth and development (Bowman & Donovan 2010; Yulianingsih et al. 2020). During the early childhood period, a child needs education (Gadsden et al. 2016; Huang et al. 2017; Oostdam & Hooge 2013). Therefore, children need a variety of services and assistance from adults to meet their physical and non-physical needs, so that children can grow and develop optimally.

However, the rapid changes in the socio-cultural structure have led to increased life needs and economies so that both parents have to work. This condition causes children to be parted from their parents and reducing the span of attention and affection to children. Thus the attachment of parents and children is then lessened. Whilst, in reality, the presence of both parents is very much needed by the children. For this reason, efforts to minimize the unfulfilled needs of children in their early childhood are required. Appropriate care and education for these children are required, as they are related to the role of child care institutions in the community as the temporary substitute of parents, one of which is Child care (TPA) (Ang 2018; Stearns 2019).

Child care is a form of non-formal early childhood education (PAUD) service that is currently growing in number. One of the TPAs in the city of Malang is TPA Melati Dharma Wanita Persatuan UM that provides childcare facilities for children whose parents are busy working outside their

---

*Corresponding author: rezka.rahma.fip@um.ac.id

DOI 10.1201/9781003178163-15

home. Services for parents for children's needs are important, especially in Covid-19 pandemic era. A policy of learning from home, including early childhood, was implemented. Therefore, services are needed for parents who support parenting activities during the Covid-19 pandemic through virtual learning so that children's needs can be fulfilled.

2 METHOD

This study used the *Research and Development (R&D)* method with 4-D (Four-D Models): *define, design, develop, and disseminate* was adopted from Thiagarajan (Dewi & Akhlis 2016). The define step, therea are several things to carry out are (1) front end analysis, it is determining the fundamental problems in TPA Melati UM during the Covid-19 pandemic, (2) analysis the characteristics users and difficulties experienced, (3) task analysis, it is identifying the main tasks performed by the users according to their needs, (4) concept analysis, it is determining the material presented on the media, and (5) objective analysis, it is formulating indicators of the application for child care services goals. The design step, what is conducted in the design and developed a mobile application-based parenting services on the *Android OS*. The development step is validation by media experts and material experts with continued revisions, and then testing or implementing media. The disseminate step is distribute media in *Google Playstore*.

3 RESULT

3.1 *The development of a mobile application for TPA Melati Dharma Wanita Persatuan UM*

The development of a mobile application for child care in TPA is a form of virtual learning facility, especially during the Covid-19 pandemic. There are 4 (four) menus available in the application including (a) the child's profile; (b) chat service for children's health; (c) child stimulation services; and (d) children's page containing identities and development reports.

The results of the assessment from media experts shows that the overall validation results from media experts are 89.52%, and the category is very feasible.

While, the results of the assessment of material experts shows the percentage of the feasibility of 89.57% and is in the very feasible category. After the media is tested for feasibility, improvements are made, and the media is ready to be tested in the learning process.

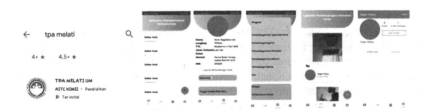

Figure 1. TPA Melati UM's application.

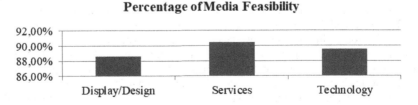

Figure 2. Percentage of media feasibility by validation experts.

Figure 3. Percentage of materials feasibility by validation experts.

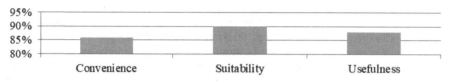

Figure 4. Percentage of media tested by parents/guardians of students as users.

The test results shows that the parents/guardian of students as user believes that the application has a very good value with a percentage of 88%. The application developed is a very feasible to use, easy, in accordance with the characteristics of the user, and useful.

These results are supported by other research that mobile technology can increase parental involvement. In this case, there is collaboration between parents and teachers which is an important step for student achievement (Beecher & Buzhardt 2016; Can 2016).

3.2 *Child care services in TPA Melati Dharma Wanita Persatuan UM*

Child care service

The child care services at TPA Melati UM are provided for children starting from the time they arrived until picked-up, including the setting of safe, comfortable, and protective facilities. In Covid-19 pandemic era, through the application has been developed, parents and teachers can take advantage of the progress report menu every week. Parent-school collaboration with mobile technology is positive to fulfill the need of children (Özdamlı & Yıldız 2014).

Education service

The educational services provided by TPA Melati UM are covering playing and learning activities both indoor and outdoor using Educative Game Tools (APE) to supports children's development. In Covid-19 pandemic era, educational services based on aspects of the development (religious and moral values, cognitive, socio-emotional, physical motor, language, and art) through the "child stimulation services" menu in application. The existence of two-way communication between parents and teachers can supports children's development (Kim 2020).

Health and nutrition service

The nutrition provided at TPA Melati UM is part of its services in the form of providing balanced nutritional food needed by children. The served food is cooked by the manager herself without artificial flavouring, and the menu was consulted with parents beforehand, according to the three pillars of service for health and nutrition: health services, nutritional intake, and psychosocial stimulation (Sadiah et al. 2020). In Covid-19 pandemic era, through a chat menu in applications, the health and nutrition services are still fulfilled and controlled. This menu helps parents to consult with a paediatricians in collaboration with TPA. This application helps various parties (the teacher, the parent, counsellors, health services, and the school management) to work together in fulfilling children's growth (Setyawan et al. 2016).

Facilities and infrastructure

The facilities and infrastructure are in the form of indoor and outdoor facilities, learning infrastructure of buildings, and multipurpose rooms that can be used for playing and studying as well as for sleeping. There are also a kitchen and bathroom, supporting facilities in the form of equipment that supports clean and healthy lifestyle. In Covid-19 pandemic, the application is a media alternative for parents to get care services in TPA Melati UM as an educational institution in implementing distance learning so that it is still carried out well (Dhawan 2020).

4 CONCLUSION

The application for child care services had been validated by media experts (89.52%) and material experts (89.57%). In general, the application for child care services received very good category (88%) from user regarding convenience, suitability, and usefulness of the application. The services provided by TPA Melati Dharma Wanita Persatuan UM can be accessed through the application so that students still get care services, educational services, health services, and infrastructure services in the Covid-19 pandemic.

REFERENCES

Ang, L. (2018). Conceptualising Home-Based Child Care: A Study of Home-Based Settings and Practices in Japan and England. *International Journal of Early Childhood*, 16.

Beecher, C., & Buzhardt, J. (2016). Mobile technology to increase parent engagement. *Interaction Design and Architecture(s)*, *28*(1), 49–68.

B. T. Bowman and S. Donovan. (2010). *Eager to Learn: Educating Our Preschoolers*. National Academy Press.

Can, M. H. (2016). Use of mobile application: Means of communication between Parents and Class Teacher. *World Journal on Educational Technology: Current Issues*, *8*(3), 252. https://doi.org/10.18844/wjet.v8i3.834

Dewi, N. R., & Akhlis, I. (2016). Pengembangan Perangkat Pembelajaran Ipa Berbasis Pendidikan Multikultural Menggunakan Permainan Untuk Mengembangkan Karakter Siswa. *USEJ*, *5*(1), 1098–1108. https://doi.org/10.15294/usej.v5i1.9569

Dhawan, S. (2020). Online Learning: A Panacea in the Time of COVID-19 Crisis. *Journal of Educational Technology Systems*, *49*(1), 5–22. https://doi.org/10.1177/0047239520934018

Gadsden, V. L., Ford, M., & Breiner, H. (2016). Parenting matters: Supporting parents of children ages 0-8. In *Parenting Matters: Supporting Parents of Children Ages 0-8*. The National Academies Press. https://doi.org/10.17226/21868

Huang, C. Y., Cheah, C. S. L., Lamb, M. E., & Zhou, N. (2017). Associations Between Parenting Styles and Perceived Child Effortful Control Within Chinese Families in the United States, the United Kingdom, and Taiwan. *Journal of Cross-Cultural Psychology*, *48*(6), 795–812. https://doi.org/10.1177/0022022117706108

Kim, J. (2020). Learning and Teaching Online During Covid-19: Experiences of Student Teachers in an Early Childhood Education Practicum. *International Journal of Early Childhood*, *52*(2), 145–158. https://doi.org/10.1007/s13158-020-00272-6

Oostdam, R., & Hooge, E. (2013). Making the difference with active parenting; Forming educational partnerships between parents and schools. *European Journal of Psychology of Education*, *28*(2), 337–351. https://doi.org/10.1007/s10212-012-0117-6

Özdamlı, F., & Yıldız, E. P. (2014). Parents' Views towards Improve Parent-School Collaboration with Mobile Technologies. *Procedia – Social and Behavioral Sciences*, *131*, 361–366. https://doi.org/10.1016/j.sbspro.2014.04.130

Sadiah, G. S., Romadhona, N. F., & Gustiana, A. D. (2020). *Penerapan Layanan Kesehatan Dan Gizi Dalam Anak Usia Dini (AUD)*. *17*(1), 50–64.

Setyawan, S. H., Absari, D. T., Limanto, S., & Andre. (2016). The design of mobile application for teacher and parents communication in Indonesian school. *MATEC Web of Conferences*, *58*, 4–8. https://doi.org/10.1051/matecconf/20165803016

Stearns, J. A. (2019). Associations of friendship and children's physical activity during and outside of school_ A social network study. *Population Health*, 10.

Yulianingsih, W., Susilo, H., Nugroho, R., & Soedjarwo. (2020). *Optimizing Golden Age Through Parenting in Saqo Kindegarten*. *405*(Iclles 2019), 187–191. https://doi.org/10.2991/assehr.k.200217.039

Development, Social Change and Environmental Sustainability – Sumarmi et al (Eds)
© 2021 Taylor & Francis Group, London, ISBN 978-1-032-01320-6

Educators' professional ability to manage online learning during the COVID-19 pandemic

S.S Pratiwi, I.H. Al Siddiq, P.P Anzari & M.N. Fatanti
Universitas Negeri Malang, Malang, Jawa Timur, Indonesia

D.F.V. Silvallana
Davao del Norte State Collage, Panabo, Philippines

ABSTRACT: The learning process during the COVID-19 pandemic requires effective and efficient communication. This research was conducted to find out the interpersonal communication provided by teachers through the level of mastery of information technology in the online learning process during the COVID-19 pandemic. The respondents of the study were teachers who were scattered in West Java. The research approach is using a quantitative approach with an explanative method. The results showed that teachers in West Java can recognize information technology tools and are able to use communication tools and applications for online learning. Mastery of teacher technology relates to interpersonal communication which is seen based on aspects of friendliness, attentiveness, openness, argumentation, and responsiveness. Teacher's ability to manage communication technology during online learning relates to optimal online learning. Thus, the teacher's communication skills are related to the ease of implementing the online learning process through available communication tools.

Keywords: online learning, COVID-19 pandemic, interpersonal communication

1 INTRODUCTION

Online learning is a policy issued by the government as a solution to continue to provide educational services to students during the COVID-19 pandemic. Technology plays a big role in organizing synchronous and asynchronous learning activities because the knowledge that has previously been prepared by teachers is transferred through the internet (Nuncio et al. 2020). The implementation of online learning conducted by teachers using various digital platforms shows that the teaching and learning process must continue during disasters (Kapasia et al. 2020). The digital transformation does cause the parties involved in education responsible for education and trying to adapt to the situation (Iivari et al. 2020). The importance of online learning implementation requires supporting facilities and infrastructure as well as the teacher's ability to operate and manage classroom technology tools to the optimum.

However, classroom management through technology requires the ability of teachers to communicate learning instructions clearly and efficiently. Teachers who cannot operate information technology and good communication skills with students will hinder the achievement of learning objectives. Besides, ineffective communication can lead to misunderstandings between teachers and students. Teachers need to carry out their functions properly. The paradigm of evolutionary change proposed by Parson states that society is composed of a set of differentiated sub-systems based on their structure and based on their functional meaning for the wider community (Ritzer & Goodman 2010). So, the teacher has a major role in online learning as a provider of knowledge, giver of direction, and a motivator when the learning process takes place.

DOI 10.1201/9781003178163-16

The learning process according to Vygotsky suggested that students be involved in active learning and the teacher played an active role in accompanying every activity carried out by students. This situation is intended so that students can work in the zone of proximal development while the teacher can still provide scaffolding for students (Anwar 2017). Therefore, teachers need to have good management of the learning environment during online learning. The teacher also needs to clearly instruct the activities that students must do during online learning.

Online learning needs to pay attention to the successful integration of humans, namely students and teachers, with non-human entities, namely learning management (Al-Fraihat et al 2020). Classroom management is also related to how teachers communicate learning material through media intermediaries. Therefore, it is necessary to further investigate how the relationship between mastery of information technology by teachers and interpersonal communication skills during online learning is implemented. This article will explain about the mastery of information technology by teachers with interpersonal communication skills.

2 RESEARCH METHOD

The research approach used is a quantitative approach with an explanative method. The research hypothesis is that there is a relationship between the mastery of information technology by teachers with the dimensions of interpersonal communication. The objective of this research is to accurately explain the relationship between one variable and another (Azwar 2019). Respondents in this study were teachers from various disciplines who tutored students at the high school level who were drawn based on random sampling techniques. The research location is in West Java Province, Indonesia. Taking into account the epidemic of COVID-19, data collection was carried out through questionnaires distributed via a Google form. To obtain basic data from the teacher, questions were formulated about the age and level of education. The analysis was carried out using a Likert Scale with the results of the questionnaire that the respondents had filled in and were analyzed, the validity and reliability of the research instruments were determined, until the testing stage of the research hypothesis. The purpose of this study was to see the relationship between teacher mastery of information technology and interpersonal communication skills during online learning.

3 RESULTS AND DISCUSSION

3.1 *Mastery of various information technologies*

Limitation of school activities due to lockdown cause students to carry out the learning process through applications available on devices (Iwata et al. 2020). Students behavior also changes rapidly, especially to restrictions on interaction in society and the learning process undertaken (Cohen et al. 2020). Viewed from the teacher's point of view, it is necessary to prepare for digital transformation, especially involving teachers, students, and parents to have the skills, competencies, and resources that support educational change. One way that teachers can do this is by mastering communication media to convey and direct the student learning process (Figure 1).

Communication tools are used for the process of delivering teaching materials, learning resources, and evaluating student learning outcomes. During online learning, the teacher can communicate face-to-face using the Google Classroom application, Zoom, and WhatsApp video call (Suni Astini 2020). Based on the research conducted email is the most widely used application during online learning. Besides, there are applications on Google and other applications that teachers use to manage their learning classes.

During online learning, teachers need to be given access to digital learning that is open source and an effective and efficient online learning management system (Kapasia et al. 2020). Learning content is created creatively. The availability of the internet also needs to be considered to support online learning (Nuncio et al. 2020). The communication system via the internet has a

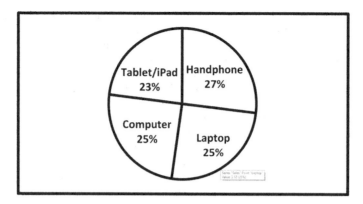

Figure 1. Use of information communication tools.

positive impact based on cost efficiency, extensive learning resources, easy management, and data integration (Puspitorini 2020). When the teacher can master the technological tools and various applications in them, their mastery has implications for the communication carried out with students during the learning process.

3.2 *The teacher ability to create interpersonal communication*

Teacher skills in communicating are social competencies that are used to achieved goals in the learning process (Siahaan 2018). Teacher competence in communicating can be considered as the capacity needed to develop student learning outcomes (Poedjiastutie 2013). The research conducted show that the teacher's interpersonal communication is based on the aspects of friendliness, attentiveness, openness, argumentation, and responsiveness.

Communication through intermediaries in the form of communication tools affects the way teachers perform during online learning. To attract students' attention or create closer relationships, it is necessary to pay attention to student characteristics and the communication tools used. Communication style can be defined as a set of characteristics of a person's speech in communicating which is an indicator of how a person arranges his social relationships (Pânișoară et al. 2015). Communication dimensions that show concern are integrative behaviors to other to facilitate the achievement of group assignments through the suggestions given (Leung & Bond 2001). In the context of learning, the interaction between communication dimensions and previously acquired knowledge affects teaching effectiveness (Liu et al. 2019). The communication that is carried out when online learning is not much different from learning in class, the teacher needs to adjust several things to support online learning.

4 CONCLUSION

The condition of COVID-19 pandemic forces teachers to use information technology as the main medium of learning. Therefore, the more proficient teachers are in using information technology, the more it will affect the effectiveness of communication. The aspects used to show the teachers interpersonal communication with students are friendliness, attentiveness, openness, argumentation, and responsiveness. Judging from the research conducted, the teacher already can operate information technology tools that support online learning. Teachers have also been able to upload subject matter, carry out the teaching process, and evaluate learning through applications during online learning. There is no significant difference when the teacher conducts classroom learning with online learning, it's just that in some cases the teacher still needs to carry out its functions optimally and adapt to the updates that occur.

REFERENCES

Al-Fraihat, D., Joy, M., Masa'deh, R., & Sinclair, J. (2020). Evaluating E-learning systems success: An empirical study. *Computers in Human Behavior*, *102*(August 2019), 67–86. https://doi.org/10.1016/j.chb.2019.08.004

Anwar, C. (2017). *Teori-teori Pendidikan*. (Y. Arifin, Ed.) (Pertama). Yogyakarta: IRCiSoD.

Aucejo, E. M., French, J., Araya, M. P. U., & Zafar, B. (2020). The Impact of COVID-19 on Student Experiencess and Expectations: Evidence From Survey. *Journal of Public Economics*. https://doi.org/10.1016/j.molliq.2020.112490

Azwar, S. (2019). *Metode Penelitian* (XVI). Yogyakarta: Pustaka Pelajar.

Boussakssou, M., Hssina, B., & Erittali, M. (2020). Towards an Adaptive E-learning System Based on Q-Learning Algorithm. *Procedia Computer Science*, *170*, 1198–1203. https://doi.org/10.1016/j.procs.2020.03.028

Choudhury, S., & Pattnaik, S. (2020). Emerging themes in e-learning: A review from the stakeholders' perspective. *Computers and Education*, *144*(September 2018), 103657. https://doi.org/10.1016/j.compedu.2019.103657

Cohen, A. K., Hoyt, L. T., & Dull, B. (2020). A Descriptive Study of Coronavirus Disease 2019–Related Experiences and Perspectives of a National Sample of College Students in Spring 2020. *Journal of Adolescent Health*, *67*(3), 369–375. https://doi.org/10.1016/j.jadohealth.2020.06.009

Iivari, N., Sharma, S., & Ventä-Olkkonen, L. (2020). Digital transformation of everyday life – How COVID-19 pandemic transformed the basic education of the young generation and why information management research should care? *International Journal of Information Management*, (June), 102183. https://doi.org/10.1016/j.ijinfomgt.2020.102183

Iwata, K., Doi, A., & Miyakoshi, C. (2020). Was school closure effective in mitigating coronavirus disease 2019 (COVID-19)? Time series analysis using Bayesian inference. *International Journal of Infectious Diseases*, *99*, 57–61. https://doi.org/10.1016/j.ijid.2020.07.052

Jouanjus, E., Lapeyre-Mestre, M., Nodot, M., Roussin, A., Franchitto, N., Boyes, J. P., ...Dupouy, J. (2019). Teaching Basic Knowledge on Substance Use Disorders: The Impact of e-Learning on Health Professionals. *Clinical Therapeutics*, *41*(10), 2154–2161. https://doi.org/10.1016/j.clinthera.2019.07.012

Kapasia, N., Paul, P., Roy, A., Saha, J., Zaveri, A., Mallick, R., ... Chouhan, P. (2020). Impact of lockdown on learning status of undergraduate and postgraduate students during COVID-19 pandemic in West Bengal, India. *Children and Youth Services Review*, *116*(June), 105194. https://doi.org/10.1016/j.childyouth.2020.105194

Leung, S. K., & Bond, M. H. (2001). Interpersonal communication and personality: Self and other perspectives. *Asian Journal of Social Psychology*, *4*(1), 69–86. https://doi.org/10.1111/1467-839X.00076

Liu, J., Zhang, R., Geng, B., Zhang, T., Yuan, D., Otani, S., & Li, X. (2019). Interplay between prior knowledge and communication mode on teaching effectiveness: Interpersonal neural synchronization as a neural marker. *NeuroImage*, *193*(September 2018), 93–102. https://doi.org/10.1016/j.neuroimage.2019.03.004

Nuncio, R. V., Arcinas, M. M., Lucas, R. I. G., Alontaga, J. V. Q., Neri, S. G. T., & Carpena, J. M. (2020). An E-learning outreach program for public schools: Findings and lessons learned based on a pilot program in Makati City and Cabuyao City, Laguna, Philippines. *Evaluation and Program Planning*, *82*(May), 101846. https://doi.org/10.1016/j.evalprogplan.2020.101846

Pânşoară, G., Sandu, C., Pânşoară, I.-O., & Duţă, N. (2015). Comparative Study Regarding Communication Styles of The Students. *Procedia – Social and Behavioral Sciences*, *186*, 202–208. https://doi.org/10.1016/j.sbspro.2015.04.066

Poedjiastutie, D. (2013). HOW DOES TEACHER S' COMMUNICATION COMPETENCE IN INDONESIA LOOK LIKE?*.

Puspitorini, F. (2020). Strategi Pembelajaran Di Perguruan Tinggi Pada Masa Pandemi COVID-19. *Jurnal Kajian Ilmiah*, *1*(1), 99–106. https://doi.org/10.31599/jki.v1i1.274

Ritzer, G., & Goodman, D. J. (2010). *Teori Sosiologi Modern*. (T. W. B. Santoso, Ed.) (6th ed.). Jakarta: Prenada Media Group.

Schunk, D. H. (2012). *Learning Theories* (Bahasa Ind). Yogyakarta: Pustaka Pelajar.

Siahaan, A. T. A. A. (2018). Keterampilan Komunikasi Guru Profesional di Sekolah. *Ijtimaiyah*, *2*(1), 1–16.

Suni Astini, N. K. (2020). Tantangan Dan Peluang Pemanfaatan Teknologi Informasi Dalam Pembelajaran Online Masa Covid-19. *Cetta: Jurnal Ilmu Pendidikan*, *3*(2), 241–255. https://doi.org/10.37329/cetta.v3i2.452

Syaripudin, T., & Kurniasih. (2013). *Pedagogik Teoritis Sistematis*. (T. Syaripudin, Ed.) (5th ed.). Bandung: Percikan Ilmu.

Development, Social Change and Environmental Sustainability – Sumarmi et al (Eds)
© 2021 Taylor & Francis Group, London, ISBN 978-1-032-01320-6

Learning style from face-to-face to online learning in pandemic COVID-19 (the case study at East Java)

Desy Santi Rozakiyah*, Indah Yasminum Suhanti & Seli Septiana Pratiwi
Universitas Negeri Malang, Malang City, Indonesia

ABSTRACT: Distance education has been an alternative education during COVID-19 pandemic. This education is undertaken by children from different economic conditions. During the pandemic, there is no difference between children from high and low-income economies. This study was designed to determine how the education during the pandemic in Indonesia differentiates from one region to another. The study employed qualitative research with a case study approach. The results showed that students received a different education apart from distance education during the pandemic. In the odd-even semester, face-to-face learning was carried out at the junior and senior high school levels. In the elementary school setting, learning activities were done in the form of small study groups with face-to-face learning activities. In the university context, learning was carried out online or referred to as asynchronous and was done using media spaces such as Zoom, Google Meet and Google Classroom as a means of delivering material.

Keywords: distance learning, learning media in pandemic

1   INTRODUCTION

The impact of SAR-CoV-2 disease pandemic known as the Coronavirus (COVID-19) has become a factor for debate in carrying out education (Pozo-Rico et al. 2020). Emile Durkheim explained that in the sociological study of education, the existence of a process in education can develop children through socialization and interaction between friends (Pavlyshyn et al. 2019). The impact of learning changes during the pandemic base on psychology experiences students were stress and difficult (Wood et al. 2012). Therefore, during the pandemic, learning requires a new habit that all people never carried out in online learning (Panigrahi et al. 2018). Changing the paradigm of thinking in this pandemic period requires hard work and learning changes from face-to-face to online learning (Neuhauser 2002). The main characteristic of online learning is using technology to participate in learning and meeting in virtual situations (Paechter & Maier 2010). Changing the paradigm of community thought or the thoughts of parents of students is very difficult because this pandemic has changed traditional learning to online learning, and this is needed as habituation in learning online, and student change their learning style from face to face to online learning. The concept of home learning has never been a discourse in national education. However, an epidemic like this forces the community to change the learning pattern to digital learning as a form of the popular education revolution in 2020 where children carry out school at home, which is a very difficult challenge for students' parents (Howland et al. 2006). The application of online learning has so far been limited to the use of internet networks, unlike in other countries, but the existence of a physical distancing policy to cut the spread of the epidemic forcing changes in formal education in school to being forced to learn from home with a national-scale online system. It means forcing parents and students to use online learning (Shalev-Shwartz 2011). For Indonesian people, using

---

*Corresponding author: desy.rozakiyah.fis@um.ac.id

online learning is indeed very difficult and requires readiness. The most important thing is parents in accompany child in learning activity although they are not ready with the digital technology in education process.the problem of internet network access is that it is not available or reliable in all areas.

2 REVIEW OF RELATED LITERATURE

Implementing an online education system is not easy. In addition to personal discipline for independent learning, some facilities and resources must be provided. Since implementing education in this pandemic era, the most important thing has become safety to reduce the risk of children and teachers being affected by the COVID-19 disease pandemic (Alauddin et al. 2020). According to (Maslow 1987) related to needs of human needs depend on basic fulfilment, how the human get information in around as to prevent direct physical contact with other people this is a from of preventing the transmission of COVID-19. (Berry et al. 2020). Little consideration is needed to predict the impact of face-to-face learning activities during a pandemic (Monto et al. 1985). Closing schools aims to reduce the transmission of the COVID-19 pandemic (Chao et al. 2010). Learning online or distance learning is indeed very difficult for the community because there are various characteristics of the environment that must be considered, especially the availability of facilities at home for learning online (Moore et al. 2011). It takes patterns and habits for students and parents to accompany online learning. In addition, the ministry of education also issued policies related to the implementation of the curriculum in educational units in special conditions since the school system during the pandemic was not operating as usual. However, with a disease pandemic like this, a change in the learning paradigm must be carried out according to environmental conditions or school climate. This learning pattern can be seen in the learning theory known as behaviorism which shifted to constructivism, meaning that students construct knowledge through learning processes not transferred from teacher to student (Deschesnes et al. 2003). The importance of learning media used by schools can also assist students in participating in learning activities. The teacher's role in providing motivation to students is due to online learning, which results in students feeling bored in learning. Thus, the importance of the role as a teacher in motivating children is so that students can follow learning as well (Rurik et al. 2011). The role of accompanying teachers and parents during the pandemic is felt by all parents of students in accompanying and carrying out education at home (Subramani & Venkatachalam 2019). From the results of research conducted by Hadi et al (Pajarianto 2020), the characteristics of learning carried out by children can cause differences in participating in learning activities. In short, it is caused by the facilities in home learning which depends on the awareness of the parents in assisting learning and the willingness to provide facilities for their children.

The prominent role of teachers and parents during the COVID-19 pandemic is to work together to succeed in distance learning. Therefore, cooperation is needed in providing motivation and learning support to children (Daniel 2011). As a form of implementing learning during a pandemic like this, teachers usually do it by applying a lot of learning models and methods, only applying student-centered learning and student creativity. These learning patterns are needed, which are called strategies in developing learning components with the aim of achieving learning. Parents' roles in schools contains humanistic behavior because they must pay attention to their students as holistic learners. Holistic learners have cognitive and affective needs, and the role of parents is to understand their children deeply, especially concerning psychological conditions (Suryani 2013).

3 METHOD

A field study is aimed to gather information from teachers, parents, and students. Thus, identifying patterns and behavior of teachers, parents and students in implementing this home learning. Thus, the results of this study examine face-to-face learning changes into online schools known as distance learning. Teachers, parents, and students were selected through sampling in the form of snowball sampling and then asked to be interviewed for 1 hour. Semi-structured interviews were conducted. Respondents were asked to explain how learning has transitioned from face-to-face to online. Interviews in the analysis used the basic theory as described by Creswell (Creswell 2009). The data collected was examined through a cooperative approach to classify the similarities and differences in the participants' perspectives involved in online learning activities. The coding process was undertaken to develop categories and themes which were carefully linked to the existing literature. In the end there will be research findings. The research credibility was obtained by prolonged involvement and intensive discussions with respondents.

4 RESULT AND DISCUSSION

Based on the findings, parents, teachers and students have difficulty following online learning and the workload of parents has also increased. Characteristics of online learning experience by students ranging from elementary school education to university levels is different because of elementary implementation learning like grouping student, while secondary school, senior high school and university get used to use online learning. The findings during the study showed the level of use of instructional media spaces used by students from elementary school to the university level, online learning media such as WhatsApp, Zoom, Google Meet, and Google Classroom were identified. For elementary education, the learning media room used was the WhatsApp learning media because parents find it easier to use and assist their children's learning activities. In addition, for schools that are in the red zone, students will be greeted by their teachers through Zoom and Google Meet. Junior high school, senior high school, and university students use WhatsApp, Zoom, Google Meet and Google Classroom. But something is interesting in high school education, which is that they carry out learning by applying odd and even student absences to take turns doing face-to-face learning at school. As for the university level, apart from the learning media space used, lecturers deliver material through videos uploaded to YouTube and podcasts as a medium for delivering material to students.

Many parents complain and cannot follow and overcome the problems experienced by their children. But it is different for the parents of students who have a higher educational background and who are younger to monitor and guide their children in carrying out learning activities. In addition, the psychology of students in carrying out online education starts from elementary school and impacts up to university levels. Students tend to be bored and lazy in following the learning that takes place. This is motivated by the teacher's many tasks in almost every subject and the fact that they have to complete the assignment given by the teacher.

Carrying out education during a pandemic is very difficult since it needs cooperation between teachers and schools and readiness in carrying out school at home (Daniel 2020). Parental support is very important for children to support learning activities during a pandemic like this. The goal is to maintain psychological and physical health. In carrying out learning activities in children (Alivernini & Lucidi 2011), psychological service readiness is also prepared to maintain the health of children and adults during a pandemic, as well as a form of concern and handling during a pandemic (Bell et al. 2020). As parents, providing support in carrying out education is not as usual because skills in assisting children in carrying out learning tasks while at home are very difficult things and need many aspects that need attention (Uchino 2009). In addition to perceived social support for predicting student perceptions, control and identification with schools to foster children's academic achievement, thereby reducing the likelihood of children dropping out of school (Fall & Roberts 2012). The existence of a platform in learning activities carried out by teachers and students in carrying out learning activities such as learning through Zoom, WhatsApp and Google Classroom as a form of teacher policy in conveying learning occurs (Thalheim et al. 2003). This is because a lockdown that affects the learning system and patterns is not implemented as school would normally be. This media is used starting from elementary school to tertiary education instead of learning the E-learning system (Lee 2006). In addition, learning during a pandemic like this is more focused on learning (student centered) and a constructivist approach. In addition, the role of the teacher uses the context of learning methods where students are required to learn independently. During a pandemic like this, the use of textbooks that teachers usually given to students are now turning to digital books as a means of development and learning (Maki et al. 2000).

5 CONCLUSION

Changes in student learning styles caused by the COVID-19 disease start from how to change the paradigm and behavior patterns of students and parents in accompanying them while home learning is in progress. It can be proven how parents and teachers need habituation and readiness to assist children in carrying out school at home. Online learning application took many risks experienced by students, starting from parents who cannot use technology, lack of internet networks and the barrier of children carrying out online learning feeling bored due to the teacher's large number of tasks to students.

REFERENCES

Alauddin, M. et al. (2020) 'How can process safety and a risk management approach guide pandemic risk management?', *Journal of Loss Prevention in the Process Industries*. doi: 10.1016/j.jlp.2020.104310.

Alivernini, F. and Lucidi, F. (2011) 'Relationship between social context, self-efficacy, motivation, academic achievement, and intention to drop out of high school: A longitudinal study', *Journal of Educational Research*. doi: 10.1080/00220671003728062.

Bell, D. J. et al. (2020) 'Health service psychology education and training in the time of COVID-19: Challenges and opportunities', *American Psychologist*. doi: 10.1037/amp0000673.

Berry, L. L. et al. (2020) 'Service Safety in the Pandemic Age', *Journal of Service Research*. doi: 10.1177/1094670520944608.

Chao, D. L., Elizabeth Halloran, M. and Longini, I. M. (2010) 'School opening dates predict pandemic influenza A(H1N1) outbreaks in the United States', *Journal of Infectious Diseases*. doi: 10.1086/655810.

Creswell, J. W. (2009) *RESEARCH DESIGN Qualitative, Quantitative, and Mixed Methods Approaches*, *SAGE Publications*. doi: 10.2307/1523157.

Daniel, G. (2011) 'Family-school partnerships: Towards sustainable pedagogical practice', *Asia-Pacific Journal of Teacher Education*. doi: 10.1080/1359866X.2011.560651.

Daniel, S. J. (2020) 'Education and the COVID-19 pandemic', *Prospects*. doi: 10.1007/s11125-020-09464-3.

Deschesnes, M., Martin, C. and Hill, A. J. (2003) 'Comprehensive approaches to school health promotion: How to achieve broader implementation?', *Health Promotion International*. doi: 10.1093/heapro/dag410.

Fall, A. M. and Roberts, G. (2012) 'High school dropouts: Interactions between social context, self-perceptions, school engagement, and student dropout', *Journal of Adolescence*. doi: 10.1016/j.adolescence.2011.11.004.

Howland, A. et al. (2006) 'School Liaisons: Bridging the Gap between Home and School', *School Community Journal*.

Lee, Y. C. (2006) 'An empirical investigation into factors influencing the adoption of an e-learning system', *Online Information Review*. doi: 10.1108/14684520610706406.

Maki, R. H. et al. (2000) 'Evaluation of a Web-based introductory psychology course: I. Learning and satisfaction in on-line versus lecture courses', *Behavior Research Methods, Instruments, and Computers*. doi: 10.3758/BF03207788.

Maslow, A. H. (1987) *Motivation and personality, 3rd ed.*, *Motivation and personality, 3rd ed.*

Monto, A. S., Koopman, J. S. and Longini, I. M. (1985) 'Tecumseh study of illness. XIII. Influenza infection and disease, 1976-1981', *American Journal of Epidemiology*. doi: 10.1093/oxfordjournals.aje.a114052.

Moore, J. L., Dickson-Deane, C. and Galyen, K. (2011) 'E-Learning, online learning, and distance learning environments: Are they the same?', *Internet and Higher Education*. doi: 10.1016/j.iheduc.2010.10.001.

Neuhauser, C. (2002) 'Learning Style and Effectiveness of Online and Face-to-Face Instruction', *International Journal of Phytoremediation*. doi: 10.1207/S15389286AJDE1602_4.

Paechter, M. and Maier, B. (2010) 'Online or face-to-face? Students' experiences and preferences in e-learning', *Internet and Higher Education*. doi: 10.1016/j.iheduc.2010.09.004.

Pajarianto, D. (2020) 'Study from Home in the Middle of the COVID-19 Pandemic: Analysis of Religiosity, Teacher, and Parents Support Against Academic Stress'.

Panigrahi, R., Srivastava, P. R. and Sharma, D. (2018) 'Online learning: Adoption, continuance, and learning outcome—A review of literature', *International Journal of Information Management*. doi: 10.1016/j.ijinfomgt.2018.05.005.

Pavlyshyn, L. et al. (2019) 'Ethical problems concerning dialectic interaction of culture and civilization', *Journal of Social Studies Education Research*.

Pozo-Rico, T. et al. (2020) 'Teacher training can make a difference: tools to overcome the impact of COVID-19 on primary schools. An experimental study', *International Journal of Environmental Research and Public Health*. doi: 10.3390/ijerph17228633.

Rurik, I. et al. (2011) 'Knowledge, motivation, and attitudes of Hungarian family physicians toward pandemic influenza vaccination in the 2009/10 influenza season: Questionnaire study', *Croatian Medical Journal*. doi: 10.3325/cmj.2011.52.134.

Shalev-Shwartz, S. (2011) 'Online learning and online convex optimization', *Foundations and Trends in Machine Learning*. doi: 10.1561/2200000018.

Subramani, C. and Venkatachalam, J. (2019) 'Parental Expectations and Its Relation to Academic Stress among School Students'.

Suryani, A. (2013) 'Home-School Interaction: Remodelling A Framework Of Parents-Teachers Relationship For Supporting Students'learning', *JURNAL SOSIAL HUMANIORA (JSH)*, 6(1), pp. 1–19.

Thalheim, B., Binemann-Zdanowicz, A. and Tschiedel, B. (2003) 'Content modeling for e-learning services', in *Proceedings of the 7th World Multi-Conference on Systemics, Cybernetics and Informatics (SCI 2003)*.

Uchino, B. N. (2009) 'Understanding the Links Between Social Support and Physical Health: A Life-Span Perspective With Emphasis on the Separability of Perceived and Received Support', *Perspectives on Psychological Science*. doi: 10.1111/j.1745-6924.2009.01122.x.

Wood, L., Ntaote, G. M. and Theron, L. (2012) 'Supporting Lesotho teachers to develop resilience in the face of the HIV and AIDS pandemic', *Teaching and Teacher Education*. doi: 10.1016/j.tate.2011.11.009.

Development, Social Change and Environmental Sustainability – Sumarmi et al (Eds)
© 2021 Taylor & Francis Group, London, ISBN 978-1-032-01320-6

Private school reform through learning community: Evidence from Muhammadiyah School

L.A. Perguna*, H. Sutanto & J.H.G. Purwasih
Universitas Negeri Malang, Malang City, Indonesia

ABSTRACT: Private schools are facing a dilemma. Schools must continue to look for students to maintain their income as well as improving education's quality, both of which required hard work. This article focuses on how private schools improve the quality of their learning through teacher learning communities on Lesson Study through the SWOT analysis. A qualitative method was used to explore schools' reformation through teachers' learning communities within junior high private schools. The results showed that the Lesson Study provided positive changes for both teachers and school development following the relationship building of trust and openness principle. Learning communities that have been formed with the Lesson Study principles provided changes not only in the learning-based process but also in schools' development. The reformation of private class to the public sphere affects schools' reformation.

Keywords: Reform, Lesson Study, Learning Community, Private School, Public Philosophy

1 INTRODUCTION

The 4.0 industrial revolution continuously echoed coinciding with the pandemic presence that has changed the entire structure of society, from bureaucracy to civil society and the education sector. Education must be ready to face the upcoming changes, including changes in learning patterns from traditional old learning systems to digital and virtual learning. All education stakeholders must act and be prepared in facing these changes. Simultaneously, education must also be vigilant to repress the negative impact of science and technology development (Stepanek 2001). At the forefront of education, schools and all their elements must be adaptive and adoptive in facing challenges in this disruptive era. The students are digital natives, which is different from the teachers who are digital immigrants. Thus, the demands to change are enormous following the bigger challenge to face (Germain-Mc Carthy 2013).

Looking through the history of Indonesia, the public and the private sector's role in education cannot be underestimated. Historically, private education had been a driving key element of education in the country. The Islamic boarding school, which is mostly managed by the *Nahdlatul Ulama* social organization, and schools managed by the *Muhammadiyah* organizations long before Indonesia independence are examples. Now, with the presence of the 4.0 industrial revolution and the pandemic, the real challenge of digitization is materialized within the learning system. This big challenge demands bigger changes, especially for private schools. Many private schools are developing and growing, but the number of private schools that started to collapse also escalates.

There are various ways for schools to improve, one of which is through Lesson Study (LS) which has been recognized by teachers and educators in many countries. LS is a professional teacher development effort to improve teaching and student learning through practice-oriented, student learning- focused, collaborative and observation-based research which is conducted by the

---

*Corresponding author: luhung.fis@um.ac.id

DOI 10.1201/9781003178163-18

teacher or the learning community (Bell & Gilbert 2004; Fernandez 2002; Fernandez & Yoshida 2004; Murata & Takahashi 2002; Wang-Iverson & Yoshida 2005). Regardless of the high number of researchers and schools using the LS as a professional development approach, LS remains relatively new in Indonesia with various additional issues, especially in private schools located on the outskirts of Surakarta city. LS's functions in the teaching learning process in schools, including its contributions to school development, are discussed in this article.

2 METHOD

The research used a qualitative descriptive approach with various data collection techniques. To collect data, researchers interacted with informants or participants and reported the observation results. Researchers conducted participatory observations on learning communities based on LS, involving teachers at school, and carried out LS learning activities from the planning stage, open lesson and reflection. The study documentation was carried out by collecting school curriculum data and school development blueprints. Focus group discussions were carried out with the related informants, while the data analysis was completed using informants' answers based on the research focus. The research location was SMP (Junior High) Muhammadiyah 2 Surakarta, Indonesia. The data were obtained purposively from the school's person in charge of the LSLC, the school's committee, teachers, students and students' parents. The data analysis was conducted by triangulation to see how LSLC impacted schools.

3 RESULT AND DISCUSSIONS

3.1 SWOT in lesson study based learning community

In the midst of high demands, private schools must be creative and innovative in developing and pursuing schools to grow more advanced. Once they are not creative and innovative, they may lose social capital and students, which results in schools' closing. In Surakarta, at least four private schools have been shut down. Failure in acquiring students becomes one of the main reasons. Besides, the collapse is also caused by many closely related factors such as lack of facilities and infrastructure, human resources factors including an institution's limited creativity and discrimination between private and public schools by the community and even the government. This became a record and reflection for the other private schools in Surakarta, including Muhammadiyah schools as part of private schools. There are 42 Muhammadiyah schools in Surakarta, ranging from elementary to senior high schools. At the junior high school level, there are 8 SMP and 1 Madrasah Tsanawiyah. All schools had experienced a fluctuating development with a different number of students. Thus, schools are required to make breakthroughs within their development.

One of the breakthroughs that have been implemented is building Learning Community (LC) with LS principles and characteristics. In March 2018, a Learning Community was formed at the school. There are two goals set for its establishment. The first goal is to facilitate teachers to learn and discuss professional development in learning. This LC also involves the school's principal not as a leader but as a member of the LC. The principle of "monologue," which the principal often used, was changed to the principle of "dialogue." After intensive discussion, LC implements ways of making the previously private class, owned by teachers with the subject being taught, becoming public property following LS's characteristics. This school's publicly owned class is the first public class of Muhammadiyah School in Surakarta. The public class allows anyone to attend and participate in the learning process. Students' parents are allowed to observe the students learning in class. This is a means of promoting the school to the public.

Several stages of LS, starting from lesson design, the open lesson to reflection, are carried out through the learning community. The preparation of lesson design is not solely conducted by the class teachers but together with the other teachers who have free time. They have a discussion

Table 1. SWOT in establishing LS-based schools

Strength	**Weakness**
Homogeneous Teacher-Student. The majority of the teachers are digital natives who have a high desire to learn and change. The principal is very supportive of school development policies, including the LS program. The lesson design is on only 1 page, which made teachers interested. Teachers get a lot of input from peer-to-peer records in LS.	Student input are the remnant from public schools. Students' families with a lower-middle economy focus on their respective Obs. Teachers are busy with administrative affairs. It takes time to change student and teacher behavior from individual to inquiry-based collaborative learning.
Opportunities	Threat
The *Muhammadiyah* Foundation fully supports school activities Schools are free to determined school development policies	Support from the government is different from that of the public schools. Stigma against private schools rather than public schools both economically and academically LSLC is yet to be a national policy

to find the best strategies and models for learning based on the observations they have done before. The principle of no students should be left behind in learning is primarily used in the process of preparing lesson design. The dialogue principle, collaborative and active education is also emphasized in its formulation. This design is made on only one sheet of paper with the main components of introduction - core activities - closing activities along with its objectives and learning indicators (Purwasih & Perguna 2018)

As the time is determined, the next step is Open Lesson. The teachers who carry out this activity are invited LC members, teachers from other schools, and students' parents in that class. Classes that are often held exclusively for students and teachers now become open. This openness is a symbol that teaching is not a monologue and didactic and is also a symbol of building trust with the public. Simultaneously, support from all parties is needed to achieve the desired quality in learning activities. Classroom learning that emphasizes inquiry activities, a two-way dialogue of students' ideas, and meaningful content exploration facilitated by the teacher is a very challenging endeavor. Invited teachers and guests observe the class focusing on student learning rather than how the teacher teaches.

After the open class, reflection is carried out to see whether students can focus on learning, whether they have difficulties in focussing and the reasons behind that. Some of these questions came up in the reflection stage. The reflection results contain several alternative solutions in learning to be followed up in the next open class with a different teacher. These three processes are new methods and have deconstructed the teacher's behavior in their comfort zone. This emphasis on student learning in the LS process reminds the teachers of the importance of understanding students' ideas and helps them to bring a reformation vision within their classrooms. Classroom reformation from private to public (micro-level) will impact schools' reformation (macro-level). In one year, the school had carried out the class reform activities for 4 LS cycles. This figure is considered high for schools that have just practiced the LS.

Researchers as observers in LS activities in school use Mead's term of the Looking Glass Self by using the SWOT analysis (Strength, Opportunities, Weakness, Threat), especially in a micro-scale that occurred in schools, as presented in Table 1.

LS-based learning facilitates value changes that have been deeply rooted in learning. Teachers are preoccupied with many school's administrative matters and rarely have the opportunity to see other teachers or even discuss their teaching. The teachers focus more on students getting good grades or being different from others. In teaching, the teacher relies on familiar, repeated routines and roles in the classroom, such as giving homework, giving assignments in class, delivering material and new skills, and asking students to practice them (McLaughlin & Talbert 2006). This was done for teachers as teaching is a personal activity. There are values and norms (cultural conservatism) that inhibit and oppose traditional teacher norms from learning from one another (Collinson & Cook 2006; Hiebert & Stigler 2017). The norms barrier is both cultural and structural. This LS community-based learning is gradually reforming the individualist, conservatism classroom to dialogic and collaborative inquiry-based learning (McLaughlin & Talbert 2006; Vescio et al. 2008). Teachers' communities are more likely to innovate efficiently, as teachers need knowledge and various pedagogical strategies for learning. This community mediates those necessities due to collegial interactions that occur through meetings and observations.

4 CONCLUSION

In the community, as homo socius, teachers interact on developing and re-developing their skills, knowledge, beliefs and philosophy of teaching and learning. The concept of learn-unlearn-relearn is carried out by teachers in the community. This study explains how Lesson Study-based learning communities, with their advantages and disadvantages, have succeeded in reforming teachers' learning. Through the community, teachers learn that teaching is an active dialogue and collaborative effort to plan the lesson designs that lead to students' success in education. This paradigm shift takes a reasonably long period of at least one year. This study provides evidence that individualism and conservatism can shift toward collectivity as long as there is goodwill from schools' principals and the foundations. The teacher and classroom reformation carries a multiplier effect for schools in becoming more open and democratic.

REFERENCES

Bell, B. and Gilbert, J. (2004) 'A model for achieving teacher development', *The Routledge Falmer reader in science education*, pp. 258–278.

Collinson, V. and Cook, T. F. (2006) *Organizational learning: Improving learning, teaching, and leading in school systems*. Sage.

Fernandez, C. (2002) 'Learning from Japanese approaches to professional development: The case of Lesson Study', *Journal of Teacher Education*. doi: 10.1177/002248702237394.

Fernandez, C. and Yoshida, M. (2004) 'Lesson Study: A case of a Japanese approach to improving instruction through school-based teacher development'. Mahwah, NJ: Lawrence Erlbaum.

Germain-Mc Carthy, Y. (2013) *Bringing the NCTM standards to life: Exemplary practices for middle school*. Routledge.

Hiebert, J. and Stigler, J. W. (2017) 'Teaching Versus Teachers as a Lever for Change: Comparing a Japanese and a U.S. Perspective on Improving Instruction', *Educational Researcher*. doi: 10.3102/0013189X17711899.

McLaughlin, M. W. and Talbert, J. E. (2006) *Building school-based teacher learning communities: Professional strategies to improve student achievement*. Teachers College Press.

Murata, A. and Takahashi, A. (2002) 'Vehicle To Connect Theory, Research, and Practice: How Teacher Thinking Changes in District-Level Lesson Study in Japan.'

Purwasih, J. H. G. and Perguna, L. A. (2018) 'MENGENALKAN LESSON STUDY MELALUI PELATIHAN GURU DI LINGKUNGAN MADRASAH ALIYAH KABUPATEN MALANG', *Jurnal Praksis dan Dedikasi Sosial*. doi: 10.17977/um032v0i0p80-86.

Stepanek, J. (2001) 'A New View of Professional Development.', *Northwest teacher*, 2(2), p. 2.

Vescio, V., Ross, D. and Adams, A. (2008) 'A review of research on the impact of professional learning communities on teaching practice and student learning', *Teaching and Teacher Education*. doi: 10.1016/j.tate.2007.01.004.

Wang-Iverson, P. and Yoshida, M. (2005) *Building our understanding of Lesson Study*. Research for Better Schools.

Development, Social Change and Environmental Sustainability – Sumarmi et al (Eds)
© 2021 Taylor & Francis Group, London, ISBN 978-1-032-01320-6

Women in education: A review of Indonesian feminism

Yuliati*, M.N.L. Khakim & Idris
Universitas Negeri Malang, Malang City, Indonesia

ABSTRACT: Suwardi Suryaningrat or better known as Ki Hajar Dewantara, is one of the legendary teachers of Indonesia. Politicians, educators, humanists, statesmen and other titles have been held by him. Few people know that his character also includes being a feminist. Ki Hajar Dewantara's thoughts about Indonesian women, especially Javanese published in Wasita Rini, should be known and used as a timeless reference. Wasita Rini emphasizes important teachings for women regarding the concept of freedom, discipline, morality and the role which contains women's rights and obligations. This teaching is useful for Indonesian girls or women to remain virtuous in utilizing their independence.

Keywords: Women, education, Indonesian feminism.

1 INTRODUCTION

The majority of Indonesian historical writings are written by men so that historical works give the existence of this country like men (androcentric). This is proven by (Purwanto & Nursam 2006) through the example of Abdurrachman Suryomihardjo's dissertation which describes social development in Yogyakarta that seems to be only carried out by men. The female historian, Darsiti Soeratman, apparently still used the male narrative when writing the World Life of Kraton Surakarta in 1930, while Djuliati Suroyo did not discuss gender inequality in revealing labor during the Cultivation Period in Kedu. Then Asvi Warman Adam, a historian at LIPI, in his essay, made clear Bambang Purwanto's statement that the three historians' dissertations were guided by a senior historian who was loyal to the field of history, namely Sartono Kartodirdjo (Adam 2007). From there, Purwanto and Nursam (2006) concluded that consciously or not, the historiographic reality of women has been neglected as part of the historical process of Indonesia. The androcentric history of Indonesia was also stated by Asvi Warman Adam, which was filled with political and military topics, which had the dimensions of male strength in wars and power struggles. Asvi Warman Adam then opened our memories of the opinion that was once expressed by Kuntowijoyo to start a business with the theme of women in historical research, (Soeri Soeroto & Frederick 1928) which had also been suggested.

Therefore, it is important to write women's histories in line with the times. This study aims to complement our previous research on the history of women in Indonesia (Yuliati et al. 2019; Khakim et al. 2020). One of the important figures who initiated education for women in the early days of Indonesian independence was Ki Hadjar Dewantara. Suwardi Suryaningrat or better known as Ki Hajdar Dewantara is known as a pioneer figure in education in Indonesia. The role of Ki Hajar Dewantara in developing Indonesian education is based on local wisdom values. During the Dutch colonial period until independence in Indonesia, education was primarily for men. However, not many people know that Ki Hajdar Dewantara has paid attention to education for Indonesian women. This article aims to discuss how education and gender equality according to Ki Hajar Dewantara became a foundation in developing Indonesian women in the future.

---

*Corresponding author: yuliati.fis@um.ac.id

DOI 10.1201/9781003178163-19

2 METHOD

The method of this research is literature study. Literature research method or literature study is a way of activities related to data collection methods, reading, reviewing and recording and analyzing research materials (Zed 2004). This research method was in accordance with the preparation of this article because it used books, journals, and articles related to Ki Hadjar Dewantara's Review about women's education in Indonesia. The researcher read all the literature on the history of Ki Hadjar Dewantara's review about women's education in Indonesia and then noted and summarized the essential parts. The results of the summary were analyzed by historical methods.

This literature study method was complemented by the historical method because the focus of this study was on Ki Hadjar Dewantara's Review about women's education in Indonesia. This historical method was properly selected because it upholds interpretation and analysis in historiography. The historical method is a way or steps in rebuilding past events, through four stages of research, namely heuristics, source criticism, interpretation, and historiography (Hamid & Madjid 2011). Heuristics or collecting reference sources on Ki Hadjar Dewantara's review about Women Education in Indonesia. It was complemented by a critique of the accuracy of relevant reference sources. Interpretation from each source was used to reconstruct Ki Hajar Dewantara's review about women's education in Indonesia. Historiography was used to write the results of reconstruction chronologically and scientifically.

3 RESULT AND DISCUSSION

The most essential women's problems that cannot be denied is their nature. Women's nature is a reality that is not undeniable, that becomes the right and a pointer if people think about women (Dewantara 1928). Women's nature in Indonesia is different from woman's nature in Europe. In Europe, women have struggled hard to get various kinds of equality with men. The aspirations that women want to achieve in Europe are indeed right, but the movement to get equality with men eventually leads to conditions that fail to match the nature of women.

The emancipation of European women fights for the equality of rights and equality in every aspect. Equality of rights is no longer becomes their single demand, but equality in various aspects, such as in dressing, getting pleasure, life, work and so forth. The description of the European women's struggle who demand equality in all fields of life at that time was considered harming their natures by Ki Hadjar Dewantara. They forget that a woman's body is different from a male body. The difference is related to the nature of women who should be mothers, get pregnant, and give birth.

Women's issues become important issues. A woman is the symbol of the perfection of human life. During the life of a woman, the divine command of God instructed to guard them, because if there is purity there is a contradiction, which can plunge women into disgrace and misery.

Problems about women for Tamansiswa are not only confusing to the realm of education but also developing into other domains, for example, politics and economics. Consequently, its effects cannot be predicted in advance. In an article addressed to the police, Ki Hajar Dewantara reminded of the duty of a police officer to maintain order and peace in the community, so that the customs of the people in charge must be known. For example, a Javanese proverb that reads "earth's smile, a bath of water, acts of death." This proverb shows us that all disputes between our communities regarding the struggle over land even though only a few inches of land and power struggles over women, even if only in the form of a forehead is usually brave. According to the opinion of Europeans who have different customs with Indonesian people, the above issue of femininity is considered as an insignificant problem, even kissing a person's wife, that are considered strange by our customs, may be judged only by a fine of 2.5 rupiahs, which is considered an unfair trial by us (Ki Hajar et al. 2002).

In the proverb above, women as the descendants that must be pure in their lives both physically and mentally. Every now and then there should not be any doubt about whom men are entitled to participate in the derivative that was born by the woman. In the multiplication, according to natural law women are the descendants of descendants, while men are the masters of descent. In this respect, the law of each country determines the rights and obligations of husband and wife, as well as father and mother. For this reason, marriage intends to eliminate the doubt as much as possible. Likewise, religious rules and traditions in the community aims to purify marriage between two humans, men and women that have been legalized by state law.

The proverb *"senyari bumi sedumuk bathuk"* contains the symbol of the immortality of human life in the world. The dead man expects his offspring to remain in the world. Consequently, it causes the derivative in human life is considered an important matter, as it seems to be "eternity" or "immortality." Since women give birth to a child, then they are considered as a symbol of immortality in the world and therefore human beings can save their lives to protect the purity of the life of women who are their dependents (Dewantara 2002).

Ki Hajar Dewantara's legacy aimed at women was Wasita Rini, a song in Javanese (*tembang*) with the song Asmarandana. Wasita Rini means advice for women. Its contents are about the teachings of decency as a provision to get personal safety. Ki Hajar Dewantara does not elaborate on this teaching in detail, with the intention that women are more flexible in giving interpretations, adapted to space and time or nature and time, so that they can think and act creatively, without leaving the subject matter.

The granting of poetry forms to Wasita Rini is intended to allow users of this teaching to easily remember its contents. Besides, the contents of the text are expected to not be easily displaced. Wasita Rini was composed around the 1940s, during which Javanese society had had several old (fiber) books containing advice for women, for example, Wulang Puteri, Wulang Estri and Wasitaning Istri (Soeratman 1996). Its complete verse is interpreted below.

1. The teachings of femininity, in ancient times and now, are both indispensable. Both of them intend to keep the women pure, safe and avoiding dangers.
2. The difference in this age is called the era of independence, where the whole community against the power and authority of others. That's how women do not like to be treated by others.
3. Remember women, independence does not just mean free from the command of others, but also must be strong and capable of self-control. Therefore, do not forget that rights and obligations are inseparable.
4. The so-called obligation is all the readiness and willingness of birth and mind. It follows the right to self-will. Remember that you have scales to weigh what is good and what is not.
5. Women who maintain the spirit of independence must know the importance of the intelligence of hope and the creation of life independence, while morality is a safety fence for the women.

In relation to the widespread expansion of free life, Ki Hajar Dewantara emphasizes this teaching on the implementation of the concept of "independence" and "morality." According to Ki Hadjar, independence is one of human nature, which is sublime and beautiful. Meanwhile, morality is the nobleness and beauty of human life. Independence which is culturally human nature has two properties of external nature that is free or loose from the coercion or other commands of the other, and the inner nature, which is independent or stand-alone (Dewantara 1964a).

Human virtue shows the nature of his inner life, for example, conviction about purity, freedom, justice, divinity, love, loyalty, order, peace, sociality and so forth. Decency or subtlety shows the subtle and beautiful outward nature of man. Teaching about nobility or attitude and morality also teaches all human rights and obligations, both as a person and as a member of society (Dewantara 1964b).

Ki Hajar Dewantara's teachings for women in the form of discourses entitled Sengkala Candra and song lyrics are part of the entire education system that applies anywhere not only in the Taman Siswa neighborhood. It uses to challenge an increasing number of elements of foreign culture borrowed, especially those from the West, including social courtesy among teenage boys and girls. The teachings used in Tamansiswa, for example, Wasita Rini can still be used as a guide. Wasita Rini, who gave the basic concepts of independence and decency, is quite flexible in its implementation following the development of society, especially the relationship between women and men who increasingly wanted freedom in the association. In this case, it is necessary to inculcate the use of rights and obligations that must be balanced under the status that is carried.

4 CONCLUSIONS

Education by Suwardi Suryaningrat was given the connotation of planting the seeds of independence, namely only independent warriors who were able to win independence. It begins by joining the Tuesday Kliwon Circle of Friends which aims to bring about the happiness of self, nation and humanity. The Circle of Friends was dissolved after its goal was realized with the establishment of Tamansiswa. For advice directed at women, Ki Hajar Dewantara has created a song entitled Wasita Rini. In Wasita Rini's lyrics, it is explicitly mentioned that the rights and obligations of someone are essentially inseparable, appearing together equally. This is the foundation of the real understanding of democracy.

In addition, Tamansiswa also established a women's dormitory, called Wisma Rini, whose management was handed over to Tamansiswa Women. Wisma Rini was a dormitory that was used as a residence for female students whose homes were far away because Tamansiswa was a school in the form of a schoolhouse. It is a school that is also used as a house for the tutors so that students could feel at home.

REFERENCES

Adam, A. W. (2007) 'Perempuan Dalam Sejarah Lelaki', *Jurnal Perempuan*, 52, pp. 7–18.
Dewantara, K. H. (1928) 'Nature of women', *Wasita*, I, p. 80.
Dewantara, K. H. (1964a) 'Azas-azas dan Dasar-dasar Tamansiswa', *Majelis Luhur Tamansiswa*, a.
Dewantara, K. H. (1964b) 'Pendidikan', *Majelis Luhur Tamansiswa*, b.
Dewantara, K. H. (2002) 'Women's Community Development Center "Nyi Hadjar Dewantara"', *Problem Women in Yogyakarta*.
Hamid, A. R., & Madjid, M. S. (2011) *Pengantar Ilmu Sejarah*. Ombak.
Khakim, M. N. L. *et al.* (2020) 'Identification of tourism potentials in Ancient Bathing Sites of Pasuruan, Indonesia', in *IOP Conference Series: Earth and Environmental Science*. doi: 10.1088/1755-1315/485/1/012099.
Ki Hajar, Dewantara & Dewantara, N. H. (2002) *Wanita*. Pusat Pengembangan Komunitas Perempuan Nyi Hajar Dewantara.
Purwanto, B. and Nursam, M. (2006) *Gagalnya Historiografi Indonesiasentris?!* Ombak.
Soeratman, D. (1996) *Dari Ki dan Nyi Hajar Dewantara sampai Pergerakan Wanita Indonesia*. BP Wanita.
Soeri Soeroto and Frederick, W. H. (1928) *Pemahaman sejarah Indonesia?: sebelum dan sesudah revolusi*. Jakarta: LP3S.
Yuliati, Y., Hakim, N. L. and Towaf, S. M. (2019) 'Kartini's Contribution in Developing the Art of Carving Macan Kurung Jepara (1903)', in. doi: 10.2991/icskse-18.2019.27.
Zed, M. (2004) *Metode peneletian kepustakaan*. Yayasan Obor Indonesia.

Development, Social Change and Environmental Sustainability – Sumarmi et al (Eds)
© 2021 Taylor & Francis Group, London, ISBN 978-1-032-01320-6

The woman's international migration: Controlling rural land by women workers

M. Zid* & A.R. Casmana
Universitas Negeri Jakarta, DKI Jakarta, Indonesia

ABSTRACT: This study aims to examine the characteristics of international migration undertaken by Indonesian women. Women's international migration generally aims to meet social-economic needs, as well as to be able to improve the quality of one's life financially. The research method used in this study is qualitative with case studies conducted in two villages, namely Panyingkiran Village and Ciherang Village. The results of this study indicate that in general, after international migration for financial needs, the average remittance obtained from abroad is used to buy land. More specifically, the land that was bought by the women workers was rice fields with an average area of one to two hectares. It aims to develop their business and as a tool for investment in the future. In addition, the destination country which is mostly used as a place to work in the Middle East country.

Keywords: International migration, women, remittances, land tenure.

1 INTRODUCTION

International labor migration by women from Panyingkiran Village and Ciherang Village-West Java can be interpreted as a socio-geography as a strategy as well as a response in facing life difficulties faced by rural households. Various difficulties faced by poor households in rural communities include inequality in ownership and ownership of agricultural land between social strata, inequality of various accesses, inequitable allocation and control of economic resources (Khoo & Yeoh 2018). Faced with various difficulties in life, each individual and household from various social strata will have different strategies. Efforts to get out of various livelihood difficulties by (Ellis 2000) is referred to as "survival strategies" and "coping strategies" which can be interpreted as a livelihood strategy undertaken a household when faced with difficulties. This economic action was intentional by households with high motivation to satisfy most basic needs, at least at a minimum level, in accordance with the social and cultural norms of the community (Ellis 2000).

Ellis (2000) explains in more detail that the strategies adopted by households to survive and improve living standards include migrating for work, both in cities and as workers abroad. For households that have limited access and agricultural land, one strategy that many family members do is to make the final choice by sending a family member. Usually, a daughter or wife - to become an international workforce overseas (Parreñas et al. 2019). Difficulties in life and the uncertainty of achieving a better life in the area of origin encourages rural women who come from disadvantaged groups, and hopes to improve their standard of living by working as a migrant in Malaysia, one of the uses of remittances used to purchase land (Butt, Ball and Beazley 2016). The rationality of an individual and family support to improve economic life and change social statuses such as getting a channel with more opportunities to become international workers in Asia Pacific countries such as Malaysia, Singapore, Hong Kong, Taiwan, South Korea, and Eastern countries Central, especially

---

*Corresponding author: aseprudi@unj.ac.id

DOI 10.1201/9781003178163-20

Saudi Arabia which still needs female workers to be employed in the domestic sector as domestic servants (PRT) which are known as jobs that are categorized as dirty, dangerous and difficult (dirty, dangerous, and difficulty) (Liao & Gan 2020).

Migrants are interested in utilizing remittances for land because of the consideration that land as a resource, for rural residents who make a living as farmers, has economic value, and at the same time high social value (Platt et al. 2016). In other words, there is a close emotional bond between the farmer and the land he owns, as stated by Spaan and van Naerssen in 2018, that there is an emotional connection between the farmer and the land. Based on this formulation, the first question in this study is: "what is the use of remittances obtained from abroad after international migration?"

2 METHOD

This research is a case study by taking two villages, namely Panyingkiran Village, Rawamerta District, Karawang Regency, and Ciherang Village, Pasawahan District, Pur-wakarta Regency. Consideration of the use of case studies that the topic examined in this research is a phenomenon that is happening now in the context of real-life in the form of international migration of women, land tenure and gender equality in rural areas, especially in the two villages where the research took place. The type of data collected is primary and secondary data. Primary data obtained directly from the results of in-depth interviews (in-depth interview) with respondents and key informants. To complete the data, an FGD was conducted, which was followed by respondents, key informants. Secondary data is data obtained from the results of searches on archives, documents ranging from the level of the research village, Rawamerta and Pasawahan sub-districts, the Department of Man-power and Transmigration, BPS Karawang and Purwakarta Districts, as well as the IPB, UI, National and LIPI libraries. In this study, the data collected was analyzed using a combination of quantitative methods and qualitative methods, with more emphasis on qualitative methods.

3 RESULTS AND DISCUSSIONS

3.1 *Utilization of remittans and land tenure*

Land tenure by women migrants and their families is the main focus of this study. Land has an important meaning for them because most of the female migrants come from families of tunakisma farmers who make a living as farm laborers and other lower-class jobs (Listiani 2018).

The 104 female migrants from the villages of Panyingkiran and Ciherang with a working period of between four to twenty-two years are able to buy land, although in a narrow size. Most of them buy land on land, with varying sizes, the smallest land that women migrants can afford is enough to cover 60 square meters, while the largest is 800 square meters. The most extensive field of rice that can be purchased by female migrants is 1 hectare at each purchase. Findings in both villages show that a migrant, in general, can only afford to buy land after going back and forth working abroad at least three times the contract period or in the seventh and eighth years of work.

The ability of a migrant to buy land occurs after the basic needs of the family and household can be met. Thus, the use of remittances sent during the first to fourth year is generally used only to provide food and to renovate or build permanent houses (Hasanah, Mendolia and Yerokhin 2017). Only migrants who are tenacious and work several times overseas can afford to buy land. Most migrants are only able to buy land in a limited size; this is because land prices are relatively lower when compared to the price of rice fields. Only 37 times the purchase of rice fields by women migrants from Panyingkiran and Ciherang Villages. The most rational reason is that the price of rice fields continues to increase from year to year, and it is impossible to reach them with the wages they receive as domestic workers (Platt 2018). It can be seen from an example of three Indonesian women who were migrating abroad.

There are three women migrants - one from a pioneer generation of migrants, and two from a generation of followers - who have managed to collect money from the sweat of their years of work in Saudi Arabia and accumulate wealth, including purchasing agricultural land in the form of rice fields. They are ITA (36 years), N.Yt (34 years), and Mas (65 years). ITA is a former female migrant from Panyingkiran Village who has managed to accumulate the proceeds of work for nine years into a variety of wealth such as land and paddy fields, which amounts to approximately 3.5 hectares, four-wheel open-air vehicles, and a shop for agricultural production facilities that provide various fertilizers and medicines.

N.Yt, a female migrant from Ciwelut-Panyingkiran village, was able to buy a 2-hectare rice field, and a land area of 600 square meters. Before leaving to become a domestic worker in Saudi Arabia, her parents' work was only as a "single" and a farm labourer for a wealthy family in her village. At present the economic conditions of the N.Yt family and parents can be categorized as "Jelema boga" or people who obtain provisions of daily food from the harvest of rice fields and the benefits of opening a stall in their village. Meanwhile, Mas, one of the pioneering migrants and the longest working in Saudi Arabia, who is 21 years old, was able to buy six units of paddy land which covers an area of approximately 2.5 hectares, and the entire paddy field has been distributed to five children who are married, so the economic condition of his children is even better when compared to his condition.

Regarding various slanted and unpleasant accusations from its neighbors, ITA only revealed the following:

> I had heard the words of my friends and neighbours which makes me uncomfortable to hear, which is when I brought quite a lot of money from the middle east, and when I took two months off in the village, I was sent money by the employer to buy tickets back to the middle east, according to proverbs, until so the subject of village discussion, he said, I was made into a mistress's wife in a rich Arab household. But my family and I have never paid any attention to it, if it is served, it hurts, and finally the slanted talk goes away" (Interview, 3/23/2011).

Mr. ITA, namely Sup, who is a retired civil servant in class II has the consideration that his son is not likely to be strong working continuously abroad, and his son must also be married. Therefore, he feels obliged to 'nyakolakeun' or manage the money sent by his son to in the form of paddy soil and a little land. All purchases are always with the knowledge of ITA, and the purchase is in ITA's own name. According to Sup, the price of paddy land in Panyingkiran Village from year to year the price continues to rise, because it includes a first-class rice field with good irrigation, so that the yield is always profitable.

The meaning of land, in this case for migrants and their families who come from the lowest strata in the countryside or in the terminology of the local community is called the "jelema teu boga" group, very crucial; this is because it has a high social and economic function among other social functions as a backup to build a house for the family, where the house is the basic needs of every family (Liao & Gan 2020). Economically, land functions as a savings when migrant families experience shocks due to various life difficulties such as a disaster. So land is one way out as a form of a coping strategy for every migrant family.

3.2 *Building a permanent house*

Being able to build a house, especially a permanent home, is the desire of all families because home is a basic need for everyone. In addition, the house is also often used as a measure of social status in society (Yuniarto 2016). One form of success of a migrant working abroad, among others, can be seen from the house which is generally built quite well for the size of the countryside. All women migrants claimed that the money from working abroad was used to repair or build houses, and that was the case with the second or third departure (Yuniarto 2016). Building a house in general in a gradual way was done. One of the remittance effects that women migrants send to families in the village of origin is the emergence of business opportunities in the non-agricultural sector (Butt et al. 2016). This was captured by those who previously owned land, especially those located around the village roadside. The emergence of stalls that sell daily necessities, food stalls, equipment kiosks and mobile phones (HP), water refill kiosks, retail gasoline kiosks are a form of business that is often chosen by migrant families. One of the migrants in Panyingkiran, who is quite successful, ITA (36 years), has a kiosk that sells a variety of agricultural production materials (saprotan) in the form of fertilizers, pesticides, spray equipment, farming equipment such as hoes, sickles and various other items needed by farmers.

The strategy of migrants is that migrants who have stalls or kiosks are building networks and emotional ties with consumers so that consumers are bound and continue to be loyal customers of their stalls or kiosks. In an interview with Cas (53 years old), a farmer in the distance of distance from Posta-Panyingkiran village, Cas claimed that for the sake of fertilizing and treating his rice fields of approximately two hectares, all were supplied by the ITA-Tas kiosk. The reason for using Cas, besides the fact that they have long known each other, ITA-Cas also allows the payment behind the alias ngebon, and pais during the harvest season, of course, with prices that have been adjusted. This condition is very helpful for Cas, because as a farmer, he has never held enough cash to capitalize his farming business. The reciprocal relationship that leads to this exchange is actually a more mutual form of protection where each party gets a balanced benefit.

4 CONCLUSION

This part contains the abstraction from the analysis previously presented, as well as to answer the questions and objectives of this study. Firstly, the socio-geographical setting of Panyingkiran and Ciherang Villages as agriculture-based villages places land tenure as an important element as capital to meet various needs, the land is also a measure of social strata in rural communities that are still agriculture-based. Secondly, this then became a motive for women in both regions, namely Panyingkiran Village and Ciherang Village to choose overseas migration even though they had to work in the domestic sector, namely as domestic servants as hazardous jobs and was known as dirty, dangerous and dangerous. Difficult (3 D) which has not been sought after and abandoned by local workers. Thirdly, this type of work in the domestic sphere is very vulnerable to exploitation from before departure, in the country of work, to return to the country. Fourthly, economic problems in the form of low tenure of agricultural land, lack of employment in rural areas, poverty, are the most determining factors in determining the motive for migrating rationality. In addition, a measure that still often does not receive attention is the socio-psychological aspect of the decision to migrate from rural women. At this level, education, skills, migrants possess, plus information about the language, culture of the destination country of work, working conditions are very influential in the individual's decision to migrate. Finally, international networks and the use of remittances are other important aspects of improving family welfare and severing dependence on international migration.

REFERENCES

Butt, L., Ball, J. and Beazley, H. (2016) 'False papers and family fictions: Household responses to 'gift children'born to Indonesian women during transnational migration', *Citizenship Studies*, 20(6–7), pp. 795–810.

Ellis, F. (2000) *Rural livelihoods and diversity in developing countries*. Oxford university press.

Hasanah, A., Mendolia, S. and Yerokhin, O. (2017) 'Labour migration, food expenditure, and household food security in eastern indonesia', *Economic Record*, 93, pp. 122–143.

Khoo, C. Y. and Yeoh, B. S. A. (2018) 'The Entanglements of Migration and Marriage: Negotiating Mobility Projects among Young Indonesian Women from Migrant-sending Villages', *Journal of Intercultural Studies*, 39(6), pp. 704–721.

Liao, T. F. and Gan, R. Y. (2020) 'Filipino and Indonesian migrant domestic workers in Hong Kong: their life courses in migration', *American Behavioral Scientist*, 64(6), pp. 740–764.

Listiani, T. (2018) 'Analysis of the Characteristics of Circular Migration: The Case of Female Domestic Workers from Rural Indonesia', *Journal of Policy Science*, 26(1), pp. 149–163.

Parreñas, R. S. et al. (2019) 'Serial labor migration: Precarity and itinerancy among Filipino and Indonesian domestic workers', *International Migration Review*, 53(4), pp. 1230–1258.

Platt, M. et al. (2016) 'Renegotiating migration experiences: Indonesian domestic workers in Singapore and use of information communication technologies', *New Media & Society*, 18(10), pp. 2207–2223.

Platt, M. (2018) 'Migration, moralities and moratoriums: Female labour migrants and the tensions of protectionism in Indonesia', *Asian Studies Review*, 42(1), pp. 89–106.

Spaan, E. and van Naerssen, T. (2018) 'Migration decision-making and migration industry in the Indonesia–Malaysia corridor', *Journal of Ethnic and Migration Studies*, 44(4), pp. 680–695.

Yuniarto, P. R. (2016) 'Indonesian Migration Industry in Taiwan: Some socio-economic implications and improvement challenges', *Jurnal Kajian Wilayah*, 6(1), pp. 17–33.

Development, Social Change and Environmental Sustainability – Sumarmi et al (Eds)
© 2021 Taylor & Francis Group, London, ISBN 978-1-032-01320-6

Analysis of population vulnerability towards the spread of COVID-19 in Malang Raya from a spatial perspective

Purwanto*, Ike Sari Astuti, Ardyanto Tanjung & Fatchur Rohman
Universitas Negeri Malang, Malang, Indonesia

ABSTRACT: This study aimed to analyze the characteristics of the population's vulnerability to the spread of COVID-19 in Malang Raya from spatial perspectives. We use an elderly population of 60+ to analyze the spatial characteristics of regional vulnerabilities and spatial analysis of the spread of COVID-19 in Malang Raya from March-June 2020. Also, we divide population vulnerability zones into two zones, by distinguishing vulnerabilities by gender. The main findings are as follows: (1) based on the analysis results, rural areas are more vulnerable to the spread of COVID-19. A strong immune system causes COVID-19 not to develop in rural areas. (2) The spatial distribution of COVID-19 in Malang Raya is still concentrated in urban areas with distribution patterns following accessibility paths. (3) Older women have a higher vulnerability level to COVID-19 than men, but women have a better awareness of spatial adaptation in using personal protective equipment.

1 INTRODUCTION

Coronavirus Disease 2019, more commonly known as COVID-19, is an outbreak of infectious diseases caused by viruses in animals and transmitted rapidly in humans (Contini et al. 2020). COVID-19 is emerging as a new disease and becoming a major health threat in every country, especially a country with a very large population. The emergence of COVID-19 originated in Wuhan, China, in December 2019 under Severe Acute Respiratory Syndrome Coronavirus 2 (SARS COV2) (Bhattacharya et al. 2020). According to a study, in addition to attacking the respiratory system in humans, researchers in Shanghai and New York reported that COVID-19 could also attack the immunity or human immune system and cause similar damage to patients with HIV (Otálora 2020).

The spread of COVID-19 throughout the world is very fast because it has moved the transmission system from human to human (Shereen et al. 2020). Lack of treatment and experience due to unknown patterns and ways the virus works made it so no vaccine has been found. One of the efforts to minimize the impact is to break the chain through various actions and policies. Lockdowns, social distancing, Large-Scale Social Restrictions (PSBB), Local Social Restrictions (PSBL), self-isolation and the use of personal protective equipment and provide legal restrictions for violators of health protocols are all forms of policies and measures to minimize the spread of COVID-19. However, the extent to which the policy is effective the results are not yet clear (Lau et al. 2020), as the current number of positive cases continues to increase.

According to some experts, lockdown policies can reduce the risk of infection and death from COVID-19. As in the UK, Lockdown was able to drop 25% a week after the policy was enacted (Thornton 2020). However, there are several problems in the socio-economic sphere, including rapidly increasing discrimination and gender violence; formal and informal business sectors, the economy, and education are hampered; loss of livelihoods and rising unemployment are causing misery, especially the urban and rural poor (Shammi et al. 2020). Oversleeping occurs, resulting

---

*Corresponding author: purwanto.fis@um.ac.id

in physical and mental health disorders such as mild depression (low mood) during lockdowns (Majumdar et al. 2020).

COVID-19 can be transmitted in various media, either through direct or indirect contact. Direct transmission is the case of direct contact with the sufferer. Transmission can occur through coughing, sneezing or splashing coming out of an infected person's mouth and nose. The particle can then also stick to objects that humans often touch. Therefore, the spread of the virus becomes very fast (WHO 2020).

Rising positive cases in various countries are causing public concern globally (Lau et al. 2020), including who (Word Health Organization) is the world health organization. Therefore, as an anticipatory action, it is necessary to perform vulnerability analysis to see a region's status, taking into account age as a vulnerability indicator. Age is the basis in determining the ratio of vulnerability to COVID-19 because of the large number of cases of death. Coronavirus can infect all age groups of the population. However, each age group has a different response to this coronavirus. The most vulnerable age groups affected by the spread of COVID-19 and at the highest risk of death are the elderly (Dowd et al. 2020; Leung 2020). The elderly population is an age group that has experienced a decrease in the immune system. It is vulnerable to respiratory tract infections, diarrhea, and pneumonia (*Kemenkes RI* 2020). This can increase the risk of Coronavirus infection and cause quite severe disorders, even causing death in the elderly population.

The vulnerability of the elderly in terms of health is also reflected in the statistical data of older adults who died due to COVID-19 in many countries. In Malaysia, elderly people who died due to COVID-19 as much as 62.6% (Astroawani 2020); 85% in Brazil, 95% in Italy, 95.5% in Spain (Escobar, Molina-Cruz and Barillas-Mury 2020); 80% in China (Detikcom 2020). Meanwhile, in Indonesia, existing information shows that most deaths due to COVID-19 are seniors aged 60 and over (Warta Ekonomi, March 23 2020). Indonesia, which has the fourth-highest population globally, is an important location to map the region's vulnerability to the spread of COVID-19. This mapping aims to provide early information to residents on the status of a region against COVID-19. The region's vulnerability is calculated by comparing the number of older adults with the current population to provide a mathematical picture of the community. Mapping the population's vulnerability on the national scale of East Java Province is the province with the second-highest vulnerability after DKI Jakarta as explained by the Task Force for the Acceleration of Handling COVID-19, which states that East Java is on the COVID-19 vulnerable list due to the high number of older adults, namely 12.64%. From the study results, it is necessary to study in-depth to see the extent of regional vulnerabilities on a local scale. The local scale is referred to in the district and city areas. In an in-depth study, Malang Raya area study, namely Malang City, Batu City, and Malang Regency.

2 METHOD

This research aims to describe the vulnerability of the Region to COVID-19 from spatial perspectives. The vulnerability of the region is analyzed based on comparing the number of older adults with the current population. Vulnerability is carried out in more detail studies taking into account gender. This research was conducted in the Greater Malang area, including Malang City, Batu, and Malang Regency. The data was collected using the surveyb123 application from ESRI Indonesia to see the adaptation of people in using personal protective equipment in response to a region's vulnerability. The analysis in this study uses descriptive analysis by comparing the region's vulnerability and the occurrence of COVID-19 in Malang Raya. Vulnerability analysis of COVID-19 is conducted using vulnerability ratio according to the Ministry of Home Affairs of the Republic of Indonesia as follows.

$$\text{Population Vulnerability Ratio} = \frac{\text{Total population Age above } 60 +}{\text{Total population}} \tag{1}$$

The levels of vulnerability are expressed in the following categories.

- <0 − 0.1 = Low
- >0.1 − 0.2 = Moderate
- >0.2 = High

(Sumber: Gugus Penangan perception COVID-19)

3 RESULT AND DISCUSSION

3.1 *COVID-19 vulnerability mapping in Malang Raya*

The mapping results show that areas are vulnerable to the spread of COVID-19 in the Greater Malang area in rural areas with a ratio of 0.15–0.19. The high vulnerability in rural areas is due to the high population of 60+ in the village. This does not close the possibility because of the good quality of the environment and a simple lifestyle. Unlike residents living in urban areas with a lower vulnerability ratio of 0.12–0.14 than rural communities, COVID-19 is spreading worse In urban area than rural area. Poor environmental quality and modern lifestyle causes city communities to have lower durability despite their awareness of using better personal protective equipment. The following is presented a map of the region's vulnerability level to COVID-19 in the Greater Malang area as seen in figure 1.

Population groups aged 60+ are one of the indicators or arguably the most vulnerable to COVID-19, as many previous studies have stated that increasing age is also followed by an increasing tendency to get sick and have physical limitations due to a decrease in physical ability that is quite drastic (Gatimu et al. 2016). Meanwhile, according to UGM Geriatric Expert, Probosuseno

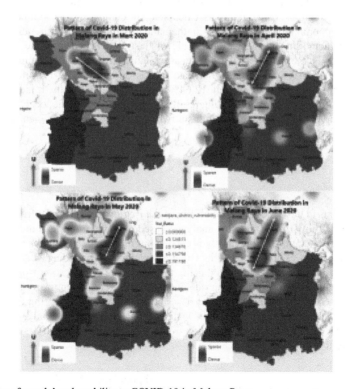

Figure 1.   Map of people's vulnerability to COVID-19 in Malang Raya.

(*Berita Harian Update Corona 21 April 2020 Terbaru Hari Ini* 2020), the factor that makes the elderly vulnerable to Contracting COVID-19 is because the elderly experience a decrease in functional capacity in almost the entire bodily system, including immunity—coupled with the number of older adults who have congenital diseases such as autoimmune disorders, diabetes, high blood pressure, cancer and heart disease. These facts show that older adults are in a vulnerable position to be infected with COVID-19 (Hakim 2020).

3.2 *Spatial pattern of COVID-19 spread in Malang Raya*

The spread of COVID-19 during the first four months shows a varied dynamic. As pictured above, the beginning of the COVID-19 incident in Malang Raya is concentrated in Malang City's area with the direction of distribution to the Northwest, namely Batu City. The spread shows the strong connection between the two Cities. In April 2020, there was a change of direction northeast towards Surabaya until June 2020. This shows a strong interaction between Surabaya as the provincial capital as well as the second highest city. The second positive case of COVID-19 has a strong impact on the spread of COVID-19 in Malang Raya. The condition is different from other Malang Raya areas, heading to Batu Kediri, Kepanjen and Blitar, and Lumajang. Based on the above conditions, it is believed that accessibility and population density have an important role in preventing the spread of COVID-19. This means that the vulnerability aspect, as the formula above, needs to be supplemented with more complex parameters such as accessibility and population density.

3.3 *Population vulnerability by gender*

Based on the results of an in-depth analysis of 2208 people in Pulungdowo village, Tumpang subdistrict, consisting of 1090 women and 1118 men with an elderly population of 60 years and above as many as 414 people. Of the 414 people of the elderly population, 200 were found by gender, and 200 were male and 214 female. The vulnerability analysis results are presented as shown in Table 1 below.

Table 1. The vulnerability ratio of Pulungdowo villagers to COVID-19.

No	Vulnerability	Total Population	Total Elderly Population	Vulnerability Ratio	Category
1.	Male	1118	200	0.1788	Moderate
2.	Female	1090	214	0.1963	Moderate
	Average vulnerability	2208	414	0.1875	Moderate

The vulnerability analysis results of the population-based on gender showed that the ratio of male vulnerability is lower compared to women. Quantitatively men have a low vulnerability if and the appeal of women is 0.1788 compared to 0.1963. Still, the facts in the field show the reverse fact, in which men dominate the ratio of positive cases of COVID-19 in Malang Raya. This is because men have a lower awareness of using personal protective equipment than women. The villagers have a moderate level of vulnerability with a very high ratio of 0.1875. Of these categories, older women had a higher vulnerability ratio than men, with a score of 0.1963. The results of the analysis are presented in table 1.

Based on the analysis of population vulnerability based on gender type in the elderly, there is a difference in vulnerability between older men and women. Previous research has suggested that men have higher mortality rates, although susceptibility rates are lower than in women. This is because of the content of enzymes in the male blood that the virus uses to infect cells, thus helping the virus survive in the lungs (Science Alert 2020). Referring to the statement, the male elderly population is more vulnerable to COVID-19 exposure than the female elderly population. Exploring the data obtained for villagers' age, the number of older men reached 200 people; the number is lower than that of older women of 214. The results that have been calculated for the vulnerability of men 0.1788% and women 0.1963%. In general, men are more at risk of COVID-19 infection because they tend to spend less time on their health care problems than women (Walter and McGregor 2020). Research on the condition of COVID-19 patients in Wuhan, China, resulted in the finding that clinically, men are more susceptible to disease and serious severity than women (Jin et al. 2020).

4 CONCLUSTIONS

Based on the results of the study above, it can be concluded that: (1) Rural areas in Malang Raya, based on the results of the analysis, have a high vulnerability ratio due to the high. The high vulnerability is reinforced by low spatial awareness related to the use of personal protective equipment. But the facts on the ground show the opposite. A simple lifestyle with agricultural work makes villagers more resistant to COVID-19. (2) The spread of COVID-19 in Malang Raya is spatially centralized in Malang, Batu, and along the lines that connect Malang with Surabaya. This is shown by the distribution pattern that extends the road to Surabaya for the last three months. (3) The vulnerability analysis results for the elderly in rural areas based on gender show that women have a higher level of vulnerability than men. However, the awareness of older women using personal protective equipment is high, causing the number of contracting COVID-19 lower.

REFERENCES

Astroawani, E. (2020) *Carian Berita Untuk English Astroawani, 16 april 2020, Astro Awani*. Available at: https://www.astroawani.com/search?q=ingglis+astroawani (Accessed: 24 January 2021).

Berita Harian Update Corona 21 April 2020 Terbaru Hari Ini (2020) *Kompas.com*. Available at: https://www.kompas.com/tag/update+corona+21+april+2020 (Accessed: 24 January 2021).

Bhattacharya, S., Basu, P. and Poddar, S. (2020) 'Changing epidemiology of SARS-CoV in the context of COVID-19 pandemic', *Journal of Preventive Medicine and Hygiene*. doi: 10.15167/2421-4248/jpmh2020.61.2.1541.

Contini, C. et al. (2020) 'The novel zoonotic COVID-19 pandemic: An expected global health concern', *Journal of Infection in Developing Countries*. doi: 10.3855/jidc.12671.

Detikcom, T. (2020) *Kasus Baru Corona 13 Mei Capai 689 Orang, Kurva Corona Menanjak Tinggi, detikNews*. Available at: https://news.detik.com/berita/d-5013585/kasus-baru-corona-13- mei-capai-689-orang-kurva-corona-menanjak-tinggi (Accessed: 24 January 2021).

Dowd, J. B. et al. (2020) 'Demographic science aids in understanding the spread and fatality rates of COVID-19', *Proceedings of the National Academy of Sciences of the United States of America*. doi: 10.1073/pnas.2004911117.

Escobar, L. E., Molina-Cruz, A. and Barillas-Mury, C. (2020) 'BCG vaccine protection from severe coronavirus disease 2019 (COVID-19)', *Proceedings of the National Academy of Sciences of the United States of America*. doi: 10.1073/pnas.2008410117.

Gatimu, S. M., Milimo, B. W. and Sebastian, M. S. (2016) 'Prevalence and determinants of diabetes among older adults in Ghana', *BMC Public Health*. doi: 10.1186/s12889-016-3845-8.

Hakim, L. N. (2020) 'Pelindungan Lanjut Usia Pada Masa Pandemi COVID-19', *Perlindungan lanjut usia pada masa pandemi COVID-19*.

Jin, J. M. et al. (2020) 'Gender Differences in Patients With COVID-19: Focus on Severity and Mortality', *Frontiers in Public Health*. doi: 10.3389/fpubh.2020.00152.

Kemenkes RI (2020) *Penelusuran Google*. Available at: https://www.google.com/search?q=Kemenkes+RI%2C+2020&oq=Kemenkes+RI%2C+2020&aqs=chrome..69i57j0l5j0i22i30l4.943j1j7&sourceid=chrome&ie=UTF-8 (Accessed: 24 January 2021).

Lau, H. et al. (2020) 'The positive impact of lockdown in Wuhan on containing the COVID-19 outbreak in China', *Journal of travel medicine*. doi: 10.1093/jtm/taaa037.

Leung, C. (2020) 'Risk factors for predicting mortality in elderly patients with COVID-19: A review of clinical data in China', *Mechanisms of Ageing and Development*. doi: 10.1016/j.mad.2020.111255.

Majumdar, P., Biswas, A. and Sahu, S. (2020) 'COVID-19 pandemic and lockdown: cause of sleep disruption, depression, somatic pain, and increased screen exposure of office workers and students of India', *Chronobiology International*. doi: 10.1080/07420528.2020.1786107.

Otálora, M. M. C. (2020) 'YULIANA', in *Parque de los afectos. Jóvenes que cuentan*. doi: 10.2307/j.ctvzxxb18.12.

Shammi, M. et al. (2020) 'Strategic assessment of COVID-19 pandemic in Bangladesh: comparative lockdown scenario analysis, public perception, and management for sustainability', *Environment, Development and Sustainability*. doi: 10.1007/s10668-020-00867-y.

Shereen, M. A. et al. (2020) 'COVID-19 infection: Origin, transmission, and characteristics of human coronaviruses', *Journal of Advanced Research*. doi: 10.1016/j.jare.2020.03.005.

Thornton, J. (2020) 'COVID-19: A&E visits in England fall by 25% in week after lockdown', *BMJ (Clinical research ed.)*. doi: 10.1136/bmj.m1401.

Walter, L. A. and McGregor, A. J. (2020) 'Sex- And gender-specific observations and implications for COVID-19', *Western Journal of Emergency Medicine*. doi: 10.5811/westjem.2020.4.47536.

WHO (2020) 'Coronavirus disease (COVID-2019) situation reports', *World Health Organisation*.

Development, Social Change and Environmental Sustainability – Sumarmi et al (Eds)
© 2021 Taylor & Francis Group, London, ISBN 978-1-032-01320-6

The distribution problem of social safety net program in Surabaya and Gresik during pandemic

Imamul Huda Al Shiddiq*, Abdul Kodir, Imam Mukhlis, Febri Kevin Aditya & Satrya Paramanandana
Universitas Negeri Malang, Malang City, Indonesia

ABSTRACT: One of the consequences of the Covid-19 pandemic that is most feared by Indonesia and even developed countries around the world is economic uncertainty. Many economic activities must be temporarily stopped in response to the implementation of efforts to prevent the expansion of Covid-19 infections. Starting from large capital companies to rural MSMEs must close temporarily. This makes various social layers affected economically. Therefore, the government implemented several Social Safety Net (JPS) programs during the pandemic to ease the burden on the affected communities. This study aims to explain the impact of JPS for the economic improvement of vulnerable groups. In addition, this study seeks to explain the level of suitability of field implementation with central government regulations. The method used in this research is a qualitative method by conducting semi-structured interviews with beneficiary communities. The results of this study indicate that the policies set by the central government have not been maximally executed in the regions. There is a difference in the nominal value of obtaining assistance in Sidoarjo municipality compared to the nominal in other cities. An example of a case in the Surabaya city and Gresik municipality was that the recipients of massive aid were mis-targeted. However, most beneficiaries admitted that with this JPS their lives were helped and fulfilled economically.

Keywords: Social Safety Network, Poverty, Vulnerable Community, Pandemic, Covid-19

1 INTRODUCTION

On March 11, 2020, the World Health Organization (WHO) declared COVID-19 as a global pandemic, taking into account the number of infections that have reached 118,000 cases in more than 110 countries and the continuing risk of global spread (Ducharme 2020). As the case curve increases, each country takes its own initiatives in order to protect their country from this pandemic. More than 80 countries have closed their borders to arrivals from countries with cases of infection, ordered businesses and public spaces to close, social distancing is echoed, and schools are closed (The Economics 2020). The economic impact of the anticipated pandemic, globally, is beyond estimation. The increase in the number of unemployed and poor families is increasing in both developed and developing countries.

Indonesia, as one of the developing countries in Asia, also feels the economic slowdown during the implementation of the national health emergency status. The Minister of Finance revealed that Indonesia's economic growth this year could fall to 2.5%, even 0% (Bayu 2020). Millions of families are vulnerable to unemployment and even poverty. As of mid-May 2020, Bappenas has calculated the unemployment rate to reach 2 to 3.7 million people (Hidayat & Rosana 2020). A projection for the poverty rate due to COVID-19, the lightest, will increase from 9.2 percent in September 2019 (see diagram 1) to 9.7 percent by the end of 2020 or 1.3 million more poor people,

---

*Corresponding author: imamul.huda.fis@um.ac.id

DOI 10.1201/9781003178163-22

the highest projection. severe, the poverty rate will increase to 12.4 percent or 8.5 million more people will become poor (Suryahadi et al. 2020).

As a result, Indonesia needs to implement a social safety net program to assist the new poor in addition to the existing poor. The scope of the definition of a social safety net varies depending on the institution defining it and the scholars researching the topic. The World Bank defines social safety nets as non-contributory assistance aimed at improving the standard of living of poor families or individuals (World Bank n.d.). The International Labor Organization (ILO) defines that social safety nets are anti-poverty assistance provided by the government (Paitoonpong et al. 2008). Meanwhile, the National Development Planning Agency (Bappenas) translates social safety nets as intervention policies to tackle or at least reduce the social impact of the crisis (Kementrian 2014). The basic definition of a social safety net that can be concluded is poverty prevention programs targeted at targets vulnerable to falling into poverty.

In this study, the limitation is taken on the social safety net that applies during the global pandemic COVID-19. It is important to investigate social safety net programs to improve the lives of vulnerable groups during a pandemic as an evaluation and reference for similar policies in the future. Evaluation is urgent given that social safety nets bear the burden of survival for vulnerable audiences. How effective the social safety nets prepared by the government are in supporting the millions of people who do not fall into poverty and those who are already poor do not go hungry needs to be measured. The hope is that if something similar happens in the future, the government is ready to take more effective policies.

2 METHOD

This study uses a qualitative method. The data collection process was carried out through interviews with the beneficiary community. The data collection process was carried out in areas with the epicenter of the spread of COVID-19 in East Java, namely Surabaya City and Gresik Regency. Both regions are at the same time the center of industry and business in East Java. So, apart from being affected in terms of public health, the three regions also felt the economic impact due to the implementation of the PSBB. Secondary data is obtained through the process of interpreting data from BPS, the Social Service, related regulations or legislation, and other supporting documents.

The analysis of this research was carried out in three stages. First, data reduction, namely the process of selecting, simplifying data, abstraction, and transforming the crude data obtained in the field. Second, the data presentation stage is a description of information conclusions that allows for drawing conclusions and taking action. Third, is the stage of drawing conclusions and verification.

3 RESULT AND DISCUSSION

3.1 *Social assistance in Surabaya*

The distribution of social assistance in Surabaya has a number of problems. Based on field research, it is stated that the social assistance budget has been disbursed by the central government as much as 172.1 trillion which should have been distributed to people affected by the Covid-19 pandemic. The research steps were started from related to social assistance to the Surabaya City Social Service and submitting research permits. The researcher also asks for data on social assistance recipients. However, the recipient data obtained is only based on the number in each subdistrict.

The results of field research through interviews with both respondents and local officials varied considerably. Research in Gunung Anyar Subdistrict has encountered problems even though it has followed licensing procedures related to social assistance research. The research team was not allowed to participate in direct interviews. However, the research team received an offer to bring in participants

Another problem is found in Gunung Anyar Tambak Village. Many admissions from kelurahan staff include insufficient human resources and forced data input overnight. This indirectly affects the accuracy of implementing and receiving social assistance. As a solution to this problem, RT and RW have sent people who deserve social assistance. However, this has not yet received a response from the central government

Research in Medayu Village that the RT acknowledges that the data sent is old data. This causes many to receive social assistance but no one. In addition, many are not on target. Apart from the mentioned sub-districts, there is also a respondent's acknowledgment. RR Hartati having her address at Jetis Wetan gang 4 no. 22 is supposed to get thrice. But in reality only once. Respondents have reported to related parties until the field visit on August 4, 2020, but there is still no response from the Surabaya City Social Service.

3.2 *Social assistance in Gresik*

Field research was also carried out in Gresik Regency. There are several findings regarding the distribution of social assistance. The Gresik Regency Social Service is cooperative, and admits that there are problems in the distribution of social assistance to the State Budget. The claim from the agency stated that the delay in some areas was because the village and hamlet had not sent the first stage of the Accountability Report.

In addition, in Abar-abir Village, problems were also found. The village has complained about the large number of gates for the implementation of social assistance distribution. This has resulted in overlapping authority and confusion over aid recipients.

The research team in the field also found that many RT and RW have proposed their residents who were really affected by the economy due to the pandemic. However, what happened was not clear from the Social Service. Meanwhile, the receipt of social assistance in each RT, hamlet and village varied. For example, in Hulaan Hamlet, many residents have received assistance twice. Meanwhile, residents in Gempol Kurung Hamlet still received one-time assistance.

The existing problems cause gaps in the distribution of social assistance. The residents felt that the distribution of social assistance was not well targeted. This is also related to data collection from the Gresik Regency Social Service. Some of the data provided by the department are not in accordance with the facts in the field.

4 CONCLUSTION

The Covid-19 pandemic in Indonesia has had an impact not only from the health aspect but also on the socio-economic side. Poverty and unemployment rates have increased due to this pandemic. Therefore the Indonesian government implemented a social safety net program. This program aims to improve the standard of living of families or individuals who are vulnerable to poverty and are manifested in social assistance. However, the reality on the ground both in the City of Surabaya and Gresik Regency is that there are problems. Obstacles that exist include procedural complexity, limited human resources, confusion of data on aid recipients and less targeted assistance.

REFERENCES

Bayu, D. J. (2020, A. 14), Jokowi: Pertumbuhan Ekonomi akan Turun Cukup Tajam akibat Corona – Katadata.co.id.

Ducharme, J. (2020, M. 11), The WHO Just Declared Coronavirus COVID-19 a Pandemic. *TIME*.

Governments are still struggling to get ahead of the coronavirus. (2020, M. 17), The Economist.

Kementrian, P., 2014. Perlindungan sosial di Indonesia: Tantangan dan arah ke depan. *Jakarta: BAPPENAS RI*.

Paitoonpong, S., Abe, S. & Puopongsakorn, N., 2008. The meaning of "social safety nets." *Journal of Asian Economics*, 19(5-6), pp. 467–473.

Suryahadi, A., Al Izzati, R., & Suryadarma, D., 2020. The Impact of COVID-19 Outbreak on Poverty: An Estimation for Indonesia, Draft. *The SMERU Research Institute*.

World Bank, The State of Social Safety Nets 2018. 2018. Available at: https://openknowledge.worldbank.org/handle/10986/29115 License: CC BY 3.0 IGO.

Development, Social Change and Environmental Sustainability – Sumarmi et al (Eds)
© 2021 Taylor & Francis Group, London, ISBN 978-1-032-01320-6

Capturing the dual role of female medical workers during the COVID-19 pandemic in Surabaya

D.W. Apriadi*, D. Mawarni & M. Saputra
Universitas Negeri Malang, Malang City, Indonesia

ABSTRACT: The aim of this study is to see the dual role of female medical worker in the family and how it has changed since the outbreak of the COVID-19 pandemic, as well as to see the views of female medical workers on the culture of the domestic realm. This research is a qualitative with purposive sampling technique. Data collection techniques used participatory observation, in-depth interviews conducted via video calls and or telephone, and supported by the literature reviews. The results showed that has led to changes in the division of duties in the domestic realm, particularly for medical personnel handling COVID-19 at their hospitals. Based on the analysis, it was found that the view of the cultural concept of the domestic realm is that the responsibility of the wife is more determined by the family where religion is the dominant factor affecting this view.

Keywords: patriarchy culture, dual role, female medical workers, COVID-19 Pandemic

1   INTRODUCTION

Women have a role in reproduction, productive economy, and community management (Zuhdi 2019). This means that women have a dual role as housewives/wives who have to do household chores and also as breadwinners to help the family economy. However, the general opinion of the community is that a woman or a mother is considered taboo or violates her nature as a woman if she is too often outside the home (Arsini 2014) .Women are considered to have only three functions, namely cooking, bearing children, decorating, or only having kitchen duties, wells and mattresses (Arifin in (Rostiyati 2018). McLellan and Uys, in 2009, conducted a study to explore how self-employed women are coping with the balance of their dual roles as mothers and entrepreneurs in Gauteng. Despite being able to earn double income, they still bear the primary responsibility for caring for the family and ensuring their welfare. Analyzes how the structural demand for female labor affects gender differences in labor force participation. They show that gender differences in labor force participation span time and space with measures of women's labor demand.

Previous research on womens dual roles has been carried out in Indonesia, including research from Qori Kartika and Rabial Canada (2017) and Syaifuddin Zuhdi (2018). Qori Kartika and Rabial Canada's research (2017) aims to describe the perceptions of women in the city of Lahat about the concept of gender equality and gender equality (KKG) in the social and cultural sphere of society in Merapi Selatan District, Lahat Regency. The results of this study indicate that: first, the role of farmers' wives in South Merapi District, East Kalimantan is concentrated in the agricultural sector. Wives' demands to meet family needs are the same as mens', so they don't only stay at home to wait and spend their husband's income from rice fields or coffee plantations, but are also involved in earning a living through piecemeal or other means. Second, the wife's participation in improving family welfare in South Merapi District is manifested in three roles, both in the home environment,

---

*Corresponding author: deny.apriadi.fis@um.ac.id

in the economy, and in society. They have to complete all their duties as mothers and wives who are naturally responsible for helping to make a living.

Syaifuddin Zuhdi's research (2018) regarding the dual role of women in the industrial era states that basically women have a main role as someone who works in the domestic sphere. Over time, the role of women has shifted from what was originally domestic, then shifted towards the public. Several reasons that make women work in the public sector are related to the economic value in the family. The shift in the role of women into a money-oriented industrial society has an impact on family conditions and social relations in society.

This research will complement previous research regarding the dual role of women, but by raising the latest issue, namely regarding the COVID-19 pandemic which has shocked the world in recent months. This pandemic began with the coronavirus which was first discovered in Wuhan, China on December 8, 2019. On January 30, 2020, the World Health Organization (WHO) declared the corona virus a global public health emergency and on February 11, 2020, WHO stipulated the mention of the corona virus replaced as COVID-19 (Corona Virus Disease 2019). Until the announcement was made, 114 countries had reported Covid-19 cases with a total of 118,000 cases (https://nationalgeographic.grid.id/read/132059249/who-tetapkan-covid-19-sebagai-pandemi-global-apa-maksudnya, 05 August 2020). There is a lot of research on the dual role of women, but it is very rare to do research on the dual role of female medical personnel. This research will highlight the dilemma of female medical personnel where they are required to provide the best service for COVID-19 patients as well as to take care of their families at home. The purpose of this study is to see the dual role of female medical personnel in the family and how it has changed since the outbreak of the COVID-19 pandemic, as well as to see the views of female medical workers on the domestic sphere which has been considered a wife's business.

2 METHOD

This research is a qualitative research. Qualitative research is aresearch which is based on the philosophy of positivism, is used to examine the conditions of natural objects, where the researcher as a key instrument and the results of research emphasize meaning rather than generalization (Sugiyono 2016). In qualitative research, what is used as the target of the study is the conditions of social life or society as a whole and comprehensive unit. This relates to the issues raised, namely regarding the socio-cultural problems of the community in the midst of the COVID-19 pandemic.

The data collection techniques used in this study were participatory observation, free and in-depth interviews conducted via video call and/or telephone, and supported by a literature review. The process of selecting informants was taken purposively, in which the selected informants were those who understood and understood the research problem raised, so that later data would be appropriate and did not deviate far from the research topic. This research was conducted on 4–28 July 2020. The informants in this study were female medical personnel who work at hospitals that treat Covid-19 patients in the city of Surabaya. This study involved 30 informants from 15 referral and non-referral hospitals for Covid-19 in the city of Surabaya.

Analysis of the data in this study through three stages, namely making field notes, doing data reduction, and drawing conclusions. The first step carried out after the interview is to make field notes (field notes), then grouped by researchers on the basis of existing specific activities and what is being researched. At the data reduction stage, data that has gone through the grouping process will be abstracted and linked to one another. others as an integrated unit of events and facts, so as to produce strong data value. Through this abstraction, it will show the prevailing social institutions in the area or community where the research is taking place (Ahimsa-Putra 2009).

3 RESULT AND DISCUSSION

Role is the part that is played in every situation, and how to behave to conform to the situation (Wolfman in (Putra 2018). Soekanto (2012) states that a role determines what a person does for society and what opportunities the community gives him. In the past, women who worked outside the domestic sphere were often belittled because they were considered to have violated their nature. However, in an increasingly modern era, many women work outside the domestic sphere for various reasons, such as: helping to fulfill the household economy, making parents happy, social status, and so on. This is also the case for female medical personnel, where they have multiple roles in the domestic sphere and outside the domestic sphere.

The work as a medical personnel is, of course, quite tiring work. This condition will be more tiring if they return home and do all the household chores. Therefore, it is necessary to divide the tasks between husband and wife in completing household chores. This is based on considerations of time and energy efficiency. In addition, the husband's awareness is needed that his wife is tired of working to help the family economy. Based on interviews, husbands are willing to help their wives in the domestic sphere. The husband's household chores are washing clothes in the washing machine, drying clothes, watering plants, cleaning the room, and sweeping the yard. While the wife does the tasks of taking care of children, cooking, washing dishes, sweeping and mopping the floors and ironing clothes. For husband and wife who live with their family, the task is lighter because it is shared with other family members. For those who have a household assistant (ART), their duties at home are only to take care of their children and husbands.

The gender equality of the Javanese ethnic transmigration community, stated that gender roles can be seen through nurture theory and nature theory. According to the nurture theory, the differences between men and women are essentially the result of socio-cultural constructions, resulting in different roles and tasks. These differences cause women to always be left behind and neglected in their role and contribution in family life, society, nation and state. Meanwhile, according to the nature theory, the differences between women and men are natural, so they cannot change and are universal. This biological difference provides an indication and an implication that the two types have different roles and tasks. In social life, there is a division of labor, as well as in family life. This is also experienced by female medical personnel in the city of Surabaya. Even though the wife and husband both work, the socio-cultural construction that considers women to be responsible in the domestic sphere makes female medical personnel have a dual role.

Working women have a heavier role than men where men are only responsible in the public sphere, while women are responsible for the domestic and public sphere. Women carry out many tasks and assume responsibilities inside and outside the home, they must learn to use their time wisely. Conditions like this will cause gender role gaps in the family, so mutual agreement is needed in the division of roles between husbands. and wife. Based on the results of interviews, most female medical personnel share roles with their husbands in the domestic sphere. Even though in practice the role of the wife in the domestic sphere is bigger than that of the husband, at least it can reduce the gender role gap in the family.

Since the COVID-19 pandemic, medical personnel working hours have changed. The working hours change during Large-Scale Social Restriction (LSSR; PSBB in Bahasa), namely morning shift at 07.00–14.00 WIB, day shift at 14.00–19.00 WIB and night shift at 19.00–07.00 WIB. However, after the PSBB ended, working hours returned to normal. Currently, for medical personnel who work in inpatients and non-COVID-19 normal rooms, the shift division is 2x morning shifts, 2x day shifts, 2x night shifts, 2x holidays, and so on. As for medical personnel on duty in the COVID-19 room, the shift division is 1x morning shift, 1x day shift, 1x night shift, 1x holiday, and so on.

For female medical personnel who are members of the COVID-19 Team, their workload is getting heavier. They must wear complete PPE while handling patients to minimize exposure to COVID-19. This also affects the performance of medical personnel, for example inserting an IV, which is usually straightforward, but when wearing PPE, it takes a while to look for blood vessels because the glasses are often dewy. The workload of the COVID-19 team is also getting heavier because all the needs of patients in the COVID-19 isolation room must be handled by the nurse or midwife on duty. This condition affects the physical and psychological aspects of medical personnel, which then affects their domestic sphere.

Each hospital in Surabaya City provides temporary housing facilities for medical personnel who have joined the COVID-19 team. However, not all COVID-19 teams choose to live there. HN (30 years old) revealed that when he first joined the Covid Team, HN lived in the mess that had been provided. This prevented HN from returning to her house, so that all household chores, including the affairs of her children, were handled by her husband and parents. HN will return home after 21 days in the hospital and take the SWAB test. If the result is negative, then the new HN will return home. This provoked protests from the children because they missed their mother at home. This condition lasts for 2 months. After that, HN decided to return home after work.

In society, of course, it is familiar to the assumption that the domestic sphere is the responsibility of the wife. Collin (Missa 2010) thinks that the family is a place of coercion, the husband as the owner and the woman as the servant. Domestic duties such as: cooking, washing dishes, sweeping, mopping, washing clothes, etc. are considered the responsibility of a wife. Meanwhile, the husband as the head of the family is responsible for fulfilling the family's needs financially. This kind of assumption is like a culture that grows and develops in Indonesian society. However, in practice, the culture that the domestic sphere is the responsibility of the wife is not fully approved by female medical personnel. Based on the results of the interview, Most of the female medical personnel consider that the roles of husband and wife in the domestic sphere are the same, so that household duties are not a burden to the wife alone. Although in practice, it is the wife who does most of the household chores.

There are two reasons why female medical personnel think that the roles of husband and wife in the domestic sphere are the same. First, the role of the wife in economic terms is balanced with the role of the husband. The wife also works to help the family economy, so that their income is sufficient to meet their daily needs and can be said to be financially secure. This then makes the position of husband and wife equal in the public sphere, so that in the domestic sphere the position of the husband must also be equal to that of the wife for a more balanced situation. This is as said by DN (26 years), a nurse from Darmo Hospital. According to DN, if a husband and wife work together, there will be more sources of income. Expenditures are borne together, so that household chores must also be done together. DN said that if a man only wants to be served without doing household chores, then he is better off not marrying any woman. This is in line with DN, YS (30 years), a midwife from Dr. Soetomo Regional Hospital, who said that a woman should be productive so that she is ready to face unexpected events, such as if one day her husband's income is no longer sufficient or if the husband experiences a reduction in income or even after being laid off, the wife could help her husband at that time. Second, the household is built together, so that all household matters are shared responsibilities. Men and women marry to build a complete household. It is impossible for a household to be built alone, without a partner. Therefore, husband and wife must help each other and cooperate in all household matters.

4 CONCLUSION

Female medical personnel have multiple roles, namely as wives/housewives and as medical personnel. Work in the hospital makes them have to divide their roles in the family and in the hospital. The demands of different roles put female medical personnel in a dilemma, so that many of them feel overwhelmed if they have to do both, especially during the COVID-19 pandemic. In the end, there is mutual awareness and agreement between husband and wife in carrying out their duties in the domestic sphere. The division of domestic roles between husband and wife means that the gender role gap in the family can still be well coordinated.

The view of female medical personnel regarding the cultural concept of the domestic realm is that the wife's responsibility is influenced by family factors. Those who grow up in a religious family have a different pattern of division of roles from those who grow up in an ordinary environment. For those who grew up in a religious family environment, the concept that the domestic realm is the responsibility of the wife is still upheld today. Meanwhile, those who grow up in an ordinary family environment think that the domestic sphere is a shared responsibility.

REFERENCES

Ahimsa-Putra, H. S. (2009) 'PARADIGMA ILMU SOSIAL-BUDAYA', *Kuliah Umum "Paradigma Penelitian Ilmu-ilmu Humaniora."* Bandung: Program Studi Linguistik Sekolah Pascasarjana Universitas Pendidikan Indonesia.

Aldianto, R. (2015) 'Kesetaraan gender masyarakat transmigrasi etnis Jawa', *Jurnal Equilibrium Sosiologi*, 3(1).

Arsini (2014) 'Peran Ganda Perempuan pada Keluarga Masyarakat Agraris: Kasus 10 Istri Buruh Tani di Desa Putat Purwodadi Grobogan', *Sawwa*.

McLellan, K.-L. and Uys, K. (2009) 'Balancing dual roles in self-employed women: An exploratory study', *SA Journal of Industrial Psychology*, 35(1), pp. 21–30.

Missa, L. (2010) *STUDI KRIMINOLOGI PENYELESAIAN KEKERASAN DALAM RUMAH TANGGA DI WILAYAH KOTA KUPANG PROPINSI NUSA TENGGARA TIMUR, MAGISTER ILMU HUKUM.*

Putra, A. (2018) 'CITRA PEREMPUAN DALAM CERITA RAKYAT WAINDHO-INDHODHIYU PADA MASYARAKAT WAKATOBI', *ETNOREFLIKA: Jurnal Sosial dan Budaya*, 7(1), pp. 20–29.

Rostiyati, A. (2018) 'PERAN GANDA PEREMPUAN NELAYAN DI DESA MUARA GADING MAS LAMPUNG TIMUR', *Patanjala?: Jurnal Penelitian Sejarah dan Budaya*. doi: 10.30959/patanjala.v10i2.373.

Sugiyono, P. D. (2016) *metode penelitian kuantitatif, kualitatif,dan R&D, Alfabeta, cv.*

Zuhdi, S. (2019) 'MEMBINCANG PERAN GANDA PEREMPUAN DALAM MASYARAKAT INDUSTRI', *Jurnal Jurisprudence.* doi: 10.23917/jurisprudence.v8i2.7327.

Development, Social Change and Environmental Sustainability – Sumarmi et al (Eds)
© 2021 Taylor & Francis Group, London, ISBN 978-1-032-01320-6

Environmental health behavior of fishing communities during COVID-19 pandemic

Singgih Susilo*, Budijanto & Ifan Deffinika
Universitas Negeri Malang, Malang, Indonesia

ABSTRACT: The chaotic settlement environmental problems, causing slum environments to be scattered in various corners of the area. This study aims to find and reveal the various conditions behind the low environmental health behavior of fishing communities in facing the COVID-19 Pandemic. This study used a quantitative descriptive approach. The population in this study were housewives who had toddlers in Pamekasan Regency fishing community, and the sample was taken purposively using in–depth interviews to gather information. The research results show that the environmental health behavior of the fishing community is in a good category. Most of them use clean water from PDAM and have a special place for disposal. The handling of the COVID-19 Pandemic in this community is in the low category. But even so, none of the fishing communities have been exposed to COVID-19, even though Pamekasan Regency is in the red zone.

1 INTRODUCTION

The quality of life of a nation among others can be measured from the death rate. Many nations have achieved low mortality rates which generally have a relatively high socio–economic level. Through improving public health, it can be expected that the survival rate of children will be higher. Evidence shows that in developed countries more than 97% of children can survive to the age of five, while in developing countries 20 to 25% of babies born die before reaching the age of five (Mosley 1984). The results of preliminary observations at the research location show that there are factors that continue to encourage the low environmental health of fishing community settlements, namely limited environmental health infrastructure and low education which results in low access to job opportunities supported by unfavorable demographic characteristics. Thus causing the low environmental hygiene in the fishing community.

The relationship between socio–economic factors and mortality cannot be direct, but must go through intermediate variables. According to Mosley and Chen (1984), the relationship be-tween these two variables will be through an intermediate variable consisting of factors related to mother-hood, environmental pollution, malnutrition, and individual illness monitoring. This phenomenon occurs in the community living in the fishing community in the village of Branta Tinggi. So on this occasion, the researcher' want to conduct research in relation to the most basic problems, namely environmental health problems. The topic raised in this research is: Environmental Health Behavior of Fishing Communities Settlements in Branta Tinggi Village, Tlanakan District, Pamekasan Regency.

This study intends to reveal the behavior conditions of the fishing community during the COVID-19 Pandemic in Branta Tinggi Village, Tlanakan District, Pamekasan Regency. With the socio–cultural characteristics that exist in the community, the results of this study will later become a reference for determining solutions for parties related to handling COVID-19 in the regions.

---

*Corresponding author: singgih.susilo.fis@um.ac.id

DOI 10.1201/9781003178163-24

2 METHOD

This study was designed with an "explanatory research and research and development" approach. This approach explains the symptoms caused by an object of research, namely the influence of socio–economic and demographic backgrounds on environmental health behavior during the COVID-19 Pandemic in the fishing community of Branta Tinggi Village. The quantitative approach is based on deductive and "inductive" theories relying on "natural" data from the field to find environmental health behaviors and health behaviors for the COVID-19 Pandemic that are applicable to fishing communities.

To determine the research location and program targets are based on: The health behavior of the fishing community in Pamekasan Regency. This area is one of the areas located in the Port Area II, Branta Tinggi Village, Tlanakan District, Pamengkasan Regency where there are fish-ing community settlements. Therefore, the selection of this area was carried out purposively with the determination of non–random research areas (non–probability sampling) which selected based on certain considerations (Singarimbun 1989).

The number of the samples taken was 300 respondents who were divided into three hamlets namely Dusun Tengah, Dusun Gedungan and Dusun Planggaran. The first thing to do to selecting the respondents is population enumeration at the location of household with children under five in the study area. Second, the researcher determined the number of samples at each specified location. Third, determine the amount of the interval done by dividing the population in each location by the number of samples 1. Then, each interval is taken by the respondent randomly. For example, the interval size (1) is 10. If in random to determine sample 1, the first respondent is selected number 5. If the selected sample doesn't meet the requirements or it isn't available, then it is replaced with the closest respondent.

The data analysis in this study was carried out using quantitative and qualitative techniques. Quantitative data were analyzed using percentage and statistical tables. To capture the information and data researcher find out about the study area condition which carried out by using maps. The household (that have children under five) characteristic information was obtained by using non–participation observation, documentation study, participatory observation, and interview.

3 RESULT AND DISCUSSION

The location of this research is in the coastal area of Pamekasan Regency, more precisely is in port area III in Pamekasan Regency which is quite far (about 8 km) from the health center (located close to the Tlanakan District health center). According to the researchers' observations, the location is a port area so that areas with relatively low elevations are always inundated by seawater and the water is relatively black, dirty and stinks. Apart from that, the results of the researcher observations and interviews with the community stated that the sanitation and environment office rarely and almost never conducts field visits to this area. The results showed that the low number of health behaviors in an area was due to behavioral factors.

3.1 *Disposal place*

Garbage Disposal Place is a facility used in everyday life related to waste generated from activities in one day. The use of these facilities reflects the management of the health behavior of each household. Prawiro (1988: 69) states that in cities it is increasingly difficult to find disposal sites and there are more waste materials, so the beach becomes an alternative as a place to dispose of waste/feces as well as being the main source for meeting water needs.

As shown in Table 1, 71.1% of the respondents already have a special place for garbage disposal. The facilities are made of rubber tires, cement (in a form of small tub), cans (in the form of small drums), woven bamboo (simpler, in the form of baskets) and others. This community group can be interpreted as having good health behavior management. They are fully aware that waste which

Table 1. Component of environmental health behavior of Pamekasan Regency Fishing Community.

A. Disposal place				C. Sanitary Place			
No	Place	f	%	No	Place	f	%
1	Beach	51	24.30	1	Beach	46	15.30
2	Water gutter	37	12.33	2	Public sanitary	89	29.70
3	Special place	212	71.70	3	Private sanitary	165	55.00
B. Household waste disposal sites				D. Clean water			
No	Place	f	%	No	Water resource	f	%
1	Beach	62	20.70	1	Water well	106	35.40
2	Open drains	182	61.60	2	PDAM	194	64.60
3	Special place	56	18.70				

consists of waste products affects the health of the population. But there are still 29.3% who use the beach (24.3%) and water gutter (5.0%) as their disposal place.

3.2 *Household waste disposal sites*

The place to dispose of household waste is a facility used in everyday life related to the waste that is generated by daily activities in the household in the form of liquid objects from washing kitchen utensils after cooking or washing clothes and so on. The use of these facilities reflects how the health behavior of each household. Household waste disposal sites are divided into three criteria, namely open channel beaches and special places.

Based on the Table 1, it shows that 61.6% of the population of waste water disposal sites generally use an open drain to a ditch, so that creates an unfavorable and dirty view. It also causes unpleasant odors and disturbs comfort. If this condition is left for a relatively long time, it will cause various kinds of diseases and unhealthy environment. Only 18.7% of households have a specific household waste disposal site, in the form of infiltration wells with a depth of about 10m above it and cast cement with a hole in the form of a pipe, such as a septic tank. The low percentage of this household group caused by the distance between the houses is too close. Resulting in no more usable land for the waste disposal absorption wells. This household group can be interpreted as having good health behavior management. They are very aware and understand that household waste which consists of waste products can affects environmental health.

3.3 *Sanitary place*

Place for defecation or sanitary (for bathing and washing) is a facility used in everyday life. The use of these facilities reflects the management of the health behavior of each household. Based on the Table 1, 55.0% of the population already has their own toilet. In daily life, the disposal of feces generally uses a goose neck toilet (100%). From the percentage, it can be concluded that the temporary findings of the majority of the community have understood the importance of health shown in managing good health behavior for family members in their household.

On the other hand, there are still 15.3% who use the beach as a toilet. It shows that there are still people who don't understand the importance of environmental health management. This group is those who do not own any sanitary and use public toilets that sometimes together with members of other societies. However, the results of investigations by researchers through in–depth interviews from this group were not only for the toilet, not including bathing and washing.

Table 2. Class of environmental health behavior of Pamekasan regency fishing community.

No	Environmental Health Behavior	f	%
1	Less	47	15.67
2	Moderate	96	32.00
3	Good	157	52.33

3.4 *Clean water*

The source of clean water is water that is consumed for daily living needs includes eating, drinking, bathing, and washing. The description of the source of clean water used is divided into two sources, namely PDAM and water wells. Furthermore, from the two sources of clean water, the western part of the Pamekasan Sumenep road mostly uses PDAM, be-cause the salty water that this area (which is located in the coastal area) have. Meanwhile, the eastern one, Jalan Raya uses a well. They're using the water well because the water tasteless.

Based on the Table 1, it shows that 64.6% of the population has used PDAM as a source of clean water for their daily lives. They assume that PDAM is undoubted because it meets health standards for consumption. But, the people who use wells as a source of clean water are still quite high at 35.4%. Based on the results of the study, it was found that most people use water wells as a source of drinking water (42%) and in terms of requirements most of them have met the health requirements, namely construction (85.72%) and depth (100%), most of which have used sanyo. On the other hand, there are still 9.7% who use the beach as a source of clean water.

Most people in this community have a good health behavior management related to the use of clean water. In accordance with the statement of Iskandar (2013: 83), people who live along the coast tend to use dirty beach water for daily purposes. However, the results of the researchers' tracing through in–depth interviews from this group were only for bathing and washing. For the purpose of eating and drinking there were some who took water from their neighbors' wells, and there were also those who said they took from springs around/on either side of the beach.

3.5 *Environmental health behavior*

Environmental Health Behavior is a phenomenon that shows how the environmental health behavior in settlements by people in these settlements. The health behavior of the residential environment shows the daily phenomenon of how to consume clean water sources, dispose of feces, dispose of garbage, and dispose of household waste. The results showed that environmental health behavior in the community is as in the Table 2:

Based on the Table 2 above, we can see that 52.33% of the population has good management of environmental health behavior. 32% of the fishing community is categorized as moderate and 15.67% is categorized as less in the management of environmental health behavior. This finding needs to be criticized because this shows that there are still community groups who have bad environmental health behavior management and do not fully understand the meaning of healthy life. The use and consumption (for eating and drinking) of water, the garbage which is left for a few days (besides causing an unpleasant odor it is also unpleasant, especially in sensitive community groups like toddlers), and the disposal of feces and household waste, it all causes bad environmental health behavior. But even so, it can be concluded that most people in the fishing community of Pamekasan Regency understand the importance of environmental health. It is shown in how they managing good health behavior for their family members in the household.

4 CONCLUSION

The health behavior of the COVID-19 pandemic apart from being related to maternal education, family income and dependency, is also related to health behavior, especially with regard to the use of clean water resources. The community tends to use springs on either side of the beach which have a large potential for having contaminated water. On the beach, we can still see waste disposals (or even household disposals) that dispose into the open drains or directly to the beach. In addition, we can see in the use of public toilets that there are also those who use the beach as a toilet.

There needs to be a high priority scale especially for community groups who still do not know good and correct health behavior, especially during the pandemic like now. There is a need for concrete steps to provide an understanding of the impact on coastal users, especially by the mjority of the population downstream.

REFERENCES

Agence Française de Développement (2020) *Resources for Managing Water & Sanitation During the Coronavirus Pandemic, Institutional Document*. Available at: https://www.afd.fr/en/ressources/resources-managing-water-sanitation- during-coronavirus-pandemic.

Ahyanti, M. (2020) 'Sanitasi Pemukiman pada Masyarakat dengan Riwayat Penyakit Berbasis Lingkungan Sanitation of Community Settlements with a History of Environmental- Based Diseases', *Jurnal Kesehatan Poltekkes Tanjungkarang*.

Atmadja, S. S. et al. (2017) 'Explaining environmental health behaviors: Evidence from rural India on the influence of discount rates', *Environment and Development Economics*. doi: 10.1017/S1355770X17000018.

BBC Indonesia (2020) *Virus Corona: Tops Terlindungi dari COVID-19 dan Mencegah Penyebaran Sesuai Petunjuk WHO, BBC News*. Available at: https://www.bbc.com/indonesia/dunia-52127080.

BPS (2020) *Hasil Survei Sosial Demografi Dampak COVID-19 2020, Jakarta: Badan Pusat Statistik*. Available at: https://www.bps.go. id/publication/2020/06/01/669cb2e8646787e52dd171c4/hasil-survei-sosial-demografi-dampak-COVID-19-2020.html.

BPS Kabupaten Pamengkasan (2020) *Hasil Survei Sosial Demografi Dampak COVID-19 Via Daring Terbaru, Kabupaten Pamengkasan: Badan Pusat Statistik*.

Butler, G., Pilotto, R. G. and Hong, Y., and Mutambatsere, E. (2020) *The Impact of COVID–19 on the Water and Sanitation Sector, International Finance Corporation*. Available at: https://www.ifc.org/wps/wcm/connect/126b1a18-23d9-46f3-beb7-047c20885bf6/ The+Impact+of+COVID_Water%26Sanitation_final_web.pdf?MOD=AJPERES&CVID=ncaG-hA.

Cooper, R. (2020) *Water Security Beyond COVID-19, K4D*. Available at: https://reliefweb.int/sites/reliefweb.int/files/resources/803_Water_security_beyond_C19.pdf.

FAO (2020) *Building Water Access for a COVID-19 Response: Multiple Water Use Systems, Water Stations, Air-to-Water Non–Conventional Technologies (Enhancing Access to Clean Water in Response to COVID–19), Land & Water*. Available at: http://www.fao.org/land-water/overview/covid19/access/en/.

Hermana, J. (2020) *Aspek Pengelolaan Infrastruktur Sanitasi Pasca COVID-19, kkp.go.id*. Available at: https://kkp.go.id/an-component/media/upload-gambar- pendukung/DitJaskel/publikasi-materi-2/penataan-wilayah/Materi 2 - Presentasi JH Webinar 18 Juni.pdf.

Iskandar, Z. (2013) *Psikologi Lingkungan: Metode dan Aplikasi*. Bandung: Refika Aditama.

Kementerian PUPR (2020) *Perilaku Hidup Bersih dan Sehat (PHBS) sebagai Upaya Mencegah Penyebaran COVID–19, Portal IBM Sanitasi*. Available at: http://plpbm.pu.go.id/v2/posts/Perilaku-Hidup-Bersih-dan-Sehat-PHBS- sebagai-Upaya-Mencegah-Penyebaran-COVID-19.

Khairani, A. I. (2016) 'Sanitasi Lingkungan Rumah dan Sosial Budaya Masyarakat Pesisir Pantai Terhadap Ke-jadian Skabies', *Jurnal Riset Hesti Medan*, 1(1). Available at: https://doi.org/10.34008/jurhesti.v1i1.7.

Moslley and Chen (1984) *Child Survival: Strategies for Research*. Cambridge: University Press.

Munir, R., Utomo, B. and Sutrisno (1992) *Morbiditas dan Mortalitas di Indonesia: Suatu penelitian di enam desa di Yogyakarta dan Lombok*. 1990 LD-FEUI.

Nursiah, A. et al. (2016) 'Environment Sanitation and Patterns of Disease in Coastal Community at Langnga Mat-tirosompe Village Pinrang Regency 2015', *International Journal of Applied Environmental Sciences*, 11(4), pp. 927–640.

Prawiro, R. H. (1988) *Ekologi Lingkungan Pencemaran*. Semarang: Satyawacana.

Purnamasari, I. and Rahayani, A. (2019) 'Preventive Health Behaviors of Community During COVID-19 Pandemic: A Descriptive Study', *Indonesian Journal of Global Health Research*, 2(4), pp. 301–308. doi: 10.37287/ijghr.v2i4.232.

Putra, Y. and Wulandari, S. S. (2019) 'FAKTOR PENYEBAB KEJADIAN ISPA', *Jurnal Kesehatan*. doi: 10.35730/jk.v10i1.378.

Saleh, M. and Rachim, L. H. (2014) 'Hubungan Kondisi Sanitasi Lingkungan dengan Kejadian Diare pada Anak Balita di Wilayah Kerja Puskesmas Baranti Kabupaten Sidrap Tahun 2013', *Jurnal Kesehatan*.

Satgas COVID–19 (2020) *Cara Melindungi Diri Terhadap virus Corona (COVID–19). Konten Berguna*. Available at: https://covid19.go.id/p/konten/cara-melindungi-diri-terhadap-virus- corona-COVID-19.

Sumertha Gapar, I. G., Adiputra, N. and Pujaastawa, I. B. G. (2015) 'HUBUNGAN KUALITAS SANITASI RUMAH DENGAN KEJADIAN PENYAKIT INFEKSI SALURAN PERNAPASAN AKUT (ISPA) DI WILAYAH KERJA PUSKESMAS IV DENPASAR SELATAN KOTA DENPASAR', *ECOTROPHIC?: Jurnal Ilmu Lingkungan (Journal of Environmental Science)*. doi: 10.24843/ejes.2015.v09.i02.p07.

Unicef (2020) *To Beat COVID–19, Hand Hygiene Must Become an Everyday Reality for All Indonesian, Press Release*. Available at: https://www.unicef.org/indonesia/press-releases/beat-COVID-19-hand-hygiene-must-become-everyday-reality-all-indonesians.

World Health Organization (2020) *WHO Coronavirus Disease (COVID-19) Dashboard*. Available at: https://covid19.who.int/.

World Health Organization (2020) *Air, Sanitasi, Higine, dan Pengelolaan Limbah yang Tepat Dalam Penanganan Wabah COVID–19, Pedoman Sementara WHO dan UNICEF*. Available at: https://www.who.int/docs/default-source/searo/indonesia/covid19/who-unicef—air-sanitasi-higiene-dan-pengelolaan-limbah-yang-tepat-dalam-penanganan-wabah-COVID-19.pdf?sfvrsn=bf12a730_2.

Yoada, R. M., Chirawurah, D. and Adongo, P. B. (2014) 'Domestic waste disposal practice and perceptions of private sector waste management in urban Accra', *BMC Public Health*. doi: 10.1186/1471-2458-14-697.

Development, Social Change and Environmental Sustainability – Sumarmi et al (Eds)
© 2021 Taylor & Francis Group, London, ISBN 978-1-032-01320-6

Social media management as optimization of tourism potential in Osing Kemiren, Banyuwangi Regency

Nur Hadi*, Elya Kurniawati & Prawinda Putri Anzari
Universitas Negeri Malang, Malang City, Indonesia

ABSTRACT: This study aims to increase the tourism potential in Osing Kemiren Village, Banyuwangi Regency. Increasing tourism potential is carried out in two ways, namely (1) increasing knowledge and skills in managing social media accounts, and (2) increasing knowledge and skills in operating social media accounts. Changing society's pattern in socializing demands the community's readiness to carry out the promotion process. The low level of community knowledge and skills in managing social accounts is the reason for this mentoring process. This community service activity is carried out through assistance with the RPA (participatory rural appraisal) approach and the AIDA (Attention, Interest, Desire, Action) model. Through this activity the community is trained to optimize the tourism potential of the Osing tribe in the traditional village of Kemiren. In order to that, the tourism potential and all tourism supporting sectors in the Osing Traditional Village increase and impact the welfare of the surrounding community.

Keywords: Management, social media, travel, Osing.

1 INTRODUCTION

The modernization of lifestyle has resulted in the formation of different patterns of action. Modern society today is very dependent on the existence of the internet. The public uses this technology in carrying out their activities, including the use of social media accounts such as Instagram, WhatsApp, Facebook, Twitter, etc. The internet has had many impacts on the way humans communicate, exchange information and improve their economy (Febriyantoro & Arisandi 2018). The life of a community such as the Osing community in Banyuwangi Regency has also been affected by the existing social changes (Made Pidata 2009)

The Kemiren Traditional Village is one of the Osing traditional community villages located in Banyuwangi Regency (*Kabupaten Banyuwangi* no date). It is one of the leading tourism destinations in Banyuwangi Regency. Emphasizing the excellence of this community in the eyes of the world is very important. Every year, the Banyuwangi Government organizes various cultural and tourism events to promote and preserve local culture (Banyuwangi (Jawa Timur 2015). The advantages and existing events will be more developed with the presence of social media accounts. Social account management and management can be done by empowering the surrounding community. Community empowerment with these activities will further optimize the potential of the Osing Tribe Village and Tourism.

Empowerment is a way so that people, communities, and organizations are directed to control or rule over their lives (Lucchetti & Font 2013). There are five factors driving change in society: (1) levels of need, (2) direct benefits, (3) competition, (4) rewards or penalties, and (5) items and novelty. As an effort to adapt to the various changes that occur in cultural elements, to get a new balance in the order of social life, individuals as members of the community concerned can

---

*Corresponding author: nur.hadi.fis@um.ac.id

DOI 10.1201/9781003178163-25

carry out various reinterpretations of the cultural elements they have. Reinterpretation can occur in aspects of appearance, meaning, benefits, and aspects of particular cultural element's function (Mardikanto & Soebianto 2012).

This Community Service is carried out as an effort to increase understanding and skills for youth as the target group in developing tourism so that the hope is that the village will become a highly competitive community (Agung 2018). The approach is carried out based on participatory rural appraisal (PRA), which means basing the needs of the villagers, and they are active in the implementation of the training. The AIDA model will be used in conducting the training, namely Attention, Interest, Desire, Action to foster participant motivation and training effectiveness. We hope that with the PRA model of community-based empowerment activities, in social account management training, optimization of the Osing tribe tourism in Kemiren Village will be better improved.

Based on the analysis of the situation, this study formulates the following problems as follows: (1) how are the upgraded operational knowledge and skills about social account management used to optimize potential village Osing Kemiren tours in Banyuwangi Regency and (2) how to increase knowledge and skills in operating social accounts to optimize village Osing Kemiren tours in Banyuwangi Regency.

2 METHOD

This study used method of increasing knowledge and skills in the form of training to solve problems experienced by the Osing community. The target group is the Kemiren traditional village apparatus and village youth totaling 40 people. Community service was carried out using the RPA (participatory rural appraisal) approach, meaning that they base villagers' needs, and they are active in the implementation of the training. This training activity used the AIDA model, namely Attention, Interest, Desire, Action. With this approach, this activity's method is carried out by means of the creation, operation and training of creating social accounts for optimization village potential Osing tribe tour in the Village Kemiren could be improved. The activities carried out are lectures, questions and answers, discussions, demonstrations, training, and assignments. In supporting the success of this activity, several methods are used, including: (1) observation methods; (2) the question and answer method; (3) discussion method; (4) practical approach; (5) demonstration method.

3 RESULT AND DISCUSSION

Osing is a traditional community located in Kemiren Village, Banyuwangi Regency. The word Kemiren comes from the number of candlenuts, durian and palm trees in the history of the area's formation. The development of time made POKDARWIS spark Kemiren as an abbreviation of Kemroyok Mikul Rencana Nyata (gotong-royong), which is also the principle of community life. This traditional tourism village was formed because Kemiren has many unique customs, arts, culture, lifestyle, culinary delights that have been preserved for a long time(*Profil desa Kemiren – Desa Kemiren Banyuwangi, Desa Adat Kemiren, Desa wisata Osing Kemiren*, no date). Various events were held to promote Osing in local and international communities (Sumarmi et al. 2020).

Promotion is the spearhead of the development of the tourism sector and the regional economy. The result of promotional media in the digital era has made social media a very effective means. It is because 56% of the Indonesian population is an active user of social media. As many as 48% of them actively access their social media through their cellphones. This phenomenon shows that modern society is indeed attached to social media and gadgets. Because of technological development, distance is not an obstacle to conveying information from one place to another. moreover, technology makes us into the new reality, compression, reduction, compaction and acceleration which makes everything close, small and not limited to distance (Piliang 1998). Social media can be a means to explore tourism potential in Kemiren so that it attracts the attention of foreign and local tourists.

The use of social media as a means of promotion should pay attention to trends in society. The social media platforms that are actively used by Indonesians are reflected in figure 2. People tend to use the internet to open YouTube (88%), WhatsApp (83%), Facebook (81%), Instagram (80%) and line (59%). As service or product providers who want to carry out a promotional activity, we should consider the available options (Websindo 2019).

Ironically, when the world's development demands mastery of technology, it turns out that not all human resources know how to control it. In the case of the Osing tribe, for example, not all levels of society, business actors, or traditional and tourism activists have the ability to operate social media accounts. Meanwhile, on the other hand, they should have the ability to manage social media accounts to promote. It is clear why, in the end, people need to increase their knowledge and skills. So that in the formulation of general development policies, Banyuwangi Regency states that from the perspective of government institutions, it seeks to make efforts to improve performance through improving human resources (*RJPMD Kabupaten Banyuwangi 2019–2024* 2019).

One way to improve performance and improve the quality of human resources is by empowering the surrounding community. Empowerment is a way that people, communities, and organizations are directed to control or rule over their lives (Sembiring et al. 2019). A community's life basically undergoes social changes, both big and small, slow and fast, and this includes the Osing community in Banyuwangi Regency. Every society's life journey is dynamic, always experiencing social transformation, both traditional and modern (Made Pidata 2009). The emergence of socio-cultural changes can occur due to the influence of internal factors that arise from the dynamics of the life of the people supporting the culture itself, or effects that come from outside (Sairin 2002).

3.1 *Increased operational knowledge and skills about social account management*

Providing operational knowledge and skills on social account management to target groups is carried out to optimize the tourism potential of the Osing community in Kemiren Village, Banyuwangi Regency. This demand was born because of changes in consumer patterns in the current millennial era. 2012 data shows that in searching for information, 52% of consumers are search engine users. This choice is made because search engines provide more relevant and useful results. Only 7% felt that the results were less relevant. Digital media is one of the media that becomes a reference for the community to get information (Mansur & Adnan 2018). Like when people want to get information about the Osing Tribe, Kemiren Village, or Banyuwangi, consumers will search the website www.osingbanyuwangi.com (*Osing Banyuwangi*, no date) or other social media that provides this information. As a service provider or product related to the potential of Osing, it must be adaptive by making changes in sharing existing information. Changes in people's lifestyles in using the internet to search for information require increased knowledge and skills (Kurniawati et al. 2019). Lifestyle becomes a feature of a modern world through development or modernization, which causes the formation of various patterns of action that differentiate one person from another, or a group from another group (Chaney 2006).

The Osing community must master technology skills such as social media accounts to get accepted today. The results of field observations indicate that the availability of available resources is even in dire need of processing and marketing through online media. The development of the idea (brainstorming) is the availability of resources at the service location to enable digital marketing training to be carried out. Multimedia-based training media in the form of videos and hands-on practice using cell phone facilities to process promotional media. In its implementation, the training is categorized into two stages with different periods, including:

a. Practice method. This method involves activities between the implementing team and the target group to create, apply and operate the activity aspects' components correctly to achieve maximum results. This training is carried out through installing simple network infrastructure, creating an account (for those who don't have a Facebook and Instagram account), and digital product marketing.

b. Demonstration method. The participants use this method to show concrete clarity about the theory and steps for operational, post-operational preparation, and results. At this stage, participants: (1) take and process images independently (2) practice the material and experiences (3) the abilities are then monitored from their respective posts on their social media to see their capabilities in promoting the product from the production stage to being presented on social media pages such as Instagram or Facebook. Through this media, besides getting direct experience in delivering products to consumers, participants also understand how to attract potential buyers. Through uploads on the participants' social media accounts, the wider community can see firsthand the goods produced independently by the Osing community.

3.2 *Group empowerment in increasing knowledge and skills in an implementation*

Empowering the target group to have knowledge and skills in an implementation manner is carried out so that the community can operate social accounts to optimize the Osing Traditional Village's tourism potential in Kemiren Village, Banyuwangi Regency. Conceptually, community empowerment is an effort to increase the dignity of layers who are currently unable to escape the traps of poverty and underdevelopment. In other words, empowering is enabling and independent community (Al Siddiq et al. 2020). Cultural dynamics that technological advances have caused through the process of development or modernization have also been able to change the idealization of humans that have resulted in mass culture, consumerism and ecstatic culture of life (Subandy 1997).

There are five factors driving change in society: (1) levels of need, (2) direct benefits, (3) competition, (4) rewards or penalties, and (5) items and novelty. As an effort to adapt to the various changes that occur in cultural elements, to get a new balance in the order of social life, individuals as members of the community concerned can carry out various reinterpretations of the cultural elements they have. Reinterpretation can occur in aspects of appearance, meaning, benefits and aspects of a particular cultural element's function (Mardikanto & Soebianto 2012).

The Osing tribe has a very potential and adaptive society in facing social change. The existing community is divided into several active working groups such as BUMDES, POKDARWIS, Karang Taruna, and UMKM. The members of each community group are actively involved in the training given. They focus on the potential that can be explored in each field. Some of them also work in synergies, such as the synergy between BUMDES and Karang Taruna in the management of Warung Kemangi, art shop, and Kemiren screen printing. The collaboration between BUMDES and POKDARWIS is carried out in managing tour package providers, managing art studios and cultural festival activities, and homestays. On the other hand, there are MSME players who focus on developing "Jaran Goyang" coffee which is the mainstay of the Osing Tribe.

4 CONCLUSION

In the Osing tribe, not all levels of society, business actors, or traditional and tourism activists can operate social media accounts. Meanwhile, on the other hand, they should have the ability to manage social media accounts for promotion. This community service was made to solve resource problems in the Osing tribe. In the first stage, the team provides operational knowledge and skills on social account management. This training is carried out through installing simple network infrastructure, creating an account (a Facebook and Instagram account) and digital product marketing. Furthermore, in the second stage, the team empowers the target group to have knowledge and skills in an implementation manner. The effect is that the community can operate social accounts to optimize the Osing Traditional Village's tourism potential in Kemiren Village, Banyuwangi Regency.

REFERENCES

Agung (2018) *Pengembangan Desa Wisata untuk Kesejahteraan Masyarakat | Universitas Gadjah Mada*. Available at: https://ugm.ac.id/id/berita/15939-pengembangan.desa.wisata.untuk. kesejahteraan.masyarakat.

Banyuwangi (Jawa Timur, I. C. and T. S. (2015) *Banyuwangi, the New Paradise of Indonesian Tourism?: Visitor's Guide Book.* Banyuwangi Regency Culture and Tourism Service. Available at: https://books.google.co.id/books?id=RqLDDAEACAAJ.

Chaney, D. (2006) 'Life Styles Sebuah Pengantar Komprehensif (terjemahan)', *Yogyakarta: Jalasutra.*

Febriyantoro, M. T. and Arisandi, D. (2018) 'Pemanfaatan Digital Marketing Bagi Usaha Mikro, Kecil Dan Menengah Pada Era Masyarakat Ekonomi Asean', *JMD: Jurnal Riset Manajemen & Bisnis Dewantara.* doi: 10.26533/jmd.v1i2.175.

Kabupaten Banyuwangi (no date). Available at: https://banyuwangikab.go.id/.

Kurniawati, E., Chrissendy, M. and Saputra, D. (2019) '93 Behavioral factor influencing indonesian micro, small and medium (msme's) owners decision-making in adopting e-commerce', *Journal of Entrepreneurship, Business and Economics.*

Lucchetti, V. G. and Font, X. (2013) 'Community based tourism: critical success factors.', *ICRT occasional paper*, (OP27).

Made Pidata (2009) 'Landasan Kependidikan Stimulus Ilmu Pendidikan Bercorak Indonesia', in *Jakarta: Rineka Cipta.*

Mansur, N. K. and Adnan, F. (2018) 'Search engine optimization: Raising the ranking of Suku Osing websites on search engine page', in *Proceedings of the 2017 4th International Conference on Computer Applications and Information Processing Technology, CAIPT 2017.* doi: 10.1109/CAIPT.2017.8320731.

Mardikanto, T. and Soebianto, P. (2012) *Pemberdayaan masyarakat dalam perspektif kebijakan publik.* Alfabeta.

Osing Banyuwangi (no date). Available at: www.osingbayuwangi.com.

Piliang, Y. A. (1998) *Sebuah dunia yang dilipat: Realitas kebudayaan menjelang milenium ketiga dan matinya posmodernisme.* Mizan Pustaka.

Profil desa Kemiren – Desa Kemiren Banyuwangi, Desa Adat Kemiren, Desa wisata Osing Kemiren (no date). Available at: https://kemiren.com/tentang-desa-kemiren/ (Accessed: 1 February 2021).

RJPMD Kabupaten Banyuwangi 2019-2024 (2019). Available at: http://bappeda.jatimprov.go.id/bappeda/wp-content/uploads/dokren/rancangan_awal_rpjmd_jatim_2019_20 24.pdf.

Sairin, S. (2002) *Perubahan Sosial Masyarakat Indonesia: Perspektif Antropologi.* Pustaka Pelajar.

Sembiring, E. B. *et al.* (2019) 'Pemberdayaan Masyarakat Kampung Rempang Cate Melalui Pelatihan Pemasaran Digital untuk Produk Unggulan Pasir Panjang', *JURNAL PENGABDIAN MASYARAKAT (AbdiMas)*, 1(2), pp. 104–117.

Al Siddiq, I. H. *et al.* (2020) 'Encouraging Economic Development Through Local Community Participation in Sidoarjo, Indonesia', in. doi: 10.2991/assehr.k.200214.022.

Subandy, I. (1997) 'Ecstasy Gaya Hidup: Kebudayaan Pop dalam "Masyarakat Komoditas" Indonesia', *Bandung: Mizan Pustaka.*

Sumarmi *et al.* (2020) 'Cultural ecology of osing in development of Kemiren Tourist Village as international tourist attraction', in *IOP Conference Series: Earth and Environmental Science.* doi: 10.1088/1755-1315/485/1/012017.

Websindo (2019) *Indonesia Digital 2019?: Media Sosial, Websindo.*

Development, Social Change and Environmental Sustainability – Sumarmi et al (Eds)
© 2021 Taylor & Francis Group, London, ISBN 978-1-032-01320-6

From pandemic to infodemic: Bias information of covid-19 and ethical consideration among Indonesian youtuber

Rani Prita Prabawangi* & Megasari Noer Fatanti
Universitas Negeri Malang, Malang, Indonesia

ABSTRACT: Since WHO declared the COVID-19 outbreak a global pandemic in March 2020, the spread of information related to this virus has become increasingly unstoppable. Indonesia is not only facing a health crisis due to the spread of COVID-19, but also false information going around on a large scale on social media. The Indonesian government has identified more than 1400 hoaxes related to COVID-19 on social media. Based on the consideration of the novelty element of the phenomenon, there are three YouTube channels that discuss COVID-19. This study uses discourse analysis and literature review method, with a corpus of data gathered through searching digital archives. The outcomes of the analysis will later be linked to the concept of free speech and journalism ethics. In the end, this research seeks to find a common formula for addressing the COVID-19 infodemic phenomenon, especially what comes about in the social media ecosystem in Indonesia.

Keywords: COVID-19, infodemic, misinformation, social media

1 INTRODUCTION

The new coronavirus pandemic – hereafter known as COVID-19, was first identified in Wuhan, Hubei, China, after several cases of mysterious pneumonia that have spread rapidly since December 2019 (Huang et al. 2020). Seeing the extent of the spread of the virus that is increasingly widespread in various countries, WHO as the world health authority finally established a global pandemic status for COVID-19 in March 2020. Shortly after the status has been determined, information pandemics are spread around the world, both by mainstream media (television, newspapers, radio and magazines) and by the Internet. Since COVID-19 is a new type of coronavirus and the exact cause of it is not yet known, the public is actively seeking information via the Internet – both on social media and on video sharing sites (YouTube). As a medium that is affordable and provides abundant information, social media has become a new space for people to share health information with each other, especially regarding COVID-19. Based on the pre-research results, some informants said that they prefer to seek information about COVID-19 through social media rather than mainstream media, because of the fast and massive nature of social media (Brennen et al. 2020).

For example, information on health protocols (keep your distance, wash your hands, and wear a mask), people actually know first information spread on the Internet – one of which is YouTube. With this information, the public can prevent and reduce the spread of the virus and reduce the burden on health care institutions in a country. Therefore, it is very important to understand the information the public receives about the coronavirus, particularly during a pandemic. The opinion refers to a previous health studies showing that YouTube has the potential to spread misinformation (Madathil et al. 2015).

---

*Corresponding author: rani.prita.fis@um.ac.id

118

DOI 10.1201/9781003178163-26

This paper aims to analyze the extent to which Indonesian YouTubers are responsible for the false information that he has already spread through their YouTube channels. While some of the videos have been removed by YouTube, the public continues to believe that the information that is being disseminated is true.

2 LITERATURE REVIEW

2.1 *YouTube is a source of health information*

There is a growing body of evidence that e-health, Internet and social media-based interventions can improve the prevention and management of chronic diseases and lifestyle-related chronic-disease risk factors (Oldenburg et al. 2015). YouTube, one of the most popular video-sharing sites on the Internet, is increasingly being used as a platform to disseminate health information and may be a tool to assist in education regarding the prevention and management of type 2 diabetes among South Asian Internet users (Madathil et al. 2015). Despite this, the quality of health information online has been a concern; a systematic review revealed that studies have documented the availability of both high- and low-quality information (Eysenbach et al. 2002). Searching for health information online is typically classified as a low-risk activity, but a review has documented cases of harm as a result of online misinformation (Crocco et al. 2002). A systematic review of 18 studies investigating health-care information on YouTube through 2013 found that YouTube contains videos that portray misleading information that contradict evidence-based reference standards. On the top, Youtube accounts such 'Lisan Hamba' and Deddy Corbuzier are able to reach more than five and three million people. While at the same time, the top reach website -Beritasatu.com- can only reach three thousand people.

2.2 *Misinformation during pandemic COVID-19*

This pandemic causes us not only have to deal with virus outbreak but also an outbreak of disinformation about COVID-19 (OECD 2020). Due to the novelty of the virus and the limited information of it, a lot of people choose to share any information they have through social media especially when new cases are found. Research finds that a meaningful spatio-temporal relationship exists between information flow and new cases of COVID-19 (Singh et al. 2020). Study in Malaysia demonstrates a desire among students to share credible and correct information with their family and friends through social media (Hashim et al. 2020). This positive result was also found in Indonesia where social media culture can educate the public about COVID-19 (Sampurno et al. 2020). The preliminary data gathered indicates that while discussions about myths and links to poor quality information exist, their presence is less dominant than other crisis specific themes (Singh et al. 2020).

However, some research also finds worrying conditions about misinformation of Covid-19. In Indonesia, despite the overflowing information about Covid-19 is, some groups of people are found to be misinformed and uninformed about the origin, transmission and preventive measures (Nasir et al. 2020). It is not surprising, because even credible sources of information are available, the ability to reach audiences is far lower than the less incredible one. Other than the source, the information about Covid-19 itself is concerning. One of misinformation that is often talked about on social media is the conspiracy behind Covid-19. Some Indonesia youtubers agree on conspiracy theory although their scenarios of conspiracy are different from one another and lack of scientific data (Wahyudi & Akalili 2020). Research on conspiracy theory shows contradictory narrative from the Chinese and the American versions. Social media in China tells of America's efforts to make Covid a biological medium warfare or biological warfare against China (Mishra 2020). On the other hand, the American version accuses China of having lost control of testing biological weapons in its lab so that America holds China accountable for this pandemic (Mishra 2020).

3 METHODS

This research using a discourse analysis and literature study from various research about misinformation, pandemic Covid-19, and information belief. Others data gathered from three channel of Indonesian's YouTuber, namely Deddy Corbuzier, ANJI, and The Hermansyah A6. The research phase begins with sampling carried out by searching for videos on YouTube by entering the keywords "COVID-19", "Indonesian coronavirus", "COVID-19 conspiracy" and searching for viral YouTuber accounts in the mass media and activating the search filter for video sequences based on relevance. From the initial sample size of 50, the author selected 6 videos and then 2 videos were selected taking into account the number of subscribers, viewers, comments, and duration of discussion of an issue. The next stage is analyzing the video using discourse analysis with an in-depth search of YouTube policies related to video uploads to the theme of COVID-19 and the snares of the ITE Law in Indonesia over the dissemination of misinformation by the YouTuber.

4 RESULT AND ANALYSIS

4.1 *Indonesian's YouTuber and misinformation of COVID-19*

Like many other social media platforms, YouTube is powered by a search algorithm and recommender system based on the principle of "collaborative filtering," designed to help users navigate the millions of pieces of content available on its site (Bendersky et al. 2014). Based on the analysis of the findings from two videos taken from the Dunia MANJI and Deddy Corbuzier channels respectively, it can be classified as content that contains junk and conspirational elements. Videos relaying verifiably false information or conspiracy theories about the origin, transmission and treatment of the coronavirus; xenophobia and denial of mainstream scientific positions as assessed against WHO public advisory information. The first video, for example, was quoted from the Dunia MANJI channel containing an interview with Hadi Pranoto, who was introduced as a professor and microbiologist containing information related to the Covid-19 drug, which received comments from 305 people and has been shared more than a thousand times. However, this information has proven to be inaccurate, disrupting the public and hampering the management of the COVID-19 pandemic in Indonesia (Garnesia 2020a)

The second video, taken from channel Deddy Corbuzier with title "CORONA HANYA SEBUAH KEBOHONGAN KONSPIRASI!!!" (CORONA IS JUST A CONSPIRACY LIE!!!) by interviewing a public figure named Young Lex. It has been viewed 10 million times and has 8.52 million YouTube subscribers. In the video, Deddy Corbuzier and Young Lex talk about COVID-19 instead of the deadly virus and the vaccine is a global human depopulation strategy. These allegations are based on unreliable sources, because both individuals are unable to provide scientific evidence of their statements (Garnesia 2020b)

4.2 *Ethics in social media environment*

The nature of user generated content (UGC) owned by social media – one of which is YouTube, frees the audience to express themselves, although there are also some rules that both media content producers and connoisseurs need to follow. In this context, YouTube is designed as a democratic media, by providing opportunities for each individual to broadcast himself, both audio and visual, and to build relationships with viewers who are accommodated in their YouTube account channel (Allocca 2018). YouTube creators compete to show off different materials and finally exclude quality control. Eventually, two videos that are the unit of analysis in this paper show that (1) the mainstream media has a big challenge in clarifying the misinformation that has already spread through social media; (2) there needs to be a regulation in Indonesia that regulates YouTube digital media content, especially health issues; (3) support and involvement of literacy activists, government and citizens to monitor YouTube content that violates information policies.

5 SUMMARY

Social media with the nature of user generated content (UGC) which opens up space and makes it easier for individuals to produce information and share it, has become an opening for misinformation, especially during the current pandemic. The phenomenon of Indonesian YouTubers uploading interview videos discussing COVID-19 is recognized by some people as having good intentions to provide information to the public in simple language, but unfortunately information that has not been verified by a credible source has already been disseminated and apparently contains misinformation. People who use social media as a reference about COVID-19 are in fact getting an incomplete understanding, especially when the information is claimed to be untrue.

The dissemination of health information, especially about Covid-19 is poor, and in particular the lack of clarification and verification, makes it even more difficult for the public to distinguish between truth and falsehood. This means that health care consumers who obtain information about COVID-19 on YouTube are poorly informed. This may lead to misconceptions about the treatment, prevention and general characteristics of the virus. We recommend that people verify the facts they learn on YouTube with more reliable sources of information such as conventional mass media, health care professionals, or online updates by WHO or Ministry of Health of the Republic of Indonesia.

As a final recommendation, we hope to see policies around the dissemination of health information through social media. Although YouTube is the platform that initiated the regulation, it appears that it has not been properly implemented within the Indonesian context. We see the need for commitment and participation from many parties, such as literacy activists, journalists and netizens, to establish rules related to health misinformation.

REFERENCES

Allocca, K. (2018) *Videocracy: How YouTube is changing the world... with double rainbows, singing foxes, and other trends we can't stop watching*. Bloomsbury Publishing.

Bendersky, M. *et al.* (2014) 'Up next: retrieval methods for large scale related video suggestion', in *Proceedings of the 20th ACM SIGKDD international conference on Knowledge discovery and data mining*, pp. 1769–1778.

Brennen, J. S. *et al.* (2020) 'Types, sources, and claims of COVID-19 misinformation', *Reuters Institute*, 7, pp. 1–3.

Crocco, A. G., Villasis-Keever, M. and Jadad, A. R. (2002) 'Analysis of cases of harm associated with use of health information on the internet', *Jama*, 287(21), pp. 2869–2871.

Eysenbach, G. *et al.* (2002) 'Empirical studies assessing the quality of health information for consumers on the world wide web: a systematic review', *Jama*, 287(20), pp. 2691–2700.

Garnesia, I. (2020a) 'Menilik Disinformasi Hadi Pranoto tentang COVID-19', *tirto.id*. Available at: https://tirto.id/menilik-disinformasi-hadi-pranoto-tentang-covid-19-fVqn.

Garnesia, I. (2020b) 'Periksa Fakta "Konspirasi COVID-19" ala Deddy Corbuzier & Young Lex', *tirto.id*. Available at: https://tirto.id/periksa-fakta-konspirasi-covid-19-ala-deddy-corbuzier- young-lex-eRVi.

Hashim, S. *et al.* (2020) 'Students' intention to share information via social media: A case study of COVID-19 pandemic', *Indonesian Journal of Science and Technology*, 5(2), pp. 236–245.

Huang, C. *et al.* (2020) 'Clinical features of patients infected with 2019 novel coronavirus in Wuhan, China', *The lancet*, 395(10223), pp. 497–506.

Madathil, K. C. *et al.* (2015) 'Healthcare information on YouTube: a systematic review', *Health informatics journal*, 21(3), pp. 173–194.

Mishra, S. (2020) 'The Post-Pandemic World Order: Nine Pointers', *New York: IndraStra Global*.

Nasir, N. M., Baequni, B. and Nurmansyah, M. I. (2020) 'Misinformation related to COVID-19 in Indonesia', *Jurnal Administrasi Kesehatan Indonesia*, 8(2), pp. 51–59.

OECD (2020) 'Combatting COVID-19 disinformation on online platforms', *OECD Policy Responses to Coronavirus (COVID-19)*, (July), pp. 1–7. Available at: http://www.oecd.org/coronavirus/policy-responses/combatting-covid-19- disinformation-on-online-platforms-d854ec48/.

Oldenburg, B. *et al.* (2015) 'Using new technologies to improve the prevention and management of chronic conditions in populations', *Annual review of public health*, 36, pp. 483–505.

Sampurno, M. B. T., Kusumandyoko, T. C. and Islam, M. A. (2020) 'Budaya media sosial, edukasi masyarakat, dan pandemi COVID-19', *SALAM: Jurnal Sosial dan Budaya Syar-i*, 7(5).

Singh, L. *et al.* (2020) 'A first look at COVID-19 information and misinformation sharing on Twitter', *arXiv preprint arXiv:2003.13907*.

Wahyudi, G. S. and Akalili, A. (2020) 'Narrative of Covids as Conspiracy on Youtube', *JCommsci-Journal Of Media and Communication Science*, 1(1), pp. 26–37.

Development, Social Change and Environmental Sustainability – Sumarmi et al (Eds)
© 2021 Taylor & Francis Group, London, ISBN 978-1-032-01320-6

How virtual fancy things build self-presentation? Consumer's acceptance and use of e-commerce

A.D. Yuniar & A.S Fibrianto*
Universitas Negeri Malang, Malang City, Indonesia

ABSTRACT: The virtual environment has been fast-growing as an ICT tool and making human life much easier. Industrial culture creates a "false need" for using ICTs because of mass production and passive consumer monopolies. The existence of "addictive behavior" about how the impact of smartphones and the internet is more complex for social change, especially lifestyle. This behavior then forms what Goffman called self-presentations. This paper used TAM grand theory of as the basis for its analysis element of perceived usefulness and ease of use which is important to consumers adopted the technology. Information richness has unlimited information as a form of unlimited consumer choices. The enjoyment of the performance industry will create a strategy that is not only informational but has an entertaining and enriching element.

Keywords: lifestyle, technology, e-commerce, society

1 INTRODUCTION

Most of modern society will answer the smartphone as a primary need. It cannot be denied when smartphones are now in line with cloth, food and shelter. After all, digital society necessities now depend on that one "smart" thing. This explanation implies that smartphones are a technology that embraces post-structuralism. This concept broadly states that technology is built-in with everything and become a part of modern society. People without hesitation in buying communication technology can be used as an investment, as evidenced by the emergence of technologies that continuously innovate, e.g., smartphones with advanced features and have high prices circulating on the broader community. The smartphone also raises attention in people seeing the extent of human efforts and following the trends they dream of. This trend can be seen when dressed up. This is reminiscent of a form of dramaturgy by Goffman. His self-presentation of everyday life sparked the term dramaturgy, which is how someone acts like they are on a stage. It implies that everyone wants to be the center of attention.

Since the existence of smartphones and social media, dramaturgy also exists in the social environment. If we do not know the latest trends which originate from social media, we can be "out of date." This drama then leads to the appearance; when people use a suitable fashion, it will be impacted through praise. (Ibrahim 2011) stated that we live where the standard of success is determined by materialistic prestige. Furthermore, (Hanson 2007) the existence of "addictive behavior" and "illusion of control" about how the impact of smartphones and the Internet is more complex for the social change of each individual, which is different on beliefs, attitudes, and values. Everyone takes part to show prestige values on how to appears *'image becomes more important than substance.'* People no longer see the basic needs values, but the satisfaction value of getting them. It all depends on the perspective; some say that looking fashionable is a form of self-respect because most people say "you are what you wear." Thus, lifestyle is not only about people with financial

---

*Corresponding author: ananda.dwitha.fis@um.ac.id

DOI 10.1201/9781003178163-27

stability, but also people from the poor too. This lifestyle can then become a profitable commodity for the appearance industry. Along with the development of new media, the appearance industry business is increasingly emerging through e-commerce (e-comm). What technology and modernization offers is something real, and no one can hinder it. Whether people like it or not, people who live with ICT development will adapt to all modern treats. For this reason, this paper will discuss e-comm strategies that stimulate the consumptive lifestyle of modern society. This paper will also discuss what factors drive this consumptive behavior, with the following questions: How the online store market strategy encourages the consumptive lifestyle of modern society?

2 METHOD

This research is a conceptual-based article with a descriptive approach. This study focuses on the concept of self-presentation (Goffman) from a consumer perspective using the analysis of the Technology Acceptance Model Theory to see the consumer acceptance side of e-comm. The primary data is obtained from some e-comm market share, namely ZL, which focuses on the fashion industry, LZ, which focuses on the smartphone industry, and Go-Glam (part of Go) focuses on the service industry (method data market share) It is undeniable; some existing e-comm has changed consumer behavior to be addictive, especially in self-prestige and self-presentation.

3 RESULT

3.1 *Technology Acceptance Model (TAM) of consumer appearance industry*

To see the process of acceptance or adoption of an innovation in information technology by the public, a Technology Acceptance Model (TAM) model, derived from the grand theory of innovation diffusion, can now be used. The TAM model's choice is because diffusion and adoption theory is quite broad for the fields of producer marketing and consumer behavior since consumers play a role as an advantage of the marketing technology system. Research on the adoption and innovation of technology on consumer behavior has been conducted by Hwang and Jeong in 2014 on "Electronic commerce and online consumer behavior" which consists of technology in the form of features presented by the E-comm platform and also in terms of changes in the form of communication in modern society. This theory consists of 2 main factors, perceived usefulness related to the uses and benefits provided to e-comm to customers and perceived ease of use related to the ease of accessing and using e-comm technology. This two elements are useful for consumers to adopt the technology.

Virtual reality is a human way of visualizing, manipulating, and interacting with very complex computers and data (Piliang 2004). This virtual reality can carry out various interactive activities daily. This virtual reality then gives rise to what (Robins 1995) calls the digital environment as a collection of all events, facts, reality into something real. The digital environment has proliferated and powerful as an ICT tool capable of making people's lives much better and more accessible. The digital era changes people to become more fluent in using digital technology and they can actualize themselves to be always up to date. Furthermore, online shopping using an e-comm platform is becoming increasingly popular because of the effectiveness and ease of use for information and society (Yuniar & Fibrianto 2019). Goffman also noted that sometimes an individual might be highly strategic in crafting an image but unaware that they create an impression as Gillette (Kucuk 2002) emphasized that the internet is playing a significant role in spurring consumerism by increasing consumer-driven market efficiency.

Perceived of usefulness, related to the uses and benefits provided to e-comm to customers. ZL can answer the needs of men's and women's fashion by offering leading brands, both local and international. ZL also always provides products that always follow the latest fashion trends that provide many choices to enhance consumer appearance. Various models of shoes, clothes, Muslim clothes, bags, accessories, batik, and sports as well as beauty & grooming products for men and women, can be easily obtained. In addition, ZL Indonesia also provides flexible pricing options and often holds special promos with attractive discount offers through the newsletter that is displayed when opening the initial website appearance. Meanwhile, the element of perceived ease of use is related to the ease of accessing and using e-comm technology. ZL reates an attractive website so that many consumers are not bored. It has many advertisements with relevant information. When a consumer opens a link, the ZL website ad link will appear. ZL created the ZL website to easily access the products offered and to display all complete information about ZL.

According to data obtained from the LZ website, the product with the most popular sales category is smartphones. If based on the value of goods, smartphones, including primary needs, are equivalent to clothing, food and shelter. Technology offered is increasingly sophisticated and makes it easier for people to mobilize. With prices that are still relatively high, people have now applied trust to e-comm without seeing the original physical appearance of the smartphone to be purchased. In the element of perceived ease of use, It presents various kinds of smartphone brands depending on the preferences of each consumer. They also provides reviews of each distributor that can be used as a guarantee of safety. Through the media website, LZ provides more in-depth and more flexible information about the form and benefits of a product. The role of website provides media to help consumers who are actively looking for the products they need. Based on the author's own experience, They create enough value and attraction for consumers who visit the site to stay and come back to make purchases. In this case continues to update their site to keep the site up to date. Whereas in the perceived usefulness element, LZ provides free shipping or cash on delivery using LZ Express for free and consumers just wait at home.

Go Glam is an extension of Go-Jek's business line that focuses on services. Initially, Go-jek focused as a facilitator between conventional motorcycle taxis and technology. However, along with market needs and the development of technology, Go expanded its business in the appearance industry. Through Go Glam, consumers don't have to bother coming to the salon and queuing for a long time. Simply by downloading the application, beauty services can be done at home or at the office. The beauty services provided by Go Glam include nail care, hair care, makeup, massage, facials, and so on. According to data obtained from the Go Glam application, the perceived usefulness for consumers includes high-quality services that guarantee the results will satisfy consumers. In addition, the operating hours are long so that whenever consumers need services, they will always be available. Then, guarantee high quality service because Go Glam works with professional beauticians who use quality products so they will provide the best service. The last benefit is that the professional partners who work with Go Glam have at least 2 years of experience and have gone through a long selection process. Whereas in the element of perceived ease of use, Go Glam provides a user-friendly application with a predominance of pink which is certainly very attractive to women. The application is also equipped with testimonials and video teasers of how Go Glam works professionally.

4 DISCUSSION

Ibrahim, in 2011, explained that the idea of a lifestyle has been corrupted by consumerism, thereby intending to commodify itself. According to Mowen and Minor (Punj 2011) consumerism is a community movement with government assistance to strengthen the rights and power of buyers in relation to sellers. Related to consumptive behavior is shopaholics in which consumers are "addicted" to shopping without thinking about the benefits of the goods they buy (Solomon & Panda 2004). Thus, from the definition described above, it can be concluded that consumerism refers to consumer protection related to the consumer protection law, while consumptive refers to deviant behavior. This consumptive lifestyle then supports the appearance industry to provide and facilitate consumers with various innovation strategies. The strategies undertaken by e-comm owners are now increasingly unique and clever in offering their products with a lure that will certainly be tempting for those who see them. It becomes a further observation, where the "temptation" that comes from the online world, with all the conveniences offered, invites consumers to do things that shouldn't exist or need what they shouldn't need. The psychological condition of society that tends to be consumptive and this novelty is then taken advantage of by the appearance industry business manufacturers.

The consumptive lifestyle of the community in doing repetitive shopping is influenced by four elements, first, time saving where the e-comm digital catalog can present a variety of choices at one time. Consumers only need to scroll the page and place an order without the need to look for parking and long queues at the checkout which can take a long time. (Comor 2000) also explains that shopping via the internet can have high-speed communication in conveying understanding to consumers straightforwardly without spending much time searching for and making transactions related to products. In the context of the e-comm appearance industry, consumers can shop while doing other activities. It is different if consumers come to the store. Such as the features presented by ZL which have categorized their products such as shirts, blazers, heels and so on. So if consumers are looking for a blazer, just click on the category, and tens or even hundreds of blazers from various brands will be displayed on the page. Then consumers can choose according to their individual preferences.

Second, money saving because so many digital catalogs are presented, consumers can compare prices with one another. Then Ettenberg, in 2002, adds that simply making payments at home or at the office through online shopping can minimize expenses from one store to another. According to my argument, money-saving here means that consumers can save a number of their expenses for certain products because there are many price and quality comparisons according to consumer desires. However, this money-saving can also stimulate consumers to make purchases related to appearance. For example, if initially what consumers need is sports shoes, but in the catalog of all branded shoe products are discounting heels, wedges, and flat shoes, consumers can easily be tempted to buy sports shoes at first because the discounts in the same catalog consumers are willing to make repayment of products they do not need.

The final element of consumptive support is enjoyment, based on the concept of the appearance industry that society now prioritizes appearance over function, if external appearance is more important than the substance itself, the performance industry players will create a strategy that does not only contain information, but also has entertaining and enriching elements. In this context, after expanding its business, this application is increasingly attached and causes consumers to become addicted in utilizing the services offered ranging from food ordering services and beauty services. The digital appearance industry provides guarantee and security for the goods sold, this also encourages people's consumption behavior in shopping.

5   CONCLUSION

The whole appearance industry: e-comm e.g LZ, ZL, and Go Glam, takes advantage of market opportunities that currently focus on style-oriented society, where appearance is everything and appearance makes their existence in society even more "recognized." The issue of lifestyle now does not only belong to people with financial stability, some of those who live mediocre also have certain lifestyles. This lifestyle can then become a commodity and a big business for the appearance industry. Competition in business makes the appearance industry provide and facilitate consumers with various innovation strategies. The strategies undertaken by e-comm owners are now increasingly unique and clever in offering their products with the lure that will certainly be tempting for those who see them.

From the description above, the strength provided by the appearance industry is able to stimulate a consumptive lifestyle because of the time saving where the e-comm digital catalog can present a variety of choices at one time. Consumers only need to scroll the page and place an order without the need to look for parking and long queues at the checkout which take a long time. Money saving is also a factor because so many digital catalogs are presented, consumers can make price comparisons with one another. Information richness has unlimited information as a form of unlimited consumer choices. The enjoyment of the performance industry will create a strategy that is not only informational, but has an entertaining and enriching element.

REFERENCES

Comor, E. (2000) 'Household consumption on the internet: Income, time, and institutional contradictions', *Journal of Economic Issues*. doi: 10.1080/00213624.2000.11506246.

Ettenberg, E. (2002) *The Next Economy: Will you know where your customers are?*

Hanson, J. (2007) *24/7: How cell phones and the Internet change the way we live, work, and play*. Greenwood Publishing Group.

Hwang, Y. and Jeong, J. (2014) 'Electronic commerce and online consumer behavior research: A literature review', *Information Development*. doi: 10.1177/0266666914551071.

Ibrahim, I. S. (2011) *Kritik budaya komunikasi: budaya, media, dan gaya hidup dalam proses demokratisasi di Indonesia*. Jalasutra.

Kucuk, S. U. (2002) 'The changing consumerism with the internet: a global perspective', *Journal of Euromarketing*, 12(1), pp. 41–61.

Piliang, Y. A. (2004) *Posrealitas: realitas kebudayaan dalam era posmetafisika*. Jalasutra.

Punj, G. (2011) 'Effect of Consumer Beliefs on Online Purchase Behavior: The Influence of Demographic Characteristics and Consumption Values', *Journal of Interactive Marketing*. doi: 10.1016/j.intmar.2011.04.004.

Robins, K. (1995) 'Cyberspace and the world we live in', *Body & Society*, 1(3–4), pp. 135–155.

Solomon, M. R. and Panda, T. K. (2004) *Consumer behavior, buying, having, and being*. Pearson Education India.

Yuniar, A. D. and Fibrianto, A. S. (2019) 'The Affect of Technical Familiarity and Consumer Protection Behavior in Using E-Commerce as Platform Online Shopping', in *Proceedings – 2019 International Seminar on Application for Technology of Information and Communication: Industry 4.0: Retrospect, Prospect, and Challenges, iSemantic 2019*. doi: 10.1109/ISEMANTIC.2019.8884265.

Development, Social Change and Environmental Sustainability – Sumarmi et al (Eds)
© 2021 Taylor & Francis Group, London, ISBN 978-1-032-01320-6

Assessing the role of mass media in information mitigation on COVID-19 pandemic issues in Indonesia: A discourse analysis on *KOMPAS* daily newspaper

Megasari Noer Fatanti*
Universitas Negeri Malang, Malang City, Indonesia

Choiria Anggraini
Telkom University, Bandung City, Indonesia

ABSTRACT: The spread of the COVID-19 outbreak caused by the novel coronavirus across continents has also garnered Indonesian media attention from a variety of perspectives. As a national newspaper, KOMPAS has regularly reported on the coronavirus that has spread from Wuhan, China since January 2020. The aim of this paper is to investigate where the media places responsibility for COVID-19 in Indonesia. KOMPAS newspaper articles have been sampled from 12 January to 18 May 2020. Investigators collected 30 news samples between January and May of 2020. The news samples were then categorized into three big themes, namely (1) prevention strategies; (2) outbreak management; and (3) the communication strategy for further analysis using reality construction theory to determine how KOMPAS narrated the COVID-19 outbreak that happened in Indonesia. As preliminary findings, the role of the media is very crucial to oversee the government to make optimal efforts in the detection, monitoring and management of handling COVID-19. In addition, the media plays a major role in shaping public perceptions of the health risks of COVID-19. However, on the other hand, some people get fed up with news related COVID-19. This is because the viewpoint of writing presented in the media considered it haunting and put pressure on the public.

Keywords: crisis communication, COVID-19, KOMPAS, mass media, media discourse

1   INTRODUCTION

For the first time in the past year, health issues has become the dominant narrative in the national print media coverage. The spread of the COVID-19 outbreak cross continents has also attracted media attention, particularly in Indonesia. Most of national media take COVID-19 as main news. Republika, for example, printed as much as 42.3 percent of COVID-19 news raised in February. This theme also become the main discussion for other media, such as KOMPAS and Media Indonesia (MI) (Kompas 2020). Print media in Indonesia use various approaches in reporting each stage of the development of COVID-19. Educational efforts were also carried out to ward off false information and calm the public regarding the COVID-19 outbreak. In this case, the efforts of several print media to provide comforting information for the public show that the mass media continue to function as information and educational media as mandated by "Constitutional Law Number 40 Year 1999 about Press" of 1999. This needs to be done so that the public can absorb complete information about COVID-19 amid the flood of information on social media. This article aims

---

*Corresponding author: megasari.fatanti.fis@um.ac.id

128

DOI 10.1201/9781003178163-28

to find out the narrative of the news about COVID-19 in the KOMPAS newspaper as a form of mitigating the health crisis during the pandemic.

2 LITERATURE REVIEW

2.1 *Risk communication in health issue*

According to (Coombs 2014) a crisis is defined as the perception of unpredictable events and has the potential to seriously threaten stakeholder expectations, and can affect the performance of an organization and produce negative output. Meanwhile, crisis communication is the collection, processing and dissemination of information needed to handle a crisis situation. Crisis communication is the most important process of managing a complex organization. Most of the crisis communication literature still discusses organizational or corporate crises with a top-down model and very limited discussion relating to interactive crisis communication during disaster conditions (Coombs 2014; Fearn-Banks 2016; Fronz 2011; Lerbinger 2012). Furthermore, the crisis communication literature is very much dominated by Western approaches which are sometimes not fully applicable in Indonesia due to different levels of disaster awareness, various levels of technology adoption, complicated bureaucratic processes, and the high influence of local culture in daily communication behavior (Gultom & Joyce 2014). Several studies that discuss crisis communication strategies in dealing with health issues or pandemics still focus on the use of media as a channel for delivering messages, not many have systematically discussed the stages of comprehensive crisis communication (Reynolds & Seeger, 2005; Reynolds & Quinn 2008).

2.2 *Roles of mass media*

Mass media or mass communication has a strategic role and function in dealing with various problems that arise in human life. Mass media is a form of communication aimed at a number of general audiences, in large numbers, and through print or electronic media, and with this form of communication, the information disseminated can reach various elements of society. Mass media is a powerful source of control, management, and innovation tools in society that can be utilized as a substitute for other strengths or resources (McQuail 1987; Rosenberry &Vicker 2017). In pandemic conditions, the mass media has an important role in conveying accurate information about the spread of the virus to increase public awareness to live clean in order to avoid transmission of the COVID-19 virus. The presence of mass media, especially newspapers and television is also a strategy to clarify the large amount of false information that has been spread through social media related to COVID-19.

3 METHODS

To develop a comprehensive description of how the mass media in Indonesia are reporting on the COVID-19 pandemic, we chose a qualitative research approach. The research method used is discourse analysis on COVID-19 news published by the KOMPAS newspaper in the January to May 2020 period. Document analysis has a similar analogy to discourse analysis, therefore we use documents in the form of news to build public health realities in context of social media in Indonesia (Zeegers & Barron 2015). The research analysis unit consists of 30 news items classified into three themes, namely: prevention strategies, health crisis management and communication strategies. Based on the interpretation of the data generated from this research, it was found that KOMPAS had a high intensity in the prevention strategy phase and the lack of available personal protective equipment (PPE) for health workers, but decreased slightly when the government's narrative regarding the crisis seemed to underestimate what was conveyed by the media. From February to March, KOMPAS coverage was more focused on economic issues as an impact from

Table 1.

No	Main Themes	Sub-Themes
1.	Prevention Strategy	1.1 Building awareness in mass media
		1.2 Screening of possible cases
		1.3 Quarantine of possible cases
		1.4 Building task force team for COVID-19
		1.5 Development of COVID-19 barrier policies
		1.6 Collaboration with another country and organization
2.	Outbreak Management	2.1 Isolation & treatment of COVID-19 cases
		2.2 Test & contact tracing of suspected COVID-19 case
		2.3 Procurement of personal protective equipment
3.	Communication Strategy	3.1 To engage the population
		3.2 To control the outbreak
		3.3 To prevent fake news (conspiracy etc.)
		3.4 Building public optimism

Source: Author, 2020

COVID-19 pandemic. Final review results in April, KOMPAS has again highlighted government policies in tackling COVID-19 transmission, such as for example urging the government to carry out the 3M movement (tracing, testing, treatment).

4 RESULT AND ANALYSIS

4.1 *COVID-19 discourse on KOMPAS daily newspaper*

Through out the beginning of 2020 to mid-February, the coronavirus attack was the central theme of coverage in six national newspapers in Indonesia (Kompas 2020). Public vigilance against the attack of the coronavirus, which is known as a deadly virus, is in line with the agenda of setting newspapers which intensively discusses it as headlines on page one. Based on the results of the content analysis of 30 headlines from the KOMPAS newspaper for the period of January to May of 2020, it shows the firmness of the news regarding the increasingly rapid spread of the virus and the weak management of the Indonesian government's crisis. The headline narrative for the January to February period emphasizes that Indonesia has entered a critical period for the COVID-19 pandemic. In addition, newspapers are also critical of the handling of COVID-19 by the government, for example in terms of providing means of personal protective equipment (PPE) and masks which are increasingly depleting for health workers. On the other hand, the newspapers appreciated the efforts of mutual cooperation from the community independently of the solidarity efforts of providing personal protective equipment (PPE) for medical personnel. Meanwhile, from March to May, news stories began to develop discussing the role of health workers in dealing with the pandemic and briefly reviewing the development of the COVID-19 vaccine in several countries.

4.2 *COVID-19 newsmaker in mass media*

For almost three months, the COVID-19 outbreak was reported on page one in six national newspapers, a number of figures were recorded by newsmakers. The newsmaker is a party in the news and is in the media spotlight because they are the ones quoted. President Joko Widodo is the newsmaker with the most quoted statements by six national newspapers regarding COVID-19. The next newsmaker is Achmad Yurianto, the government spokesman for the handling of COVID-19. The role of Achmad Yurianto, explaining to the press regarding the development of the handling of COVID-19, places him as an official source of information or a reference that is forwarded by the press to the news. If traced further, the attributes of the resource persons will also focus on the President and ministers or ministerial staff related to handling COVID-19. Next, community members rank next as sources who are consistently consulted by newspapers for their opinions or statements.

5 SUMMARY

Preventive efforts against COVID-19 are currently the joint responsibility of the government and society. No matter how strong the instructions from the government to limit themselves, even to the level of quarantine, without the active role of citizens to work together to protect themselves by maintaining health, efforts to suppress the spread of COVID-19 will be in vain. Effective public communication in times of crisis does not only rely on digital media, but must optimize the combination of digital and conventional media. For example, the use of traditional or local communication channels, mass media, social media, chat applications and creative networks (Ramadani 2019). It also relies on opinion leaders (opinion leaders, influencers), educational institutions (campuses, schools), religious, social, local bureaucracy (RT, RW), and so on. The use of communication channels between individuals and groups, as well as direct communication interventions in the field, are needed in order to absorb community responses and accelerate the delivery of information from the government. In reference to Kriyantono and Sa'diyah, 2018, one of the reasons for the failure of government communication in dealing with crises is the lack of understanding of communicators in managing communication and public culture.

REFERENCES

'Constitutional Law Number 40 Year 1999 about Press' (1999).
Coombs, W. T. (2014) *Ongoing crisis communication: Planning, managing, and responding.* Sage Publications.
Fearn-Banks, K. (2016) *Crisis communications: A casebook approach.* Routledge.
Fronz, C. (2011) *Strategic management in crisis communication: A multinational approach.* Diplomica Verlag.
Gultom, D. I. and Joyce, Z. (2014) 'Crisis communication capacity for disaster resilience: Community participation of information providing and verifying in Indonesian volcanic eruption', in *ANZTSR 2014.*
Kriyantono, R. and Sa'diyah, H. (2018) 'Kearifan Lokal dan Strategi Komunikasi *Public Relations* di BUMN dan Perusahaan Swasta', *Jurnal ILMU KOMUNIKASI.* doi: 10.24002/jik.v15i2.1480.
Lerbinger, O. (2012) *The crisis manager: Facing disasters, conflicts, and failures.* Routledge.
McQuail, D. (1987) *Mass communication theory: An introduction.* Sage Publications, Inc.
Ramadani, T. (2019) 'The Implementation of Public Communication Management Policy at Ministry of Energy and Mineral Resources', *Jurnal Borneo Administrator.* doi: 10.24258/jba.v15i1.369.
Reynolds, B. and Quinn, S. C. (2008) 'Effective communication during an influenza pandemic: the value of using a crisis and emergency risk communication framework', *Health promotion practice*, 9(4_suppl), pp. 13S-17S.
Reynolds, B. and Seeger, M. W. (2005) 'Crisis and emergency risk communication as an integrative model', *Journal of Health Communication.* doi: 10.1080/10810730590904571.
Rosenberry, J. and Vicker, L. A. (2017) *Applied mass communication theory: A guide for media practitioners.* Routledge.
Zeegers, M. and Barron, D. (2015) *Milestone Moments in Getting your PhD in Qualitative Research, Milestone Moments in Getting your PhD in Qualitative Research.* doi: 10.1016/C2014-0-02299-X.

Development, Social Change and Environmental Sustainability – Sumarmi et al (Eds)
© 2021 Taylor & Francis Group, London, ISBN 978-1-032-01320-6

The levels of empowerment of forest farmer group in coastal village development in South Malang, Indonesian

Kukuh Miroso Raharjo*, Sucipto, Zulkarnain, Hardika & Monica Widyaswari
Department of Nonformal Education, Faculty of Education, Universitas Negeri Malang

ABSTRACT: This study aims to determine the level of empowerment of the Forest Farmers Group (KTH) through the implementation of nonformal education programs in the South Malang region. This study used a mixed research approach (mixed methods). The quantitative method is done by survey methods, while in-depth interviews support the qualitative. The results of the research as a whole show that the level of empowerment of the Forest Farmer Group (KTH) through the implementation of nonformal education in the South Malang region is good with a percentage of 79.56%. These results are supported by the suitability of the results for each sub variable, namely sub-variables (1) power within; (2) power to; (3) power over; and (4) power with. The level of empowerment is influenced by factors including the intensity of group counselling which is expected to provide life skills for KTH members and make it easier to obtain information related to the forest area development.

Keywords: Community Empowerment, Forest Farmers Group, Nonformal Education, Coastal Village Development

1 INTRODUCTION

Community development is something that must be taken in order to create independent human resources. Community development will be more effective and productive if regional development is based on the geographical condition, character and talents of the community concerned as an influencing factors in village development (Yilmaz et al. 2010). Therefore, the village development mechanism needs to be endeavoured based on a portrait of regional potential, as potential natural resources as well as human resources. To make this happen, it requires hard work from all elements of the village community who can describe the physical condition of the village as the potential and talent of the community in understanding and managing specific potentials.

Building a strong community cannot be separated from the community's habit, therefore efforts are needed to equip oneself with knowledge. This is based on the increase in human resources not only focused on physical development. Therefore, the readiness of the community must also be improved, the community is also required to be able to take advantage of their potential, considering that society also has dynamics that make them able to survive in difficult circumstances. This is a potential that can be developed to improve their standard of living. The existence of development with this approach is known as bottom-up development. The development is considered more meaningful for the community, because it fully involves the community (Brem & Wolfram 2014; Khadka & Vacik 2012; M'hamdi & Nemiche 2018).

The empowerment of coastal village communities cannot be separated from their local wisdom. Therefore, socio-cultural institutions must be the main foothold. Community empowerment will

---

*Corresponding author: kukuh.raharjo.fip@um.ac.id

not be well received by coastal village communities if they do not pay attention to local socio-cultural aspects (Rukin et al. 2018).The Forest Farmers Group or KelompokTaniHutan (KTH) is a community group under the auspices of the Ministry of Environment and Forestry (KLHK) of the Republic of Indonesia which is currently being optimized in implementing activities to form and develop social forestry management in the form of groups or individuals living in forest areas and managing the area. Forestry workers have collaborated and obtained permits with the Ministry of Environment and Forestry. Following this, the Ministry of LHK has issued a decree number SK.945/MENLKH-PSKL/PKPS/PSL.O/3/2018 dated March 5, 2018, concerning the granting of Social Forestry Forest Utilization Permits/IPHPS to the KTH Bangkit Sejahtera and KTH Tunggul-Wulung areas: 3,102 Ha (2,393 Ha in Permanent Production Forest Area; and 709 Ha in Protected Forest Area), and location of Gajahrejo and Tumpakrejo Villages, with 2,200 KTH Members.

One of the people who live in the forest area is the people of Bajulmati, Gajahrejo Village, Gedangan District, Malang Regency. The condition and culture of the people of Gedangan District who work as farmers. With the collaboration between Perhutani and the community living in forest areas, it provides opportunities for the community to manage the forest. One form of management is through the Social Forestry Business Group (KUPS). Forest management is a system that can guarantee the realization of the sustainability of forest functions and benefits from economic, ecological and social aspects. Sustainable forest management does not only talk about cutting forest products but can also create an ecosystem where people live in forest areas which further serve as a form of coastal village development.

This research was conducted in Gedangan District, Malang Regency. Due to the formation of empowerment for the community through the Forest Farmers Group, efforts to protect the environment and develop the community to take advantage of the potential that exists around them. The condition of community empowerment is closely related to the science of nonformal education, namely in community empowerment, it is hoped that this program will create human resources who can overcome problems such as social, economic, and community independence.Based on the description, the researcher wants to examine the level of empowerment of The Forest Farmers Group through the implementation of nonformal education programs in the development of coastal villages in the South Malang region.

2 METHOD

This study used a mixed research approach (mixed methods). The mixed-methods approach used in this study is a quantitative approach supported by a qualitative approach. The quantitative approach is carried out with a survey method using a questionnaire instrument. At the same time, the qualitative approach in this study is used to reinforce the quantitative data obtained and to find out what factors could influence the level of empowerment of the Forest Farmers Group in developing coastal villages through the implementation of nonformal education programs. The instrument used in the qualitative approach is in-depth interviews using interview guides, observation and related documentation (see above).

3 RESULTS AND DISCUSSION

The development of a coastal village in was the ongoing efforts community empowermentto help local communities find their problems, needs, potentials and resources, develop development plans and assist development implementation over a while so that people can do it on their own. This independence includes independence to think, act and control what he does (Freudenberg DrPH et al. 2011).

The characteristics and procedures of nonformal education programs for community empower-ment are: "generally nonformal education for empowering is an educational approach which learns to gain a greater understanding of and control over social, economic, and political forces through

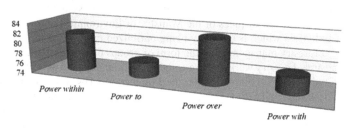

Figure 1. Comparison of the four level of empowerment indicators.

learning process and working collaboratively to solve mutual problems" (Kindervatter 1979). The perspective of nonformal education is a manifestation of goals to build a learning society, which is based on four pillars: learning to know, learn to do, learn to be and learn to live together (Hadiyanti 2016). Not only do humans have the potential to develop, but systems and mechanisms also develop on their own through a process of interaction (a lifelong learning process) in the environment (Ratanakosol et al. 2016).

To measure the level of empowerment of the Forest Farmer Group through the implementation of nonformal education programs in the development of coastal villages in the South Malang region, the researcher used indicators or parameters of the level of empowerment which consisted of four indicators. The four indicators are: power over, power to, power with and power within (Galiè & Farnworth 2019; Zamenopoulos et al. 2019).

Based on the results, it can be concluded that the overall level of empowerment of The Forest Farmers Group through the implementation of nonformal education programs in the development of coastal villages in the South Malang region shows good results with a percentage of 79.56%. These results are supported by the conformity of the results for each sub variable and the calculations are presented in figure 1.

The success of the development of coastal villages in South Malang, East Java is inseparable from several factors support the implementation of this program; there are: (1) availability of resources has the potential to be developed; (2) the existence of forming a climate that allows the community to develop by awakening the community and motivate them to develop; (3) there is the involvement of other stakeholders who support the performance of implementer and his involvement is in the form of socialization, training, and seminars to improve the performance of implementers; (4) facilitate of lower and middle groups through strengthening access by creating access and technical strengthening. Besides, need to protect the people and partiality for the weak are fundamental in the concept of community empowerment; and (5) active community participation is not only about receiving information but also providing opinions, ideas and thoughts to improve community welfare and resilience, which is pursued by physical and non-physical development. This participation can also be used as a means of communicating the desire of the community to take control of development activities. People believe more in a development program if they feel involved in the development process, so they have a sense of belonging (Cavalieri & Neves Almeida 2018).

The coastal village program is used as a source of community welfare. The manifestation of this is that the community is invited to contribute to developing coastal villages. The existence of community participation in the development of coastal villages in the South Malang region as a form of development is also supported by a variety of activities carried out through the intensity of group counselling to provide life skills for the Forest Farmer Group members and make it easier to obtain information related to the forest area development. Involvement of group members in decision making and technical group management and development in increasing capacity and innovation in social forestry enterprises. There is an increasing impact on people's access and knowledge in managing the environment, and it can increase the life capacity of coastal communities both in terms of economic and life capabilities. Besides, the public awareness of environmental problems has grown. This is following the principle of sustainable development that starts from the perspective of environmental protection to maintain the progress and development of society. This relationship needs to be cultivated in harmony with the environment (Lijing et al. 2011).

4 CONCLUSION

The overall level of empowerment of The Forest Farmers Group through the implementation of nonformal education programs in the development of coastal villages in the South Malang region is influenced by several factors including learning intensity for the community through counselling and training, increasing life capabilities in the field. Economic and social, and community involvement in overcoming problems of life and environmental sustainability in forest areas. In percentage terms, the level of empowerment of The Forest Farmers Group through the implementation of nonformal education programs in the development of coastal villages in the South Malang region showed good results of 79.56%. From these results, the empowerment of The Forest Farmers Group needs to be increased through learning programs with the community through nonformal education.

REFERENCES

Brem, A. & Wolfram, P., 2014. Research and development from the bottom up – introduction of terminologies for new product development in emerging markets. *Journal of Innovation and Entrepreneurship*, 3(1).

Cavalieri, I.C. & Neves Almeida, H., 2018. Power, Empowerment and Social Participation- the Building of a Conceptual Model. *European Journal of Social Sciences Education and Research*, 12(1), p.189.

Freudenberg DrPH, N., Pastor PhD, M. & Israel DrPH, B., 2011. Strengthening Community Capacity to Participate in Making Decisions to Reduce Disproportionate Environmental Exposures. *American Journal of Public Health*, 101(S1), pp.S123–30. Available at: https://search.proquest.com/docview/ 906290143? accountid=6180 http://dw2zn6fm9z.search.serialssolutions.com?ctx_ver=Z39.88-2004&ctx_enc=info:ofi/ enc:UTF-8&rfr_id=info:sid/ProQ%3Apais&rft_val_fmt=info:ofi/fmt:kev:mtx:journal&rft.genre=article& rft.jtitle=Ame.

Galiè, A. & Farnworth, C.R., 2019. Power through: A new concept in the empowerment discourse. *Global Food Security*, 21, pp.13–17.

Hadiyanti, P., 2016. A Group Approach in a Community Empowerment?: A Case Study of Waste Recycling Group in Jakarta. *Journal of Education and Practice*, 7(29), pp.157–167. Available at: http://www.iiste.org/Journals/index.php/JEP/article/view/33611/34804.

Khadka, C. & Vacik, H., 2012. Comparing a top-down and bottom-up approach in the identification of criteria and indicators for sustainable community forest management in Nepal. *Forestry*, 85(1), pp.145–158.

Kindervatter, S., 1979. Nonformal education as an empowering process with case studies from Indonesia and Thailand.

Lijing, Y., Niu, Y. & Xu, Y., 2011. Sustainable development and formation of harmonious nature. In *Energy Procedia*. pp. 629–632.

M'hamdi, A. & Nemiche, M., 2018. Bottom-Up and Top-Down Approaches to Simulate Complex Social Phenomena. *International Journal of Applied Evolutionary Computation*, 9(2), pp.1–16.

Ratanakosol, K., Pathumcharoenwattana, W. & Kimpee, P., 2016. Learning process for creating community identity. *SHS Web of Conferences*, 26, p. 01067.

Rukin et al., 2018. Coastal Rural Community Economic Development As a Poverty Reduction Efforts. *The International Journal of Social Sciences and Humanities Invention*, 5(4), pp. 4627–4633.

Yilmaz, B. et al., 2010. Factors affecting rural development in turkey: Bartın case study. *Forest Policy and Economics*, 12(4), pp. 239–249.

Zamenopoulos, T. et al., 2019. Types, obstacles and sources of empowerment in co-design: the role of shared material objects and processes. *CoDesign*.

Development, Social Change and Environmental Sustainability – Sumarmi et al (Eds)
© 2021 Taylor & Francis Group, London, ISBN 978-1-032-01320-6

Digital activism through online petition: A challenge for digital public sphere in Indonesia

Kun Sila Ananda* & Megasari Noer Fatanti
Universitas Negeri Malang, Malang, Indonesia

ABSTRACT: The increased use of internet not only for business, education, or entertainment but also for expressing opinion and digital activism signified that public sphere could also take place virtually through the internet. This paper aims to explore the digital activism done by Indonesian netizens through online petitions, and how it challenged the possibility of online petition as a form of the digital public sphere in Indonesia. The methods used is literature study on various works of literature and recent petitions in Change.org. This research shows that online petition provides a space for interaction between the marginalized groups, netizens, and the government. Online petitions also facilitate a new form of protest with more dynamic characteristics, including fast and effective communication. Online petition also gives the same right for every citizen to express their concern. However, online petition did not provide much space to promote a critical and deliberative public debate for public.

Keywords: Internet, Digital, Public Sphere

1 INTRODUCTION

Late in 2015, social media was buzzing about GoJek's ban on operations, online motorcycle taxi services, and similar businesses. The topic of GoJek heated up on social media until President Joko Widodo had to intervene. In just one night, Jokowi was able to undo the regulations made by The Minister of Transportation Ignasius Jonan. This kind of social movement is not only happening in Indonesia. Social media such as Facebook, Twitter and YouTube were considered to hold the key to student protests in Britain at the end of 2010. Social media also played a crucial role in the Tunisian and Egyptian revolutions, as well as mass protests on Wall Street about global capitalism in the United States (SEN 2012). This phenomenon revives the debate about the concept of the digital public sphere.

However, until now, the search for the public sphere that is considered ideal in the digital realm is never over. Experts have always compared the concepts of the public sphere in the digital world to the concept of the public sphere that Jurgen Habermas first used. Meanwhile, with the development of information and communication technology, the community continues to evolve along with the development of ways to communicate. Even today, it can be said that Indonesian society has not only entered the digital age but has entered the era of social media which is characterized by the use of social media as one of the primary media to communicate, as well as the use of social media that has become a significant and essential part of everyone's life.

This paper, therefore, tried to explore the digital activism done by Indonesian netizens through online petitions, and how it challenged the possibility of online petitions as a form of digital public sphere in Indonesia.

---

*Corresponding author: kun.ananda.fis@um.ac.id

2 LITERATURE REVIEW

2.1 *Online petition*

Lindner and Riehm (2011:3) define petitions as requests to public authorities, usually governmental or parliamentary institutions. Petitions aim, among other things, to change public policy or encourage specific actions by public institutions (Lindner & Riehm 2011:3). With the development of communication and information, technology presents online petitions as a new form of traditional petition. The presence of these online petitions has the same functionality as traditional petitions, but also offers a wider range of access in shorter time periods. Online petitions improve the democratic process, connect citizens with the government, and facilitate citizen involvement (Panagiotopoulos & Al-Debei 2010:3).

2.2 *Digital activism*

Earl and Kimport (2008: 452–453) describe some form of online activism online. The four forms of online activism are petitions, boycotts, e-mailed letters of objection and campaigns. Of these forms of online activism, all are forms of interaction between netizens and those who have power. From various forms of events that occur, individuals as self-respond to such events into the form of confirming the truth of the information, translating information into individual expressions and then making decisions on whether this information will be acted upon as action.

2.3 *Habermas' public sphere*

Jurgen Habermas describes the concept of public space as an independent and separate space from the state and market where every citizen has equal access to public opinion. Habermas believes that the concept of the public sphere is an ideal concept for the prospects of democracy today (Subijanto 2014). With the development of information and communication technology, as well as the emergence of the internet, of course, the structure of public space is no longer the same as the first used by Habermas. Here are some comparisons between public spaces in Habermas time and public spaces that existed in the virtual world (cyberspace).

One of the most striking difference between the concept of Habermas public room and public space in virtual space is that in virtual public spaces, participants are not only dominated by one particular person. Participants in virtual public spaces are also not limited by spaces, such as country and place borders. In the virtual realm, anyone can participate in discussing issues that they find interesting. Not only has the shape of public space changed, the concept of citizens as 'residents' of public spaces has also changed. Anyone can participate in a virtual public space, be it a citizen of a country abroad, or a citizen of the world who wants to give an opinion on an issue in a country.

3 METHODS

The methods used is literature study on various works of literature. The secondary data also collected from Change.org as an online platform by exploring recent petitions in Change.org including petition such as Reject RKUHP Bill, Amnesty for Nuril, Reject Music Bills, also petitions with hashtag #ReformasiDikorupsi. This research also analyzes the statement by Change.org representatives in online media news as secondary data.

4 RESULT AND ANALYSIS

4.1 *Online petition as digital activism*

What netizens do through their change.org is one form of online activism. Change.org petitions cannot be separated merely as a stand-alone form of a petition. The electronic petition (e-protest) here describes a combination of other forms of activism, such as letters of objection, campaigning by e-mail and of course some cases are open boycotts. One example is a petition demanding the concern of the Indonesian government and the Malaysian government in Wilfrida Soik's release in the alleged corruption of her employer in Malaysia. The petition, written by Anis Hidayah, an activist for Migrant Care is an attempt to represent how information obtained through the Migrant Care network in the area managed to find the facts about age forgery, moratorium violations and alleged mental disorders experienced by Wilfria Soik. All media works, including social media such as Facebook, Youtube, Twitter and Path. All of this is a form of cooperation between the organs of society in managing information, changing it in the form of expressions and actions that correspond to their respective capacities. In change.org, the whole strategy is combined into a real movement.

We see that change.org is not solely a form of spatial space or a medium of regular interaction. Some sociologists who paid attention to the conception of space such as Simmel, Foucault and Lefebvre reintroduced space as a form of spatial consciousness. Here Lefebvre (1991:26) believes that space is socially produced and becomes the centre of attention in the theory of social sciences. With the idea of spatial awareness, we can translate the space as a tool of thought and at the same time as a tool of action (action) be it in production, surveillance (control), dominance and power. Therefore, we see the change.org as a space of spatial awareness as conveyed by Lebfevre. In change.org, individuals not only product information, but also become an information management room that acts as a tool of thinking (in the form of discussion and discursus) as well as a new tool of struggle called e-protest which refer to a revolutionary stage in the issues of social movements in Indonesia.

4.2 *Public sphere in Indonesia*

Based on Subijanto (2014), in Indonesia post-1998, two institutions are often considered manifestations of the public sphere, namely media and non-governmental organizations (NGOs). But as an institution supported by donor institutions from developed countries and even transnational corporations, there are political and economic motivations that can influence the performance of NGOs following the interests of donor institutions. Also, NGOs become apolitical public spaces and are not used to criticize the government following public views and interests.

Meanwhile, the emergence of the television industry then also gave rise to discourse about the public sphere in the form of mass media. In 1989, after Habermas's work was translated into English, the public sphere defined as an area accessible to everyone without restrictions. Public space is no longer physical but becomes a virtual community with the same function, which is to play a critical role in politics. However, considering that television and other media are still controlled by corporations and are still profit-oriented organizations, it is hard for television to be a neutral public sphere. Besides, the mass media also does not meet the egalitarian nature of Habermas's public spaces.

Furthermore, as digital media technology evolves, the internet and social media again give hope as a potential platform to become a public sphere. DiMaggio et al. (2001:319) revealed that the advent of the internet gave the possibility of an up-to-date public sphere. The enthusiasm found early evidence that the internet could form a more deliberative community and a more engaged public. The advent of the internet does provide people with easy access to information, including political information, as well as providing space to express their opinions freely.

4.3 *Online petition as a public sphere*

Online petitions are a form of political participation that connects people with the government. Petitions always related to mass movements or social movements. It is because the essence of the petition is the gathering of public opinion as well as the fundraising of support that allows for change, whether in terms of policy or other. Social movements can also be referred to as movements born from and on the initiative of society to demand changes in both the realm of institutions and government policy.

Founded in 2007, change.org was initially used as a social network for social activities, then turned into a blog, and changed again to an online petition website in 2011. In Indonesia itself, change.org has opened a representative office in Indonesia on June 4th, 2012. Up till now, its membership increased rapidly to 71,000 people and continued to increase to this day. Every petition uploaded and signed will go to government e-mails or state officials, among others are the e-mails of the President, the police chief, and some members of Commission III of the House of Representatives. Campaigns and fundraisers through this petition are usually also spread through social media for maximum results.

When compared to the concept of public space from Habermas, online petition platforms such as change.org have some advantages and disadvantages. As a non-profit platform, change.org does not sponsor a particular petition, or attempt to popularize petitions. By using the internet and social media, online petitions can also reach more audiences, and efforts to gather support are relatively easy. Internet users only need to click "sign the petition," and their support is immediately counted. Also, another advantage that online petitions have that in line with Habermas' public space structure is the equality in it. Anyone can create a petition and sign a petition. Change.org also fulfill the anonymity element in Habermas's public spaces.

However, online petitions also have drawbacks, including only supporting one-way communication. Change.org does not allow for deliberative and critical discussions between users. Another drawback of change.org is the lack of openness from change.org management to users, such as the placement (display) of petitions. Some petitions are placed in front of a large, easy-to-see display, while others are not. The placement criteria (display) of this petition are not yet known. Social media can complement the shortcomings of the change.org online petitions and the alternative public space in this virtual world. Social networks such as Facebook and Twitter can not only be used to popularize a petition. Therefore, online petitions and social media can be two types of complementary platforms to become alternative public spaces in Indonesia. Combined, the use of both could meet Habermas public space criteria such as egalitarian, critical and deliberative discussions, anonymity or equality between users, censorship-free, and openness

5 SUMMARY

Netizen participation in giving their opinion about social and political issues increased over the years. The online petition provides a space for interaction between the marginalized groups, netizens, and the government and facilitates a new form of protest with more dynamic characteristics. These aspects of online petition fulfil Habermas's concept about the public sphere, which mobilizes public concern and participation openly, equally and anonymously. However, in other aspects, the online petition did not provide much space to promote a critical and deliberative public debate for the public, and the lack of openness of change.org as a platform creates a bias on popular or promoted petitions.

REFERENCES

DiMaggio, P. et al. (2001) 'Social implications of the internet', *Annual Review of Sociology.* doi: 10.1146/annurev.soc.27.1.307.

Lindner, R. and Riehm, U. (2011) 'Broadening Participation Through E-Petitions? An Empirical Study of Petitions to the German Parliament', *Policy & Internet*. doi: 10.2202/1944-2866.1083.

Panagiotopoulos, P. P. (2010) 'Engaging with Citizens Online?: Understanding the Role of ePetitioning in Local Government Democracy', in *Internet Politics Policy 2010 An Impact Assessment*.

Sen, A. F. (2012) 'The social media as a public sphere: The rise of social opposition', in *International Conference on Communication, Media, Technology and Design*.

Subiakto, Henry and Ida, R. (2014) *Political, Media, and Democratic Communication*. 2nd edn. Jakarta: Kencana Prenadamedia Group.

Subijanto, R. (2014) *Public Spaces Then and Now*. Available at: http://indoprogress.com/2014/04/ruang-publik-dulu-dan-sekarang/ (Accessed: 1 January 2016).

Development, Social Change and Environmental Sustainability – Sumarmi et al (Eds)
© 2021 Taylor & Francis Group, London, ISBN 978-1-032-01320-6

Philanthropy movement's response to government policy in negotiating COVID-19 in Indonesia

Nanda Harda Pratama Meiji*, Abdul Kodir, Sumarmi, Ardyanto Tanjung & Annisa Fathin Dianah
Universitas Negeri Malang, Kota Malang, Indonesia

Muhammad Asyrofi Al Kindy
Nalanda University, Rajgir, India

ABSTRACT: The COVID-19 pandemic has spread throughout the world, including Indonesia. This problem becomes important and raises concerns for the Indonesian people. The government has an essential role in protecting the community. Besides, policies are also needed for prevention and negotiating of COVID-19 so that the impact that is felt does not spread. This study aims to explain the response of the philanthropic movement to government policies in dealing with COVID-19 in Indonesia. This study used qualitative research methods. The data collection process was carried out through interviews with the COVID-19 response team, NGOs, and local communities. The results of this study indicate that the policies set by the government have not been maximized in dealing with the impact of COVID-19, especially the problems associated with basic needs and health facilities for the community. The Negotiation of COVID-19 in Indonesia, which seemed terrible, finally prompted various philanthropic movements to help others and improve the capabilities of people who affected by COVID-19.

Keywords: Policy, Negotiating COVID-19, Philanthropy Movement, Response, Government

1 INTRODUCTION

The pandemic coronavirus disease (COVID-19) is a problem that is being faced in more than 200 countries in the world. Indonesia was also severely affected by COVID-19, where the death rate reached 8.9% at the end of March 2020 (WHO 2020). Concern for public health and social action must be taken by individuals, institutions, communities, local and national governments and international agencies to slow or stop the spread of COVID-19. Unfortunately, the pandemic has been spread into the micro-condition of society.

Indonesia and the United States initially underestimated severe COVID-19 dangers. Meanwhile, other countries, such as Vietnam and Singapore, chose to act quickly by warning the public about the risks of the virus. They even imposed strict rules to protect their people. Vietnam, which since early January has set a lockdown and provided incentives for the low and lower-middle class. Likewise, the Chinese state imposed a lockdown during the Chinese New Year celebrations. These countries are not waiting for the COVID-19 pandemic to turn into a disaster and have taken strategic steps to overcome the outbreak (Hidayat et al. 2020).

Meanwhile, the Indonesian government does not even want to set a regional quarantine, one of which is because the government objected to covering the living costs of residents and livestock during the quarantine period. This makes many low-economic or informal workers still have to struggle to make a living amid the pandemic (Nasruddin & Haq 2020). The government has

---

*Corresponding author: nanda.harda.fis@um.ac.id

DOI 10.1201/9781003178163-31

prioritized handling the economic impacts that may occur due to the epidemic. This can be seen from the government's action of disbursing 103 billion Rp to promote the tourism sector for fear of reducing foreign tourists due to this pandemic.

But social strength is present in Indonesia precisely because of the weak role of the state (Djalante et al. 2020). A survey from Alvara Research of 1,223 respondents showed that 50.4% of them said the government was slow to respond to COVID-19. Even 60% of survey respondents also felt that the information provided by the government was unclear. Another survey from the Saiful Mujani Research Center found that the central government is perceived to be slower to move than local governments. This shows that the government's movement has not been optimal, either from education or direct action to respond to COVID-19 (Mujani & Irvani 2020). The negotiating of COVID-19 in Indonesia, which seems terrible, has finally led to the emergence of various philanthropic movements. On social media, the community enlivened the action by using #rakyatbanturakyat, a form of community solidarity in helping others amid the COVID-19 pandemic. This shows that there is still a strong social awareness and sensitivity in the community in anticipating the COVID-19 pandemic.

2 METHODS

This study used qualitative research methods. This research focuses on several areas connected to community solidarity to erase the pandemic. The data collection process was carried out through several stages, namely, direct interviews and telephone calls, considering that currently access to several areas was limited, observation, and literature study. The interview process was carried out in-depth and openly using a purposive sampling technique. Some of the informants that will be interviewed include the COVID-19 Response Team, NGOs, and local communities.

Meanwhile, a focused discussion group process was carried out with several local communities and local communities who took the initiative to make efforts to reduce the impact of COVID-19. The data analysis in this study used thematic analysis. This analysis was carried out through several stages (Bryman 2012). First, examining the results of the interview transcripts. After that, coding the results of the interview transcripts from several discourses and classifying the results of the interviews based on the topics discussed. And the last one is to interpret findings from predetermined ideas.

There are several questions that will be answered in this research, including First, has the government in general been successful in dealing with the impact of the COVID-19 pandemic? Second, how do people assess government policies on quarantine and PSBB? Third, are government actions that prioritize economic stability understandable? Last, what role should the government play in dealing with the impact of COVID-19?

3 RESULT AND DISCUSSION

Based on the data, the number of COVID-19 cases continues to increase, and the government has an essential role in handling COVID-19. The number of COVID-19 cases in Indonesia has not yet decreased, which is the concern of various parties. Various regulations issued by the government, one of which is: Government Regulation Number 21 of 2020 concerning Large-Scale Social Restrictions (PSBB) in the Framework of Accelerating COVID-19 Negotiating and issued by the Ministry of Health through Minister of Health Regulation number 9 of 2020 concerning Guidelines for Large-Scale Social Restrictions In the Context of Accelerating COVID-19 Negotiation. With the issuance of this policy, it is hoped that it can reduce the increase in the number of COVID-19 cases. Still, in fact, until now (22 June 2020), the number of COVID-19 cases in Indonesia has continued to increase (Djalante et al. 2020; Nasruddin & Haq 2020).

In handling the COVID-19 problem, the Indonesian government prefers a two-way policy path, namely its substantive policy (prevention) while focusing on economic improvement policies. Two approaches that are implemented simultaneously cause their implementation to be less than optimal and inconsistent, and even there tends to be a miscoordination between the central government and regional governments (Astuti & Mahardhika 2020). In the end, the two goals to be achieved, namely breaking the chain of the spread of the virus and improving the economy could not be reached; in fact, it tends to get worse.

Such government actions sacrifice people instead of saving the investment climate. The government should stop the spread of COVID-19 by guaranteeing health services for the people and providing adequate facilities for health workers while ensuring the people's basic needs. The economy is not only about winning, selling and accumulating profits, but also about mutual cooperation to humanize people. We should give them hope for a better life in the future.

The crisis due to COVID-19 is currently coinciding, so that the impact is intensely felt by vulnerable groups who are getting worse, including business groups that need crowds, groups of casual daily workers, street vendors, workers affected by layoffs, farmers, the poor, and so on. In this situation, it is understandable that the government does not dare to take lockdown steps in this phenomenon, because the risk leads to an economic disaster, which automatically has implications for other social impacts (Abodunrin et al. 2020). It may not be worse than the economic crisis in 1998, but the government at least need to give safety and prosperity in basic needs.

This is an unfortunate thing because in the midst of the dilemma faced by the community to remain silent and limit their social movements, the government does not provide basic needs to the community, especially marginalized people who really need help (Indradi et al. 2020). In the long term, this crisis underscores the need for individual states to expand Medicaid and for federal and state governments to take coordinated action to strengthen their insurance markets, expanding healthcare facilities and provider capacities focused on underserved and developing populations and geographic areas (Millett et al. 2020).

Everyone has the potential to be affected by COVID-19, both upper class and lower-middle-class economic people. Meanwhile, there are many deaths due to hunger every year, not even inferior to COVID-19. But the case is not that busy, because it does not attack the middle class and above. In this context, the pandemic strikes anyone regardless of their social and economic level. The case is that the effects are different. For the upper-middle class, they can hoard a lot of food when they have to carry out self-isolation or quarantine. Meanwhile, the middle and lower level, which is vulnerable groups have no choice to get some food without quarantine. If they want to stay at home, there are two threats that will be faced. Firstly, the danger of death from hunger, and second, the threat of dying from a pandemic.

Unfortunately, PSBB does not provide the social security needs of the people. People are restricted from leaving their homes without a guaranteed life. Even though Indonesia has a quarantine qaw where the government has an obligation to secure the lives of its citizens and livestock. This means that if you use a quarantine policy, citizens will receive economic guarantees. PSBB is, on the contrary, the government recommends physical distancing and social distancing, but residents must think for themselves how to find food.

PSBB is precisely the reason for companies or factories to unilaterally terminate their employment, even if they do not get severance pay. From this situation, the government is proven to have failed to guarantee the lives of its people. Work from Home (WFH) is impossible for those who work in the informal sector. PSBB limits residents who daily survive looking for daily income, such as pedicab drivers who are empty of passengers, street vendors in various places who can no longer work, and most of the people affected by COVID-19 who have jobs that require direct interaction. For example, pedicab drivers, masseuse workers, hawkers and scavengers who do not get income because of how many areas have been locked down.

Another thing is the intergenerational context that sometimes plays a role in the social realm. In fact, if you look deeper, both the younger and older generations have an equally important role in dealing with the pandemic. However, the narrative that develops on social media actually seems to describe a younger generation who is more indifferent to the epidemic and has made the spread of COVID-19 even more out of control. Whereas on the other hand, if we look at social communities in reducing the risk of a pandemic, it appears from the creative ideas of young people who are then supported by the older generation in the context of policy or financial aspects. On the one hand, this also shows that youth have a role in every era where there is chaos or happiness in society (Meiji 2016; Anderson 2019). The emergence of social communities in the midst of a pandemic shows that social capital, both young and old, is still vital in the context of solving problems at the grassroots.

This problem is the main reason for some community solidarity movements in various big cities in Indonesia to help others in the form of donations, building people's kitchens and food solidarity. Citizen volunteerism should not be considered a panacea to meet public needs (Bovaird et al. 2016) or an opportunity for the state to cancel responsibility (McLennan et al. 2016).

4 CONCLUSION

Every day the COVID-19 numbers of cases and victims who die due to the pandemic in Indonesia continue to grow. The social and economic impacts are felt by the people of Indonesia. However, the Indonesian government was slow to respond to the COVID-19 pandemic until it was finally declared a national disaster. The government, which prioritizes economic recovery rather than fulfilling the welfare of the community, has resulted in implementing inoptimal policy implementation. Such government action is at the expense of the people. The government should stop the spread of COVID-19 by guaranteeing public health services, providing adequate health worker facilities while ensuring the people's needs. This phenomenon has triggered the emergence of philanthropic movements in various big cities in Indonesia to show solidarity and initiatives to help others, especially those affected by COVID-19.

REFERENCES

Abodunrin, O., Oloye, G. and Adesola, B. (2020) 'Coronavirus Pandemic and Its Implication on Global Economy', *International Journal of Arts, Languages and Business Studies (IJALBS)*.

Anderson, B. (2019) *REVOLOESI PEMOEDA: Pendudukan Jepang dan Perlawanan di Jawa 1944 – 1946*. Jakarta: Marjin Kiri.

Astuti, P. B. and Mahardhika, A. S. (2020) 'COVID-19: How does it impact to the Indonesian economy?', *Jurnal Inovasi Ekonomi*. doi: 10.22219/jiko.v5i3.11751.

Bovaird, T. et al. (2016) 'Activating collective co-production of public services: influencing citizens to participate in complex governance mechanisms in the UK', *International Review of Administrative Sciences*. doi: 10.1177/0020852314566009.

Bryman, A. (2012) 'Social research methods Bryman', *OXFORD University Press*.

Djalante, R. et al. (2020) 'Review and analysis of current responses to COVID-19 in Indonesia: Period of January to March 2020', *Progress in Disaster Science*. doi: 10.1016/j.pdisas.2020.100091.

Hidayat, R. et al. (2020) 'Test, Trace, and Treatment Strategy to Control COVID-19 Infection Among Hospital Staff in a COVID-19 Referral Hospital in Indonesia', *Acta medica Indonesiana*.

Indradi, A. R. I. S. A. H. et al. (2020) 'Politik Hukum Pemerintah dalam Penanganan Pandemi COVID-19', *Universitas Gajah Mada*.

McLennan, B., Whittaker, J. and Handmer, J. (2016) 'The changing landscape of disaster volunteering: opportunities, responses and gaps in Australia', *Natural Hazards*. doi: 10.1007/s11069-016-2532-5.

Meiji, N. H. P. (2016) 'Pendidikan Politik dalam Kuasa Simbolik: Kajian mengenai Dinamika Politik Anak Muda yang Tergabung dalam Partai Politik di Kota Malang', *Jurnal Sosiologi Pendidikan Humanis*. doi: 10.17977/um021v1i22016p103.

Millett, G. A. et al. (2020) 'Assessing differential impacts of COVID-19 on black communities', *Annals of Epidemiology*. doi: 10.1016/j.annepidem.2020.05.003.

Mujani, S. and Irvani, D. (2020) 'Sikap dan Perilaku Warga terhadap Kebijakan Penanganan Wabah COVID-19', *Politika: Jurnal Ilmu Politik*. doi: 10.14710/politika.11.2.2020.219-238.

Nasruddin, R. and Haq, I. (2020) 'Pembatasan Sosial Berskala Besar (PSBB) dan Masyarakat Berpenghasilan Rendah', *SALAM: Jurnal Sosial dan Budaya Syar-i*. doi: 10.15408/sjsbs.v7i7.15569.

WHO (2020) 'Coronavirus disease (COVID-2019) situation reports', *World Health Organisation*.

Development, Social Change and Environmental Sustainability – Sumarmi et al (Eds)
© 2021 Taylor & Francis Group, London, ISBN 978-1-032-01320-6

Facilitating communities to identify local potential and hazards through P-GIS and FGD

L.Y. Irawan*, Sumarmi, S. Bachri, M.M.R. Devy, R. Faizal & W.E. Prasetyo
Universitas Negeri Malang, Malang City, Indonesia

ABSTRACT: Beach tourism plays the most important role in the economic sector of Desa Gajahrejo. So far, tourism activity is developed without actual planning. The duties of each tourism actor have yet to be incorporated. Moreover, Desa Gajahrejo has numerous unidentified and undeveloped tourism potentials. This research aims to facilitate Desa Gajahrejo's regional potential identification as the base of tourism planning through community participation. The purpose of the planning is to create integration between 1) community group coordination, 2) tourism planning development, 3) environmental preservation actions, and 4) disaster risk management. This is a qualitative, descriptive research. The data was collected using P-GIS and FGD community service agendas. SWOT analysis is used as the basis of the planning. P-GIS and FGD are effective to involve community participation in creating the tourism planning of Desa Gajahrejo. It also provides an excellent data source for potential identification. However, ecological-based tourism practices need to be incorporated in the activity as it has a coastal disaster hazards. Therfore, Desa Gajahrejo needs to develop a regional planning that takes both economy and ecology into account.

Keywords: Coastal, Tourism, Hazard, P-GIS

1   INTRODUCTION

Malang is one of the areas with tremendous coastal tourism potential in East Java, Indonesia (Sukmaratri 2018; Ridhoi 2020). It is supported by the natural, social, and cultural landscapes of the area which connected one to another (Hardini 2018). There are plenty of beaches in Kabupaten Malang, making it being referred to as "a city with thousand beaches" (Putri & Amalia 2020). They are mainly managed by local groups and thus creating a social cooperation within them to sustain the tourism activity. As living side by side with the ocean, the coastal community holds inherent values of respective culture to the sea. There are several annual cultural events which are a potential tourist attraction for the area. Desa Gajahrejo is no exception.

Desa Gajahrejo, Kecamatan Gedangan is located in the southern coastal area of Kabupaten Malang. Beach tourism plays the most important role in the economic sector of Desa Gajahrejo. Some of the tourist destinations are Ungapan Beach, Watubolong/Bajulmati Beach, Batu Bengkung Beach, and Jolangkung Beach. So far, tourism activity is developed without actual planning. The duties of each tourism actor have yet to be incorporated. Moreover, Desa Gajahrejo has numerous unidentified and undeveloped tourism potentials.

Regarding tourist safety, the tourism planning of Desa Gajahrejo also needs to take disaster hazards into account. It is due to the existence of multi-disaster hazards in the area, namely tsunamis, earthquakes, tidal waves and floods. It can bring damage to the environment, human beings and property. Moreover, tidal waves can give rise to an abrasion process and sea turtle hatching habitat loss. Coastal areas have highly dynamic human-environment interactions and thus

---

*Corresponding author: listyo.fis@um.ac.id

DOI 10.1201/9781003178163-32

to damage one aspect is to affect the other (Ali & El-Magd 2016; Link et al. 2018; Chu et al. 2020). Therefore, it is prominent to design a visionary coastal tourism planning.

This research aims to facilitate Desa Gajahrejo's regional potential identification as the base of tourism planning through community participation. The purpose of the planning is to create integration between 1) community group coordination, 2) tourism planning development, 3) environmental preservation actions, and 4) disaster risk management. It is essential for the sustainability of the tourism activity itself and, most importantly, for the sustainability of the environment. Community involvement on the planning also needs to be highlighted since the efforts can provide the information about local knowledge, expertise, and practicality (Okada et al. 2018; Hidayat & Syahid 2019; Wheeler & Root-Bernstein 2020). Therefore, the identification result can generate further planning which is both applicative and effective.

2 METHOD

This is a qualitative-descriptive research which was held in Desa Gajahrejo, Kecamatan Gedangan, Kabupaten Malang, East Java, Indonesia. The research was conducted as a community service agenda. The community service agenda was split into two main agendas, which area Participatory-Geographic Information System (P-GIS) and Focus Group Discussion (FGD). The agenda was done in order to facilitate planning communication within community groups and village government. The collected data was analyzed using strength-weakness-opportunity-threat (SWOT) analysis. Then, the analysis was explained descriptively.

The implementation phase of P-GIS was carried out in a participatory manner between community groups through FGD activities which then trigger interests in exchanging knowledge, ideas, and opinions regarding information related to regional maps (Boateng 2012; Indrizal 2014; Williamson 2018; Sim & Waterfield 2019). Displaying or presenting a map can serve as a prompt for a group to discuss a specific region (Hung & Chen 2013; Verplanke et al. 2016; Radil & Anderson 2019). P-GIS assists in gathering information related directly to regional development plans (Brown & Fagerholm 2015; Bitsura-Meszaros et al. 2019). The combination of data collection through the participatory mapping meth-od (P-GIS & FGD) is an effective and convenient method in making decisions regarding community-based regional development (Zolkafli et al. 2017; Álvarez Larrain & McCall 2019). The use of maps with spatial data, Google View satellite imagery and area information is one method that is easy for the public to understand. The markings marked on the map are a form of participation and knowledge of community groups. The final result, in the form of markings, is used to update the information and expectations of community groups in regional development.

SWOT analysis is an advanced stage in regional development when all data sources have been obtained. SWOT analysis is needed in data management because it relates to conditions of strengths and weaknesses in attracting regional attention (Al-Mayahi & Mansoor 2012; Delita et al. 2017). SWOT analysis was developed to identify opportunities and threats that originate from external and to understand the level of strengths and weaknesses that come from internal/organization (Agarwal et al. 2012; Kantawateera et al. 2013; Ahmadi et al. 2016). SWOT comes out as a strategic data analysis method and thus is often used in research studies to comprehensively understand the research data (Lidstone & MacLennan 2018).

3 RESULT AND DISCUSSION

The community service agenda was held in Ungapan Beach in August 2020. The community service was divided into two main agendas, which are P-GIS (Participatory-Geographic Information System) and FGD (Focus Group Discussion). The agenda was attended by 17 people. They are the representative of 6 community groups of Desa Gajahrejo, namely 1) village government, 2) public figure of the community (tokoh masyarakat), 3) LMDH (Lembaga Masyarakat Desa Hutan or

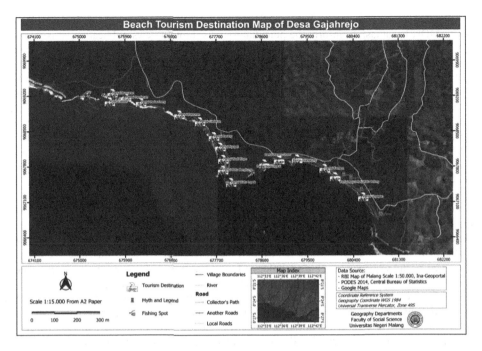

Figure 1. P-GIS result.

Forest Village Community), 4) POKMASWAS (Kelompok Masyarakat Pengawas or Superintendent Society Association), 5) BSTC (Bajulmati Sea Turtle Conservation) and 6) the SAR (Search and Rescue) team. The purpose of the agenda was to identify the marine and coastal potentials as the basic of further planning for the area. Therefore, it needed broad points of views from each community group.

The P-GIS agenda was started by explaining the physical and non-physical conditions of Desa Gajahrejo. It was done by a facilitator. The aim was to trigger the community to provide the information needed. After that, the community responded to the given map. The community was excitedly involved in the agenda.

Firstly, the participants examined the Coastal Area of Desa Gajahrejo Map. They noticed the toponymic differences on some beach tourism destinations. Then, they started to mark the name of the beach with the local names. One of the beaches is Watu Bolong Beach, which is written as Bajulmati Beach on the map. On some beaches, the local and national toponymies are unmatched. The corrected version of the beach tourism destination map of Desa Gajahrejo is shown in Figure 1.

After that, the participants talked about disaster hazards in the area. In particular, they talked more about tidal wave disasters. They said that tidal wave disasters are common in the area. They also said that the disaster has a return period that gives a great impact to the tourism activity. As a consequence, it impacted the economic stability of Desa Gajahrejo.

After identifying the disaster hazards in Desa Gajahrejo, the P-GIS agenda was followed by FGD. It was focused more on the marine and coastal potentials of the area. The purpose was to create awareness in the community that they live in a physical landscape that can be both beneficial and threatening (Mishra 2016).

From the SWOT analysis, Desa Gajahrejo has a valuable social capital as one of its strengths. Desa Gajahrejo has a good relationship and cooperation between local community groups to improve the tourism activity in the area. In particular, they have a coping capacity to respond to a tidal wave disaster. BSTC indirectly contributes to the physical environment improvements by planting Casuarina equisetifolia and Pandanus odorifer as a wave-breaker vegetation. POKMASWAS ensures conformities of the area. The SAR Team handles the coastal disaster mitigation on Ungapan Bay. LMDH has a task to inform the potential tourists through news publication. It is related to the working operations in the tourist destination whether it is still closed due to the disaster or is already open.

Another strength of Desa Gajahrejo is the excellent 3As in four developed beaches. Those are Ungapan, Jolangkung, Batu Bengkung, and Bajulmati beachs. They are all white-sanded beaches with distinct attractions on each beach, namely: 1) coastal estuary in Un-gapan Beach, 2) flat coral formation in Jolangkung Beach, 3) natural saltwater pond in Ba-tu Bengkung Beach, and 4) green swamp, karst cave (Wil Cave) and sea turtle conservation activity in Watubolong/Bajulmati Beach. The accessibility is helped by the presence of Jalur Lintas Selatan (JLS) Jawa or Southern Java Cross Lane that allows tourists to travel only for 3 hours from the center of Malang City. Some of the amenities provided in the tourism area are public restrooms, food stalls, praying rooms, signages, roads, selfie-spots, emergency services, etc.

Despite the strengths, Desa Gajahrejo has big waves due to the oceanographic factors in the area. The coastal area of Desa Gajahrejo is directly facing the Indian Ocean, which blows strong winds and thus generates big waves. It implicated one of the weaknesses of the coastal tourism in the area. Tourists are not allowed to swim on the beaches of Ungapan Bay. The big waves are worsened by the v-shaped beach morphology of the area. It is able to form a rip current which is strong enough to dangerously drag tourists offshore (Nejad & Nazmi 2019).

Another weakness of Desa Gajahrejo is the lack of participation from the village government on the tourism activities as well as planning. The tourism activity is fully managed by LMDH. The involvement of village government can better understand the needs of the tourism actors to develop the tourism activity (Kubickova 2018). Therefore, the response actions to that can be implemented efficiently (Khan et al. 2020). Unsupportive vertical communication can hinder both the planning and development efforts (Vieira et al. 2016). This is the main reason why Desa Gajahrejo has yet to develop structured and documented planning despite the plenty of potential, which are described in the next paragraph.

There are still 12 beaches that still need further tourism development, which are: Bunca-ran, Randanan, Padas Ireng, Pawonan, Gladakan, Pasang, Ngopet, Wedi Klopo, Watu Lepek, Kajaran, Nglengguk, and Parang Dowo Beach. From the FGD agenda result, the community plans to develop the tourist destination sustainably. It is supported by the sea turtle conservation efforts in the area, which can also be developed as a new tourist attraction. Therefore, the activities can be managed with an ecoedutourism system (Osland & Mackoy 2012; Sander 2012; Sakellari & Skanavis 2013).

Desa Gajahrejo also has cultural tourism potential. The coastal community holds suroan, larung ketupat, petik laut and adus gaman annual cultural festivals. These festivals are common to coastal communities all across Indonesia, especially in Java Island. It is developed as they live side by side with the sea for generations.

One of the marine potentials of Desa Gajahrejo is the plenty of fishing spots in the area. So far, it is only considered as fishery activity to sustain the life of the local community. In fact, it is also a tourism potential. As stated by the tourism actors at FGD agenda, they are planning to develop the fishing spots as a new tourist attraction. In addition, shrimp farming is prospective to play a bigger part in the economic activity of Desa Gajahrejo. The development of these potentials can raise broader tourist segments which are going to increase the tourist visits to the area.

Desa Gajahrejo also faces some threats, such as multi-disaster hazard and unmanaged fishing zones. Some of the hazards are tsunami, earthquakes, tidal waves, and floods. Tidal waves are the most hazardous. Directly, they can give an environmental impact to the area. Some of them are abrasion and property damage. Indirectly, the disaster is also able to give an economic and social impact. As the attractions and amenities are unsuitable for tourism activities, the number of visitors is going to decrease—coming to a dormant economy. It is because the tourism sector has a strategic position in the economy of Desa Gajahrejo.

Another threat of Desa Gajahrejo is the unmanaged fishing activities in the area. To protect the marine potentials for a long term, there needs to be a special management for the activity. Until now, the activities are still uncontrolled. Fishermen gather in large groups to catch fish near the shore, including non-local fishermen. The urgency increases as the tourism actors plan to develop fishing spots as one of the tourist attractions.

From the SWOT analysis, it indicated that Desa Gajahrejo needs to develop a regional planning that takes both economy and ecology into account. It needs to be started from the ecological aspect. In other words, the environmental preservation and conservation actions need to be applied first. The actions can both sustain the economic activities and reduce risk of tidal wave disaster. Furthermore, Desa Gajahrejo needs to consider the development of ecoedutourism in the area. The purpose is to create sustainability economically and ecologically.

4 CONCLUSION

From the community service agenda in Desa Gajahrejo, it can be concluded that P-GIS and FGD are effective to gather comprehensive information about local potentials as it provides a broad point of view from all community groups. Moreover, it indirectly increases the community participation in creating an applicative planning for the area. Based on the analysis, Desa Gajahrejo needs to develop a regional planning that integrates the economic and ecological aspects of the area. The planning needs to be versatile enough to be implemented by all community groups according to their tasks and functions. Therefore, it needs incorporation both horizontally and vertically. It is not only environmentally beneficial; sustainable tourism development planning can also benefit the community economically in a longer term.

REFERENCES

Agarwal, R., Grassl, W. and Pahl, J. (2012) 'Meta-SWOT: Introducing a new strategic planning tool', *Journal of Business Strategy*. doi: 10.1108/02756661211206708.

Ahmadi, M., Dileepan, P. and Wheatley, K. K. (2016) 'A SWOT analysis of big data', *Journal of Education for Business*. doi: 10.1080/08832323.2016.1181045.

Al-Mayahi, I. and Mansoor, S. P. (2012) 'UAE E-goverment: SWOT analysis and TOWS Matrix', in *International Conference on ICT and Knowledge Engineering*. doi: 10.1109/ICTKE.2012.6408556.

Ali, E. M. and El-Magd, I. A. (2016) 'Impact of human interventions and coastal processes along the Nile Delta coast, Egypt during the past twenty-five years', *Egyptian Journal of Aquatic Research*. doi: 10.1016/j.ejar.2016.01.002.

Álvarez Larrain, A. and McCall, M. K. (2019) 'Participatory Mapping and Participatory GIS for Historical and Archaeological Landscape Studies: a Critical Review', *Journal of Archaeological Method and Theory*. doi: 10.1007/s10816-018-9385-z.

Bitsura-Meszaros, K. et al. (2019) 'A PGIS-Based Climate Change Risk Assessment Process for Outdoor Recreation and Tourism Dependent Communities', *Sustainability*. doi: 10.3390/su11123300.

Boateng, W. (2012) 'Evaluating the Efficacy of Focus Group Discussion (FGD) in Qualitative Social Research', *International Journal of Business and Social Science*.

Brown, G. and Fagerholm, N. (2015) 'Empirical PPGIS/PGIS mapping of ecosystem services: A review and evaluation', *Ecosystem Services*. doi: 10.1016/j.ecoser.2014.10.007.

Chu, L. et al. (2020) 'Monitoring long-term shoreline dynamics and human activities in the Hangzhou Bay, China, combining daytime and nighttime EO data', *Big Earth Data*. doi: 10.1080/20964471.2020.1740491.

Delita, F., Yetti, E. and Sidauruk, T. (2017) 'Analisis Swot Untuk Strategi Pengembangan Obyek Wisata Pemandian Mual Mata Kecamatan Pematang Bandar Kabupaten Simalungun', *Jurnal Geografi*. doi: 10.24114/jg.v9i1.6037.

Hardini, H. K. (2018) 'Government Strategic Collaborative Partnership in Tourism Affairs A study in Malang and Batu City Governments', *Jurnal Studi Pemerintahan*.

Hidayat, D. and Syahid, A. (2019) 'Local Potential Development (Local Genius) in Community Empowerment', *Journal of Nonformal Education*. doi: 10.15294/jne.v5i1.18343.

Hung, H. C. and Chen, L. Y. (2013) 'Incorporating stakeholders' knowledge into assessing vulnerability to climatic hazards: Application to the river basin management in Taiwan', *Climatic Change*. doi: 10.1007/s10584-013-0819-z.

Indrizal, E. (2014) 'Diskusi Kelompok Terarah', *Jurnal Antropologi: Isu-Isu Sosial Budaya*. doi: 10.25077/jantro.v16i1.12.

Kantawateera, K. et al. (2013) 'A SWOT analysis of tourism development in Khon Kaen, Thailand', *Asian Social Science*. doi: 10.5539/ass.v9n17p226.

Khan, A. et al. (2020) 'Tourism and development in developing economies: A policy implication perspective', *Sustainability (Switzerland)*. doi: 10.3390/su12041618.

Kubickova, M. (2018) 'The Role of Government in Tourism: Linking Competitiveness, Freedom, and Developing Economies', *Czech Journal of Tourism*. doi: 10.1515/cjot-2016-0005.

Lidstone, J. and MacLennan, J. (2018) 'The SWOT Analysis', in *Marketing Planning for the Pharmaceutical Industry*. doi: 10.4324/9781315249674-4.

Link, P. M. et al. (2018) 'Coast to coast: current multidisciplinary research trends in German coastal and marine geography', *Journal of Coastal Conservation*. doi: 10.1007/s11852-017-0578-5.

Mishra, L. (2016) 'Focus Group Discussion in Qualitative Research', *TechnoLearn: An International Journal of Educational Technology*. doi: 10.5958/2249-5223.2016.00001.2.

Nejad, S. G. and Nazmi, A. (2019) 'Study of rip currents as one of the causes of swimmers' drowning in the Caspian Sea', *Journal of Injury and Violence Research*. doi: 10.5249/jivr.v11i2.1143.

Okada, N., Chabay, I. and Renn, O. (2018) 'Participatory Risk Governance for Reducing Disaster and Societal Risks: Collaborative Knowledge Production and Implementation', *International Journal of Disaster Risk Science*. doi: 10.1007/s13753-018-0201-x.

Osland, G. E. and Mackoy, R. D. (2012) 'Education And Ecotourism: A framework and analysis of education in ecolodges in Costa Rica and Panama', *European Journal of Tourism, Hospitality and Recreation*, 3(1), p. 77.

Putri, G. S. and Amalia, A. M. C. (2020) 'Model Komunikasi Pemasaran Terpadu Sport Tourism di Kabupaten Malang', *Expose: Jurnal Ilmu Komunikasi*. doi: 10.33021/exp.v3i1.968.

Radil, S. M. and Anderson, M. B. (2019) 'Rethinking PGIS: Participatory or (post)political GIS?', *Progress in Human Geography*. doi: 10.1177/0309132517750774.

Ridhoi, R. (2020) *Potensi Edutourism di Pesisir Selatan Malang, Jawa Timur*.

Sakellari, M. and Skanavis, C. (2013) 'Sustainable tourism development: Environmental education as a tool to fill the gap between theory and practice', *International Journal of Environment and Sustainable Development*. doi: 10.1504/IJESD.2013.056316.

Sander, B. (2012) 'The importance of education in ecotourism ventures: Lessons from Rara Avis ecolodge, Costa Rica', *International Journal of Sustainable Society*. doi: 10.1504/IJSSOC.2012.049408.

Sim, J. and Waterfield, J. (2019) 'Focus group methodology: some ethical challenges', *Quality and Quantity*. doi: 10.1007/s11135-019-00914-5.

Sukmaratri, M. (2018) 'Kajian Pola Pergerakan Wisatawan Di Objek Wisata Alam Kabupaten Malang', *Jurnal Pariwisata Pesona*. doi: 10.26905/jpp.v3i1.2048.

Verplanke, J. et al. (2016) 'A Shared Perspective for PGIS and VGI', *Cartographic Journal*. doi: 10.1080/00087041.2016.1227552.

Vieira, I. et al. (2016) 'The role of local government management of tourism in fostering residents' support to sustainable tourism development: Evidence from a Portuguese historic town', *International Journal of Tourism Policy*. doi: 10.1504/IJTP.2016.077967.

Wheeler, H. C. and Root-Bernstein, M. (2020) 'Informing decision-making with Indigenous and local knowledge and science', *Journal of Applied Ecology*. doi: 10.1111/1365-2664.13734.

Williamson, K. (2018) 'Questionnaires, individual interviews and focus group interviews', in *Research Methods: Information, Systems, and Contexts: Second Edition*. doi: 10.1016/B978-0-08-102220-7.00016-9.

Zolkafli, A., Liu, Y. and Brown, G. (2017) 'Bridging the knowledge divide between public and experts using PGIS for land use planning in Malaysia', *Applied Geography*. doi: 10.1016/j.apgeog.2017.03.013.

Development, Social Change and Environmental Sustainability – Sumarmi et al (Eds)
© 2021 Taylor & Francis Group, London, ISBN 978-1-032-01320-6

Optimizing village assets for rural tourism development in South Malang

Joko Sayono*, Lutfiah Ayundasari, Nasikh & Febri Kevin Aditya
Universitas Negeri Malang, Malang, Indonesia

ABSTRACT: This study discusses the optimization of village assets for the development of rural tourism in South Malang. This research is motivated by the many cases of mismanagement of village assets that have led to criminal acts of corruption since the enactment of law No. 16 2014 on villages. Whereas on the other hand this law gives broad authority to the village to manage assets for improvement of community welfare. The purpose of this research is to design a village asset optimization for the development of rural tourism. The research method used is descriptive qualitative research with data collection techniques through observation, interviews and documentation. The data obtained were analyzed through three stages. The results of this study recommend that the management of village assets in South Malang be carried out in optimal, professional, and modern in accordance with statutory regulations and still consider the success factors of rural tourism development.

Keywords: village, rural, tourism

1 INTRODUCTION

The village is a homogeneous and egalitarian social unit that has experienced a process of socio-economic differentiation since the colonial era (Shohibuddin 2016). This raises two major problems, namely internal (within the village) and external (rural-urban) economic disparities. This problem is common in developing countries. Over the past 2 decades Malaysia has established programs to narrow the progress gap between rural and urban areas, improve living standards and the socio-economic conditions of rural communities, especially for the poor (Fauziah & Hamzah 2012). Meanwhile in Indonesia, the resolution of this problem has received legality since the enactment of Law No. 6/2014 on villages. The de-centralized system established in this law allows villages to design regulations, plan village development, and manage finances independently where this authority was previously held by a higher authority (Susan & Budirahayu 2018).

In addition to opening up new opportunities, this regulation also presents a big challenge for village governments, especially in practicing good governance values such as anti-corruption, transparency, participation and accountability considering that it is generally known that the majority of human resources at the village level still have primary and secondary education backgrounds with limited governance knowledge (Prasetyo & Muis 2015; Azbihardiyanti & Ma'ruf 2016). This is evident from the many cases of corruption that arise not because of embezzlement of funds but because of ignorance in financial management as found by Setiawan that 44.8% of corruption at the village level is caused by low understanding of village officials on accountability for fund management (Ismail et al. 2016; Setiawan & Yuliani 2017). This is in line with ICW's monitoring which states that the amount of corruption in villages has continued to increase since 2015 due to large budget management, but its implementation at the village level is not accompanied by the

---

*Corresponding author: joko.sayono.fis@um.ac.id

DOI 10.1201/9781003178163-33

principles of transparency, participation and accountability in political governance, development and village finance (*Outlook dana desa 2018 potensi penyalahgunaan anggaran desa di tahun politik* 2018).

These governance problems not only have an impact on the increasing number of corruption crimes, but also the reluctance of the village government to take innovative steps to develop the village economy, especially those related to the management and use of village assets. Even though the government has launched the Sipades (Village Asset Management System) application, in its implementation there are still not optimal obstacles experienced by Village officials in using the SIPADES application such as the system that often errors, lack of understanding of village officials in using SIPADES, and there is no sustainable assistance if village officials encounter difficulty in using the application (Q. & Raharso 2020). The management of village assets is an important instrument in bringing prosperity and happiness to the villagers (Anwar & Angga 2018). Departing from these problems, this article seeks to provide an overview of the design of optimizing village assets for regional economic development through rural tourism.

2 METHOD

The research method used is descriptive qualitative research. Collecting data in this study using observation, interview and documentation techniques. Observations were made to 11 sub-districts in South Malang, this was done to see the condition of the community and to examine village assets that have the potential to become rural tourism destinations. Meanwhile, interviews were conducted with sub-district or village leaders in the research location. Furthermore, documentation is done by analyzing the documents available at the Central Bureau of Statistics, Malang Regency. The collected data is tabulated and processed by analysis through three stages, namely the stage of data reduction, data display, and conclusions.

3 RESULT AND DISCUSSION

3.1 *Village assets and potential for improving community welfare*

Based on Village Law 6/2014 the original village wealth (point a) is village treasury land, village market, animal market, boat moorings, village buildings, fish auctions managed by the village, agricultural product auctions, village owned forests, owned springs. villages, public baths, and other original village assets. Village assets are one of the village's original sources of income that have the potential to increase the community welfare if it well managed ('Undang-Undang Nomor 6 Tahun 2014 tentang Desa' 2014; Andari et al. 2017).

Previously, the concept of welfare was only seen as an economic phenomenon. However, along with the development of thought, the manifestation of prosperity is increasingly diverse, including economic, social, cultural and environmental sustainability. Community independence is an important indicator of measuring welfare. The village community has this independence capital because they have original village income that comes from village assets. Basically, village independence - including independent asset management, is a manifestation of village autonomy whose existence is protected and regulated in laws and other legal products (Permatasari & Pratiwi 2013). However, if the principle of independence is not balanced with the existence of qualified village resources, it will only hinder village development and the welfare of its people. The problem that occurs is that there are not sufficient resources to assess the potential of each village asset. Whereas the assessment of village potential is included in the planning stage which is important in providing an orientation for the management of village assets so that they can run effectively. Other welfare indicators include economic conditions, housing conditions, development opportunities, social security, environment, and psychology (Bao et al. 2018). All of these things will be realized in accordance with the mandate of the law through the optimization of village assets, especially for the implementation of reliable rural tourism.

3.2 *Rural tourism potential in South Malang*

South Malang or the southern part of Malang Regency covers 11 districts with a total of 125 villages. This area covers an area of approximately 1399.70 km2 (BPS Malang Regency 2020). The contours of the southern Malang region are mountainous and hilly. In some places, you can find beautiful forests, waterfalls, and springs. In addition to the hilly contours, there is also a landscape in the form of a stretch of coast that stretches from Donomulyo District to Ampelgading District. The beaches face directly to the Indian Ocean.

Regional geographical conditions in such a way constitute the superior potential of South Malang in the tourism sector. This can be seen from the dominance of the types of natural tourism in South Malang. However, the tourism potential in South Malang is not only natural tourism but also includes socio-economic and socio-cultural conditions. Tourism potential based on the socio-economic conditions of the community, among others, is agro-tourism, tourism villages, and other artificial tourism. Meanwhile, tourism potential that comes from socio-cultural conditions includes religious and cultural tourism, historical heritage, and culinary tourism.

The majority of tourism potential management in South Malang is managed by villages and village Pokdarwis (tourism awareness group), the rest are managed by other asset owners such as individuals, Perhutani, or PD Jasa Yasa. The tourism potential that can be managed by the village is the one whose status is a village asset. Rural tourism depends on various natural and cultural resources, both publicly owned (village assets, etc.) and private, as well as the existence of related infrastructure and supporting facilities, such as road access, transportation, provision of accommodation, and restaurants.

Each sub-district in South Malang has the potential for rural tourism, both natural tourism and artificial tourism. In the category of natural tourism, beaches have a strong dominance as the tourism image of South Malang. Based on BPS 2020, there are 45 beach at-tractions. The number of beach tourism managed by the village reaches 27 objects. Sum-bermanjing Wetan sub-district occupies the top position with a total of seven village beach tourism objects. Coastal tourism is supported by easier access with the construction of the Southern Cross Route (JLS) in South Malang so that coastal tourism, both managed by villages and other stakeholders, has good prospects.

3.3 *Village asset optimization design as a tourism pillar in South Malang*

The increasing need for alternative tourism opens opportunities for villages to plan and develop village tourism by utilizing village assets they have. The rural tourism is a "rural experience" that offer a variety of attractions and activities in agricultural or non-urban areas. The types of activities include nature holidays and ecotourism, walking, climbing and riding holidays, adventure, sport and health tourism, hunting and angling, educational travel, arts and heritage tourism and, in some areas, ethnic tourism (Irshad 2010). This activity has many advantages for the village for the growth of employment opportunities, expansion of the economic base, social progress, and the revitalization of local crafts. The development of rural tourism is a complex multilevel process and is related to the restructuring of the economy in general (Van Der Ploeg et al. 2017). The development of this tourism will be even more interesting if it is connected with the roots of the historical traditions of the community which offer direct involvement in the daily life of the community (Herawati et al. 2014). This management must also be done optimally, professionally, and modernly to improve efficiency, effectiveness and create added value in managing assets (Heriningsih et al. 2015). In addition, in its development, it is necessary to consider factors that affect the success of rural tourism, including awareness of community tourism, management assistance, and sustainable training (Irshad 2010; Ajri et al. 2019; Larasati & Kurrahman 2019).

The optimal development of village tourism is carried out by careful planning, first, mapping tourism potential based on assets owned. Several village assets that have potential include village treasury lands, fish auctions, forests, springs, public baths and coastlines. Second, a SWOT analysis is carried out to deter-mine the Strengths, Weaknesses, Opportunities and Threats and SOAR to identify the situation and position faced by the village in the tourism business competition according to internal strategic factors owned by the village and external factors facing the village. Third, determining the tourism development strategy according to each potential. While professional development is carried out by carrying out good management, namely first (Anggraeni 2016). Second, managed independently involving youth and communities who have expertise in their fields because they are important elements in this development (Ezeuduji 2015; Van Der Ploeg et al. 2017). Third, using integrated information technology for planning, management (production and distribution), and reporting so that management runs transparently and accountably (Kayumova 2017). The development of modern village tourism is carried out by designing destination designs and products according to market needs that meet quality, ethical, and easy factors. This convenience takes the form of IT-based travel guides and promotions.

Apart from the managerial factors, another social factor is needed, namely tourism awareness. The community must become the subject and object of village tourism development so that they have a sense of belonging and are aware that they are an important part of developing tourism in their environment (Raharjana 2012; Putri & Manaf 2013). If possible, this form of involvement will be in the form of CBT (Community Based Tourism) which combines several variables, namely social, economic and environ-mental (Herawati et al. 2014). This CBT will be successful if the community is able to bring up the uniqueness of the location, facilitation of grants for the embryos of existing activities, there are driving figures and links to important stakeholders (Putri & Manaf 2013). An example of the uniqueness that can be presented is food. Typical food can be a tourist attraction seen from the point of view of consumer behavioral theories, the "experience economy" and the "intimacy" model. Typical foods serve to reinforce personal identity, the search for fresh-ness, taste and authenticity, support for local producers, and environmental concerns (Baldacchino 2015; Sidali et al. 2015). Local food and its associated culture can help sustain rural tourism partic-ularly and rural communities generally. One of the potential food and beverage products in South Malang is coffee originating from the slopes of Semeru (Dampit) which has been famous since the Dutch colonial government. The last but also very important is the continuous management and training assistance. Village communities are basically not people who understand the ins and outs of the tourism industry so that in management they must be accompanied by third parties such as government agencies, universities, and other social institutions. This is done to optimize management, avoid conflicts between residents fighting over assets, and avoid corruption due to ignorance of governance.

The implementation of strategies and success factors that determine the development of village tourism is expected to be able to lead people to prosperity according to the mandate of the law. In order to achieve a successful tourism village, development planning and implementation need to be evaluated based on the seven successful aspects of rural tourism community involvement: proximity to a generating market or gateway, product development (Tourism planning, infrastructure, and activities), a visitor center, partnership collaboration/cultural heritage, welcome centers, a quality brand, a regional label brand and funding (Irshad 2010). Although it is quite difficult, this must be started immediately, because it has been proven that many villages have succeeded in managing their assets such as Pangkah Kulon Gresik Village, villages in Dieng Plateau, a village in Jogjakarta (Putri & Manaf 2013; Astuti & Issundari 2016; Chomariyah et al. 2016). In addition, real examples in Malang can be seen in Pujon Kidul Tourism Village, Sumber Maron Tourism Village, Boon Pring Tourism, etc.

4 CONCLUSION

Based on this study, it can be concluded that village assets as a source of village income can be used to improve community welfare as long as it is well managed. South Malang is a region that is rich and has village assets that can be used optimally for economic improvement and community welfare. The village assets are in the form of village treasury lands, fish auctions managed by the village, agricultural product auctions, village owned forests, village springs, public baths, and coastlines. This management must be carried out in an optimal, professional, and modern manner in accordance with statutory regulations and still consider the success factors in the development of rural tourism, including awareness of community tourism, management assistance, and continuous training.

REFERENCES

Ajri, M. *et al.* (2019) 'Pengembangan Desa Jomboran sebagai Desa Agrowisata Mandiri Melalui Model Pembanguna Karakter, Model Tetrapreneur, dan Pemetaan Potensi Desa Berbasis Pertanian', *Jurnal Pengabdian kepada Masyarakat (Indonesian Journal of Community Engagement)*, 4(2), p. 198. doi: 10.22146/jpkm.30912.

Andari, I. G. A. R. D., Sulindawati, N. L. G. E., Atmadja, A. T., & SE, A. (2017) 'Optimalisasi Pengelolaan Pendapatan Asli Desa Untuk Meningkatkan Pembangunan Perekonomian Desa Pada Desa Pejarakan, Kecamatan Gerokgak, Kabupaten Buleleng', *JIMAT (Jurnal Ilmiah Mahasiswa Akuntansi S1)*, 7(1). doi: 10.23887/jimat.v7i1.9674.

Anggraeni, M. R. R. S. (2016) 'PERANAN BADAN USAHA MILIK DESA (BUMDES) PADA KESEJAHTERAAN MASYARAKAT PEDESAAN STUDI PADA BUMDES DI GUNUNG KIDUL, YOGYAKARTA', *MODUS*, 2(3), pp. 225–237. doi: 10.24002/modus.v28i2.848.

Anwar, M. Z. and Angga, R. D. (2018) 'PEREMPUAN, ASET DESA, DAN SUMBER PENGHIDUPAN: Studi Kasus Desa Gadungan, Blitar, Jawa Timur', *Musãwa Jurnal Studi Gender dan Islam*, 16(1), p. 81. doi: 10.14421/musawa.2017.161.81-96.

Astuti, M. and Issundari, S. (2016) 'Desa wisata sebagai aset soft power Indonesia', *Masyarakat, Kebudayaan dan Politik*, 29(2), p. 68. doi: 10.20473/mkp.v29i22016.68-78.

Azbihardiyanti, A. and Ma'ruf, M. . (2016) 'OPTIMALISASI PENGELOLAAN ASET DESA STUDI DI DESA SIMOREJO KECAMATAN KEPOHBARU KABUPATEN BOJONEGORO Apriva', *Publika*, 8(1).

Baldacchino, G. (2015) 'Feeding the Rural Tourism Strategy? Food and Notions of Place and Identity', *Scandinavian Journal of Hospitality and Tourism*, 15(1–2), pp. 223–238. doi: 10.1080/15022250.2015.1006390.

Bao, H. *et al.* (2018) 'Investigating Social Welfare Change in Urban Village Transformation: A Rural Migrant Perspective', *Social Indicators Research*, 139(2), pp. 723–743. doi: 10.1007/s11205-017-1719-9.

Chomariyah, Hudi, N. and Ariyanto, B. (2016) 'Participation Principle On The 2014 Village Law In Coastal Village', *International Journal of Business, Economics and Law*, 10(4), pp. 33–40.

Ezeuduji, I. O. (2015) 'Strategic event-based rural tourism development for sub-Saharan Africa', *Current Issues in Tourism*, 18(3), pp. 212–228. doi: 10.1080/13683500.2013.787049.

Fauziah, C. L. and Hamzah, M. R. (2012) 'Homestay tourism and pro-poor tourism strategy in Banghuris Selangor , Malaysia', *Elixir Geoscience*, 45(March 2012), pp. 7602–7610.

Helmy Syahrizal, A. (2018) 'Strategi Optimalisasi Pengelolaan Kekayaan (Aset) Desa Dalam Pembangunan Desa (Studi Kasus Di Desa Sambiroto Kecamatan Kapas Kabupaten Bojonegoro)', *Publika*.

Herawati, A., Purwaningsih, A. and Pudianti, A. (2014) 'Rural Tourism Community Empowerment Based on Local Resources for Improving Community Welfare: Case on Pentingsari Village, Yogyakarta, Indonesia', *Review of Integrative Business & Economics Research*, 3(2), pp. 88–100.

Heriningsih, S., Sudaryati, D. and Fitriyani, L. Y. (2015) 'Analisis Tata Kelola Dana Desa (Studi di Kecamatan Banguntapan Kabupaten Bantul)', *FEB UPN Vyk*.

Irshad, H. (2010) 'Rural Tourism – an Overview October 2010', *Journal of Sustainable Tourism*, (October), pp. 1–30.

Ismail, M., Widagdo, A. K. and Widodo, A. (2016) 'Sistem Akuntansi Pengelolaan Dana Desa', *Jurnal Ekonomi dan Bisnis*, 19(2), pp. 323–340.

Kayumova, M. (2017) 'The Role of ICT Regulations in Agribusiness and Rural Development', *The Role of ICT Regulations in Agribusiness and Rural Development*. doi: 10.1596/29041.

Larasati, D. C., & Kurrahman, Y. T. (2019) 'PERAN PEMERINTAH DESA DALAM MENGELOLA WISATA HUTAN PINUS UNTUK MENINGKATKAN PENDAPATAN ASLI DESA DI DESA BENDOSARI, KECAMATAN PUJON, KABUPATEN MALANG', 9, pp. 161–167.

Maria Rosa Ratna Sri Anggraeni (2016) 'Peranan Badan Usaha Milik Desa (Bumdes) Pada Kesejahteraan Masyarakat Pedesaan Studi Pada Bumdes Di Gunung Kidul, Yogyakarta', *Modus*, 28(2), pp. 155–167.

Outlook dana desa 2018 potensi penyalahgunaan anggaran desa di tahun politik (2018) *Indonesian Corruption Watch*. Available at: www.antikorupsi.Org.

Permatasari, K., Pratiwi, R. N., & S. (2013) 'OTONOMI DESA DALAM PENGELOLAAN ASSET DESA (Studi Kasus Pada Desa Sitirejo Kecamatan Wagir Kabupaten Malang) Kartika Permatasari, Ratih Nur Pratiwi, Suwondo', *Jurnal Administrasi Publik*, 1(6), pp. 1213–1219.

Van Der Ploeg, J. D. *et al.* (2017) 'Rural development: From practices and policies towards theory', *The Rural: Critical Essays in Human Geography*, 40(4), pp. 201–218. doi: 10.4324/9781315237213-11.

Prasetyo, A. and Muis, A. (2015) 'Pengelolaan Keuangan Desa Pasca UU No. 6 Tahun 2014 Tentang Desa: Potensi Permasalahan dan Solusi', *Jurnal Desentralisasi*, 13(1), pp. 16–31. doi: 10.37378/jd.2015.1.16-31.

Putri, H. P. J. and Manaf, A. (2013) 'Faktor Â Faktor Keberhasilan Pengembangan Desa Wisata Di Dataran Tinggi Dieng', *Teknik Perencanaan Wilayah Kota*, 2(3), pp. 559–568.

Q., M. R. and Raharso, M. (2020) 'Evaluasi Kesuksesan Implementasi Sistem Pengelolaan Aset Desa (SIPADES)', *Jurnal Manajemen Aset Infrastruktur & Fasilitas*, 4(1), pp. 33–42. doi: 10.12962/j26151847.v4i1.6831.

Raharjana, D. T. (2012) 'Membangun Pariwisata Bersama Rakyat: Kajian Partisipasi Lokal Dalam Membangun Desa Wisata Di Dieng Plateau', *Jurnal Kawistara*, 2(3), pp. 225–237. doi: 10.22146/kawistara.3935.

Setiawan, N. D. and Yuliani, N. L. (2017) 'Pengaruh Pemahaman dan Peran Perangkat Desa Terhadap Akuntabilitas Pengelolaan Dana Desa', *Urecol*, pp. 205–210.

Shohibuddin, M. (2016) 'Peluang dan Tantangan Undang-undang Desa dalam Upaya Demokratisasi Tata Kelola Sumber Daya Alam Desa: Perspektif Agraria Kritis', *MASYARAKAT: Jurnal Sosiologi*, 21(1), pp. 1–33. doi: 10.7454/mjs.v21i1.5021.

Sidali, K. L., Kastenholz, E. and Bianchi, R. (2015) 'Food tourism, niche markets and products in rural tourism: combining the intimacy model and the experience economy as a rural development strategy', *Journal of Sustainable Tourism*, 23(8–9), pp. 1179–1197. doi: 10.1080/09669582.2013.836210.

Susan, N., & Budirahayu, T. (2018) 'Village Government Capacity in the Implementation of Village Law No. 6 of 2015 in Indonesia', *Sustainable Future for Human Security*, pp. 17–27.

'Undang-Undang Nomor 6 Tahun 2014 tentang Desa' (2014). doi: 10.1145/2904081.2904088.

Development, Social Change and Environmental Sustainability – Sumarmi et al (Eds)
© 2021 Taylor & Francis Group, London, ISBN 978-1-032-01320-6

Zoo management for animal welfare through sustainable tourism principles

A. Demartoto*
Universitas Sebelas Maret, Surakarta City, Indonesia

ABSTRACT: This article aims to describe manager and stakeholder behavior in managing zoo using sustainable tourism principles for animal welfare. This study enriches previous research concerning zoo management and sustainable tourism principles. This case study design employed typology analysis to interpret written data, interview, and observation on manager and stakeholder behavior of Surakarta Zoo with Parsons' structural functionalism theory. The result shows that management applies sustainable tourism principles and The Five Freedoms less optimally. Problems such as budget, organization, supervision and control obstacles in managing zoos existed. The findings of this study shed light on putting zoo as a conservation institution and suggest the importance of education, environmental enrichment, and regulation for sustainable tourism and animal welfare.

Keywords: zoo, management, animal, tourism

1 INTRODUCTION

At least there are three functions of zoo: conservation, education and research. But not all people realize those functions, moreover they only know zoo as tourism place where we can see wild animals more closely than watching them on television (Patrick & Tunnicliffe 2013). Zoos' function as conservation indicates how tourism sustainable existence is important to management (Dávid 2011; Hosey et al. 2013; Iswandono et al. 2016). Sustainable tourism existence in zoo management suggests that sustainable ecology is the most significant point except economic value. Therefore, it must be vital step to take animal welfare aspect as first priority, yet the fact indicates differently, because it has not been understood by all zoo managers in Indonesia.

World Society for the Protection of Animals (WSPA) and Pro Fauna explains that the condition of animals in 10 zoos all around Indonesia generally are in less good and satisfied condition. Various events become the proof, like in July of 2013 there were 105 animal deaths in Surabaya Zoo and recently a 3 year old komodo dragon died and was found by a keeper in its cage on Saturday the 1st of January, 2014 in the morning (Indonesia 2014) and other cases happened in Surakarta Zoo or Taman Satwa Taru Jurug (TSTJ) and in Bandung Zoo. Those realities were getting worse with zoo visitor impacting adversely the fauna survival, such as throwing any kinds of food for animals.

The sustainability concept starts to develop as a new perspective in development in 90's. Reaching highest, in 1992 on UN Conference on the Environment and Development (UNCED) in Rio de Janeiro and sounding loudest in effecting development model until sustainable development paradigm born. Sustainable tourism is the part of sustainable development implementation in the tourism sector, therefore needing huge attention (Sharpley 2002; Jayawardena et al. 2008; Demartoto 2009; Hanna 2013). Sustainable tourism is an effort to develop tourism by noticing and integrating economy, social (participation and society interest) and ecology aspects equally (Crouch 2002; Dávid 2011; Davies 2012). Moreover, zoo contexts of all biological resources are part of

---

*Corresponding author: argyodemartoto_fisip@staff.uns.ac.id

DOI 10.1201/9781003178163-34

interesting tourism attraction for visitors to come (Patrick et al. 2007; Tyrrell & Johnston 2008). As the expression of moral, animal welfare concept has been developed sufficiently in activist and international animal lover circle. All humans are responsible for pets and wild animals (Webster 2007; Davies 2012). Animal welfare theory contains human care and treatment to animal and how society can increase animal living quality. Every kind of wild faunas and animal must live freely in nature (Röcklinsberg et al. 2014; Cudworth 2015).

In Indonesia, the animal welfare concept is neither popular nor applicable. Indonesian people are less familiar with that, because generally the welfare term is identical with human matters. Nevertheless, Non-Governmental Organization activists who are concerned for animal welfare try to socialize society to understand that the welfare concept is not only for human matters, but also for animals (Eccleston & KE 2009). Animal welfare was revealed firstly by Major C. W. Hume known not only as "father" of animal welfare movement but also as the founder of University of London Animal Welfare Society (ULAWS) in 1926. Human attempts to convince the scientific community to be more humane in treating animal and animals have personalities like people, have emotion, enjoy playing, and have other behaviors similar to humans (Haynes 2008). In animal welfare principle, all people are motivated to be empathic and to appreciate animal (Davies 2012; Mellor 2016).

To gain animal welfare, an international method is needed with particular indicators, such as The Five Freedoms. The Five Freedom Principles are: freedom from hunger and thirst by giving enough food and beverage to guarantee animal health; freedom from discomfort by giving proper care and a gratifying environment for the animal; freedom from pain, injury and disease by preventing illness possibilities and suffering wounds as much as possible, and if the animals still get ill they must be examined by a veterinarian and cured; freedom to behave normally by giving the animals a large environment, which makes them act naturally and gather with other animals and freedom from fear and distress by guaranteeing animal conditions and treatment in order to prevent boredom, stress, fear and worry about threats (Ohl & van der Staay 2012) (McCulloch 2013).

Animal welfare should get attention and be applied to zoos, being one of tourism objects and attractions to run conservation (Catibog-Sinha 2008; Wardhani 2008; Appleby et al. 2011). Flora and fauna conservation in Indonesia has been confirmed with establishment of the conservation institution under various rules and constitutions, for example, part I, first paragraph number 3 of Republic of Indonesia's Minister of Forestry's regulation number P.53/Menhut-II/2006 about conservation institutions. Animal welfare is organized under Indonesian Government Regulation Number 95 in 2012 about Veterinary Society Health and Animal Welfare.

A zoo, in its management system, needs to be supported by a subsystem including actors or managers and stakeholders related to the government, non-government or private sector and society (visitors), goals, situations and conditions as well as normative standards. Structural functionalism theory from Talcott Parsons is a sociological and anthropological perspective defining society as a structure belongs to many related parts and addressed to particular fulfilling need directions and systems. There are four absolute rules to have in order to turn on society function: Adaptation, Goal Attainment, Integration and Latency (AGIL) (Sciortino 2015). Action in zoo conservation indirectly and absolutely must gain animal welfare. More than that, animal welfare needs to be proposed to support various zoo function itself and assure sustainable tourism's role as development model. This research attempts seriously to investigate TSTJ management as an object and tourism attraction and also as conservation place and enrich study about sustainable tourism, especially animal welfare.

2 METHOD

This study used qualitative research with case study being research strategy (Yin 2003). Primary data was obtained directly from the sources including TSTJ manager and stakeholders (tourist or visitor, seller vendor around the zoo, Tourism and Culture Department, Education and Sport Department, Agriculture and Animal Husbandry Department in Surakarta, private sector and academician). Secondary data was obtained from books, the internet, files and documentation related to this tourism object. The data obtained such as written documents or in-depth interview records and observations were analyzed using a typology analysis technique (Yin 2003; Jenner et al. 2004). To avoid or to minimize possibility bias, the author must crosscheck the interview result from an interviewee with that from another and from TSTJ documents manager (Miles et al. 2014).

3 RESULT AND DISCUSSIONS

3.1 *Narration of management and tourism potential*

TSTJ is one of the main tourism places in Surakarta and famous enough. Historically, this zoo is called Sriwedari Zoo is a part of Sriwedari Park located in Sriwedari administrative village Laweyan Surakarta. TSTJ was built in Sri Susuhunan Paku Buwono X era on 17th July 1901 and developed as public recreation place, as well as announced officially as tourism place in 1976. In addition, there was a park in other place, Jurug Park. The construction of Sriwedari Stadium made fauna collection in Sriwedari Zoo moved to Jurug Park. Since 1983 it called as TSTJ and managed by Bengawan Permai Company as deposit site of Regency Government of Surakarta before then returned to government through Bina Satwa Taru Jurug foundation in1986-1997, but the management has not been done professionally and the funding was less for developing and building. Briefly, based on Regional Government's Regulation Number 6 of 2010 about Taman Satwa Taru Jurug Regional Building Company, the government built TSTJ Regional Company to support regional economy growth until now. Since that time TSTJ is an object and tourism attraction for society, moreover after it fixed and developed many facilities. TSTJ is not only tourism place but also conservation and research place. It has about 263 animas in its collection coming from local and foreign locations such as Sumatran Tigers, Lions, orangutans, komodo dragons, camels, elephants, snakes, and various plants such as casuarinas, Poinciana, acacia and other trees.

3.2 *Representation of conservation insitutions*

TSTJ, as a recreation, conservation and research place, shows more specialty than other tourism places. TSTJ aims to be committed to flora and fauna conservation, education, rescue and development in social, cultural, entertainment aspects, as well as upgrading regional income. TSTJ conservation department cooperates with the Conservation of Natural Resources House in Semarang and also the Indonesia Forestry Minister. TSTJ puts forward its tourism potential to attract tourist to visit. TSTJ operational management carry out structured coordination related to Conservation Institution. The result of observation shows many improper, rusty and broken cages in TSTJ. Additionally, many faunas have no buddy or partner in the cage, despite the fact that such companionship functions significantly to carry out reproduction and to prevent the animal from being stressed. A way to fulfill the animal welfare principle is to provide partners for breeding fauna, so the conservation department creates a network with the Surakarta government, private sector, personal, community and institution like as the Zoos Association in Indonesia. To carry out cleaning the cages and environment, it cooperates with Sebelas Maret University students, except daily cage cleaning done by the cleanliness department.

In conservation efforts, TSTJ also cooperates with all stakeholders to add fauna collection through grants, such as for orangutans. A veterinarian said there are 34 single (with no partner) animals out of 263 in TSTJ. The existence of a partner becomes an indicator in raising animal welfare. Internal environments inside also contribute to TSTJ management. In previous management, there were many problems related to the management's less optimal and minimal commitment to showing how TSTJ can be interesting to visitors. Human resource utilization, which belongs to TSTJ, has not been run optimally. In the work environment nowadays, there is a good shift in manager and stakeholder commitment in TSTJ development. One of each department starts to innovate by extending outside network to provide education packages through social media, such as through Facebook, Twitter, Instagram and the plazatamanjurug.com website. TSTJ also cooperates with a third party to fix animal parks, because it has little budget only to repair tools and infrastructure. But human resource development has been run poorly due to no promotion or reward system for staff, but only punishment for the staff breaking the rules. It results in non-maximal staff performance. There are changes in financial resources from tax, rides, and government capital and funds from marketing cooperation. Now, the director of TSTJ regional company is trying to ask tax cutting from Surakarta Government. Therefore, there are efforts in TSTJ management to abide by the sustainable tourism principle for animal welfare. Integration from all parts comes from actor, tool and infrastructure; situation, condition and budget caused TSTJ developed. Instead of it tends to be dynamic but the change not always run well, despite stopped in the certain pattern.

3.3 *Challenges of synergy animal welfare and sustainable tourism*

The management system of TSTJ is in less optimal rank and eventually will be unable to gain sustainable tourism and maintain animal welfare standards. Therefore, a new TSTJ management is needed with sustainable tourism principle and animal welfare being its foundation, meaning that sustainable tourism will smooth the achievement of (Jahja 2016). TSTJ has chosen its direction and tried to gain the fixed goals. The actors of TSTJ management with sustainable principle of animal welfare consist of personal or a group, manager and worker in the zoo, visitor or tourist, seller around the zoo and those related. Society participation is very vital in planning work program. Periodically monitoring and evaluation have been implemented but less optimal. Animal welfare in the zoo will be gained if sustainable tourism principle becomes the foundation of its management. The first step to achieve this is to repair tourism potential aspect, natural resources, human resources and financial resources in TSTJ management system. Those aspects become the key to consider comprehensive management system and expected outcome based on sustainable tourism principle for animal welfare (Talcott & Turner 2013; Ingenbleek et al. 2012) .The improvement of human resource aspect can be done by giving education about sustainable tourism principle and animal welfare for TSTJ workers and visitors. It can also be done using an environmental enrichment method which is a method to create conditions and particular treatment based on natural animal life, including (1) structural enrichment; (2) object enrichment; (3) social enrichment; and (4) food enrichment (Beaver 2010; Appleby et al. 2011). In addition, transparency is also important in the term of money, water, land uses and others. Balance should be created between tourist need and society (Mojo et al. 2015). TSTJ must be capable of creating quality of life local society, giving quality of opportunity to service providers in tourism industry and the point is creating quality of experience from tourists. TSTJ can grow because of its difference, uniqueness, and locality in the term of nature, flora, fauna or even culture as creativity, credibility, taste and man's mind.

4 CONCLUSION

TSTJ, as a system, has limitation viewed from the created subsystems, such as actor, tool and infrastructure, situation and condition as well as budget subsystems. Some efforts need to be made to create systemic and comprehensive zoo management: (1) human resource capacity improvement by giving education about sustainable tourism principle and animal welfare for the staff and visitors; (2) using enrichment methods (tool and infrastructure); (3) making regulations related to animal welfare, such as tightening accompanied with straight sanctions implementation for visitor who feed the animals improperly, disturb composure and make stress to animal and pollute or litter in the TSTJ area.

REFERENCES

Appleby, M. C., Hughes, B. O., Mench, J. A., & Olsson, A. (2011) 'Animal Welfare, 2nd ed', *UK: CAB International Publishing.*
Beaver, B. V (2010) 'Welfare of animals: Introduction'.
Catibog-Sinha, C. (2008) 'Zoo tourism: Biodiversity conservation through tourism', *Journal of Ecotourism,* doi: 10.1080/14724040802140527.
Crouch, D. (2002) 'Critical sociologies of tourism', *Sociology*, 36(3), pp. 743–749.

Cudworth, E. (2015) 'Killing animals: Sociology, species relations and institutionalized violence', *The Sociological Review*, 63(1), pp. 1–18.

Dávid, L. (2011) 'Tourism ecology: towards the responsible, sustainable tourism future', *Worldwide Hospitality and Tourism Themes*.

Davies, G. (2012) 'Caring for the multiple and the multitude: Assembling animal welfare and enabling ethical critique', *Environment and Planning D: Society and space*, 30(4), pp. 623–638.

Demartoto, A. (2009) *Pembangunan pariwisata berbasis masyarakat*. Sebelas Maret University Press.

Eccleston, K. J. and KE, A. (2009) 'Animal Welfare di Jawa Timur: Model Pendidikan Kesejahteraan Binatang di Jawa Timur', *Australian Consortium For In-Country Indonesian Studies Angkatan Ke-28*.

Hanna, P. (2013) 'A break from "reality": An investigation into the 'experiments with subjectivity' on offer within the promotion of sustainable tourism in the UK', *Journal of Consumer Culture*, 13(3), pp. 366–386.

Haynes, R. P. (2008) *Animal welfare: competing conceptions and their ethical implications*. Springer Science & Business Media.

Hosey, G., Melfi, V. and Pankhurst, S. (2013) *Zoo animals: behaviour, management, and welfare*. Oxford University Press.

INDONESIA, B. (2014) 'No Title', *bbc indonesia*. Available at: https://www.bbc.com/indonesia/berita_indonesia/2014/02/140201_kbs_komodo#:~:text=
Seekor satwa kembali mati di,(01%2F01) pagi.&text=Seekor singa Afrika berumur 18 bulan awal Januari juga mati.

Ingenbleek, P. T. M. *et al.* (2012) 'EU animal welfare policy: Developing a comprehensive policy framework', *Food Policy*, 37(6), pp. 690–699.

Iswandono, E.- *et al.* (2016) 'Traditional Land Practice and Forest Conservation: Case Study of The Manggarai Tribe in Ruteng Mountains, Indonesia', *KOMUNITAS: International Journal of Indonesian Society and Culture*. doi: 10.15294/komunitas.v8i2.4945.

Jahja, R. S. (2016) 'Developing Environmental Education Model Based on Local Wisdom', *KOMUNITAS: International Journal of Indonesian Society and Culture*. doi: 10.15294/komunitas.v8i1.4936.

Jayawardena, C. *et al.* (2008) 'Sustainable tourism development in Niagara', *International Journal of Contemporary Hospitality Management*.

Jenner, B. *et al.* (2004) *A companion to qualitative research*. Sage.

McCulloch, S. P. (2013) 'A critique of FAWC's five freedoms as a framework for the analysis of animal welfare', *Journal of agricultural and environmental ethics*, 26(5), pp. 959–975.

Mellor, D. J. (2016) 'Updating animal welfare thinking: Moving beyond the "Five freedoms" towards "a Life Worth Living"', *Animals*, 6(3), p. 21.

Miles, M., Huberman, A. and Saldanþa, J. (2014) 'Sampling: Bounding the collection of data', in *Qualitative Data Analysis: A methods Sourcebook*.

Mojo, E., Hadi, S. P. and Purnaweni, H. (2015) 'Saminist's Indigenous Knowledge in Water Conservation', *Komunitas: International Journal of Indonesian Society and Culture*.

Ohl, F. and van der Staay, F. J. (2012) 'Animal welfare: At the interface between science and society', *Veterinary Journal*. doi: 10.1016/j.tvjl.2011.05.019.

Patrick, P. G. *et al.* (2007) 'Conservation and education: Prominent themes in zoo mission statements', *The Journal of Environmental Education*, 38(3), pp. 53–60.

Patrick, P. G. and Tunnicliffe, S. D. (2013) *Zoo talk, Zoo Talk*. doi: 10.1007/978-94-007-4863-7.

Röcklinsberg, H., Gamborg, C. and Gjerris, M. (2014) 'A case for integrity: Gains from including more than animal welfare in animal ethics committee deliberations', *Laboratory Animals*. doi: 10.1177/0023677213514220.

Sciortino, G. (2015) 'AGIL, History of. In International Encyclopedia of the Social and Behavioral Sciences', pp. 381–393.

Sharpley, R. (2002) 'Tourism: a vehicle for development?', *Tourism and development: Concepts and issues*, pp. 11–34.

Talcott, P. and Turner, B. S. (2013) *The Social System, The Social System*. doi: 10.4324/9780203992951.

Tyrrell, T. J. and Johnston, R. J. (2008) 'Tourism Sustainability, Resiliency and Dynamics: Towards a More Comprehensive Perspective', *Tourism and Hospitality Research*. doi: 10.1057/thr.2008.8.

Wardhani, L. K. (2008) 'Masa DepanSatwa Liar Indonesia Akankah Segera Punah...?'

Webster, J. (2007) *Animal Welfare: Limping Towards Eden: A Practical Approach to Redressing the Problem of Our Dominion Over the Animals, Animal Welfare: Limping Towards Eden: A Practical Approach to Redressing the Problem of Our Dominion Over the Animals*. doi: 10.1002/9780470751107.

Yin, R. K. (2003) 'Case study research: design and methods (ed.)', *Applied social research methods series*, 5.

Development, Social Change and Environmental Sustainability – Sumarmi et al (Eds)
© 2021 Taylor & Francis Group, London, ISBN 978-1-032-01320-6

Development strategy sustainability of historical and cultural tourism in Pacitan

Lutfiah Ayundasari*, Ari Sapto, Wahyu Djoko Sulistyo, Ronal Ridhoi & Ulfatun Nafiah
Universitas Negeri Malang, Malang, Indonesia

ABSTRACT: The purpose of this research is to design a historical and cultural tourism strategy in order to improve the community welfare and sustainability of historical tourism in Pacitan. The research method used is descriptive qualitative with PEST analysis. Sustainable tourism development strategy is analyzed based on political, economic, social and technological conditions that accompany the development of historical and cultural tourism in Pacitan. Data shows that as long as the stakeholders in Pacitan have not yet integrated various tourism potentials, each site is managed separately such as cave and beach tours. While historical and cultural potential has not been optimally developed in order to support tourism sector. The results of this study recommend the "sustainability" historical and cultural tourism development strategy as the basis for optimizing the tourism sector in Pacitan as well as to foster national identity through an understanding of local identity.

Keywords: sustainable, historical and cultural tourism, Pacitan

1 INTRODUCTION

The tourism industry has developed with various innovations such as geotourism, eco-histourism, edu-tourism, and other thematic tours (Farsani et al. 2011). The combination of optimizing the potential and innovation in the tourism sector has led to the success of cities and villages in contributing foreign exchange, increasing the welfare of the community, and developing rural areas (Macdonald & Jolliffe 2003; Vogt & Andereck 2000). One rural area that is struggling to develop tourism potential is Pacitan. A barren area on the south coast of Java. This region has a variety of potentials that have not been managed much, especially historical and cultural tourism, because so far the government's focus has been limited to traces of ancient human heritage tourism, regional potential for food policy, and the development of Klayar beach tourism (Santoso 2009; Faturahman 2017; Ratnasari 2015).

Therefore, this article tries to offer a strategy for developing historical and cultural tourism in Pacitan. This strategy is needed because basically the tourism sector is a very com-plex activity and requires good organization (Hume 2013). Based on the case that occurred in Russia the integration of historical and cultural tourism has helped improve the socio-economic community, increase regional attractiveness and promote the development of urban services, infrastructure and cultural organization (Ismagilova et al. 2015). In addition, this tour can provide an identity for an area and attract tourists who are ultimately able to contribute to regional economic development (Varfolomeyev et al. 2015).

---

*Corresponding author: lutfiah.fis@um.ac.id

162   DOI 10.1201/9781003178163-35

2 METHOD

The method used for this research is descriptive qualitative method with PEST analysis. Strategic analysis in accordance with the development of historical and cultural tourism in Pacitan is the PEST method by integrating two tourism concepts, namely sustainable tourism and rural tourism. This method was adapted from business strategy management developed by (Ward & Peppard 2002). PEST analysis looks at several external factors that affect a business plan, namely political, economic, social and technological. Ward and Peppard (2002), see that careful monitoring of these factors may lead to significant business opportunities or identification of potential threats in time to take action to mitigate the effects. The data obtained in this study were divided into four categories in PEST. The results of the data classification were analyzed and adjusted to the strategy for developing historical heritage tourism. Based on the results of this analysis, weaknesses and strengths and what actions would be taken in order to develop historical heritage tourism in Pacitan were found.

3 RESULT AND DISCUSSION

3.1 *Pacitan and its potentials historical heritage*

Pacitan is a district located at the southern tip of East Java Province. Geographically, this district is bordered by Ponorogo Regency (East Java Province) – North; Trenggalek Regency (East Java Province), Timur; Indian Ocean; and Wonogiri Regency (Central Java Province) – West. The landscape of this area mostly consists of hills and mountains, steep ravines and includes the Thousand Mountains stretching along the island of Java. Administratively, Pacitan Regency consists of 12 districts, where the distance between the district center and the administrative center of Pacitan Regency is between 7–72 km. Most of the morphology of Pacitan Regency (49%) is a somewhat mountainous area with a land slope of >40, and others are land with a flat-wavy area (slopes 0–8%) which occupy an area of 17%, Wavy land (8–15%) occupies ±2.5% area and slightly hilly land (slopes 26–40%) which occupies ±28% area. The Pacitan government divides villages/wards into five categories, namely Tepi Laut Villages/Kelurahan, non-seaside villages/wards, slope/peak villages/wards, valley villages/wards, and plain villages/wards.

Based on the ecological environment, there are two tourism potentials, namely natural tourism and artificial tourism. Natural resources of tourism include beaches and caves, while artificial tourism is historical, cultural and rural tourism. So far, the type of tourism that has been successfully managed with the help of investors and scientific institutions is nature tourism. The most famous destinations are Klayar beach and Goa Gong tours. Meanwhile, artificial tourism (history, culture, and rural areas) has not received good management. Based on the research results, Pacitan has at least 32 historical and cultural tourism potentials that can be combined with rural tourism which is spread across 9 sub-districts as presented in table 1.1.

Based on the condition of the area and the distribution of the potential, the development of historical heritage tourism in Pacitan can be integrated with the concept of rural tourism. This is because tourism utilizes nature and rural human objects as tourist attractions. Besides that, it is also very dependent on natural beauty, the environment, architecture, culture and other sources in rural areas, holidays and tourism activities that are based on experience and traditional rural tourism (Zhang 2012). Pacitan is generally known as a hilly area with a wide area distribution. Administratively, this area is not referred to as a city but a district with areas that are mostly located in the hills far from the center of government. So that people's lives are found in rural communities. In addition, almost all the potential for historical and cultural tourism is in these villages. This is a big capital in historical heritage tourism, so it requires the development of an appropriate strategy and which is fully supported by the surrounding community (Okazaki 2008).

163

Table 1. The spread of historical and cultural tourism in Pacitan.

No.	District	Tourism Potentials
1	Donorojo	Wayang Beber, Ceprotan Ceremony
2	Punung	Song Continued, Song Keplek, Song Gupuh, Ngrijangan, Baksooka River, Archaeological Laboratory, Museum of Buwana Keling, Tabuhan Cave
3	Pringkuku	–
4	Pacitan	Mantu Kucing Ceremony, Kanjeng Jimat Tomb
5	Kebonagung	Tetaken Ceremony, Baritan Ceremony, tomb of Ki Ageng Buwono Keling
6	Arjosari	Jaranan Pegon, Clean Village, Pondok Tremas
7	Nawangan	Kethek Ogleng Dance, Monument of Jenderal Soedirman
8	Bandar	–
9	Tegalombo	Ngreco Site, Badut Sinampurno, earth alms,
10	Tuakan	Monument and home of Jenderal Soedirman
11	Ngadirojo	–
12	Sudimoro	–

This participation consists of efforts to share roles proportionally, sharing knowledge about self-development (tourism), sharing benefits and costs, and deliberation in decision making (Connell 1997).

3.2 Title, author and affiliation frame recent strategies and tourism policy in Pacitan

The seriousness of the Pacitan government in managing tourism is shown by Perda No.7 of 2013 concerning the implementation of tourism which legally covers all tourism operations, especially transportation services, travel, food and beverage provision, accommodation, entertainment and recreation. The development of the tourism sector is assisted by foreign investors and institutions, such as the development of Klayar beach tourism and the revitalization of Songontin. From this it can be seen that the historical heritage plans have not been reflected in government policies. In addition, the government is also building road access. Based on 2015 data, there are 3 types of roads in Pacitan, namely state roads, provincial roads and district roads. The average access to tourist areas is a district road along 798,000m, but 362,188m is in heavily damaged condition. Another tourism business undertaken by the government is the publication of a map consisting of 23 destinations. In the map only four historical and cultural tourist destinations are listed, even though there are around 32 in Pacitan. This means that there are 28 destinations that are not included in the tourist map list. Even though this destination is a potential historical heritage that reflects the peculiarities of Pacitan such as Wayang Beber and various traditional ceremonies.

From this research it is known that the tourism supporting system sector is still not evenly distributed. There are 27 hotels scattered in Pacitan, Nawangan, and Ngadirojo and 30 in Pacitan, Punung, Pringkuku, Arjosari and Tegalombo). In order to overcome the spread of hotels and restaurants, one of the proposals offered is the provision of traditional homestays. This is done with the main objective of providing easy access from lodging to tourist destinations, in addition to providing new tourist experiences that are sought after by tourists. Other tourism support capacity is a gift shop, which in this case is managed by individuals such as Batik Saji, Pak Ran Tuna Tofu, agate crafts and Putra Samudra.

3.3 Sustainability strategy of historical heritage tourism in Pacitan

Sustainable historical heritage tourism in this study aims to maintain, preserve historical heritage, disseminate historical heritage information through tourism activities, and take advantage of the existence of historical heritage as a means of cultural heritage and identity. The development of this strategy uses PEST analysis, namely political, social, economic and technological analysis. The use of the concept of sustainable tourism is carried out in order to preserve the potential of historical heritage that is widely spread in Pacitan, from prehistoric times to the physical revolution. According to (Lane 2009) the development of a tourism sustainability strategy needs to pay attention to four things, namely; social, economic, and ecological analysis skills; broad consultations between various stakeholders; openness; and continuous implementation. Meanwhile, the concept of rural tourism is seen in accordance with the conditions and potential of Pacitan which has rural characteristics. In order to analyze this potential, it is important to pay attention to the existence of ownership of natural and cultural resources, multidirectional relationships among stakeholders and the existence of integrative management (Cawley & Gillmor 2008).

The first step is a political strategy carried out by preparing real policies and programs capable of stimulating and providing opportunities for the development of historical heritage tourism. In addition, it also designs real stakeholder participation programs, such as forming historical and cultural tourism awareness groups at the village and sub-district levels. To make it easier, this group can be initiated from members of the Ka-rangtaruna who regularly receive assistance from academic groups and the government.

The second step is an economic strategy. There are various ways to do this, for example running a culinary business that serves typical Pacitan food such as tiwul rice, chicken vegetables in spicy coconut milk, ointment, and grilled tuna. Serving local food in tourism is seen as important for the purpose of presenting attachment to nature, resilience to glob-alization, strengthening personal identity, seeking freshness, taste and authenticity and for support for local producers (Sidali et al. 2015).This facility will be more complete if the local government is able to provide new tourism experience services such as homestays in people's homes. In addition, to get memories of tourist attractions, it is necessary to design unique crafts and souvenirs. These two goods are among the highest consumption of tourists (Hume 2013) which can contribute to the provision of jobs.

The third step of social strategy includes fostering tourism behavior, fostering an entre-preneurial spirit, and a group approach (Vogt & Andereck 2000). The tourism behavior in question is an awareness of the importance of the tourism sector as a livelihood as well as a guardian of identity. This tourism behavior can be manifested in simple actions such as not destroying historical heritage by committing vandalism, preserving historical and cultural values, and making innovations in the context of disseminating historical and cultural information. Meanwhile, cultivating an entrepreneurial spirit is a simultaneous action between the community and the government on an ongoing basis because without innovation, commitment and the courage to take risks, no tourism can develop (Wilson et al. 2001).

The fourth step of the technological strategy is one of them is developing a historical e-tourism which contains integrated information, especially those related to transportation and accommodation (Varfolomeyev et al. 2015). This begins with data collection and assistance to people who provide these services, including traditional homestays, so that information on the presence of tourists can be coordinated easily.

4 CONCLUSION

Based on the results of the research and discussion in this article, it can be concluded that Pacitan has a lot of historical and cultural tourism potential that needs to be managed properly. Data shows that, so far, the Pacitan government has focused more on developing natural tourism such as beaches and caves, while the development of historical and cultural tourism has not been touched much. This is reflected in several things, including only four historical and cultural tourism sites that are included in the official Pacitan tourist map, minimal access to historical and cultural tourism sites and lack of transportation and accommodation facilities at sites that are potential historical tourism and culture.

REFERENCES

Cawley, M. and Gillmor, D. A. (2008) 'Integrated rural tourism: Concepts and Practice', *Annals of Tourism Research*, 35(2), pp. 316–337. doi: 10.1016/j.annals.2007.07.011.

Connell, D. (1997) 'Participatory development: An approach sensitive to class and gender', *Development in Practice*, 7(3), pp. 248–259. doi: 10.1080/09614529754486.

Farsani, N. T., Coelho, C. and Costa, C. (2011) 'Geotourism and geoparks as novel strategies for socio-economic development in rural areas', *International Journal of Tourism Research*, 13(1), pp. 68–81. doi: 10.1002/jtr.800.

Faturahman, B. M. (2017) 'Pemetaan Potensi Wilayah untuk Menunjang Kebijakan Pangan Kabupaten Pacitan', *Jispo*, 7(2), pp. 43–62. doi: 10.15575/jp.v7i2.2271.

Hume, B. D. L. (2013) 'Tourism Art and Souvenirs?: The Material Culture of Tourism Chapter One Introduction', (October), pp. 1–25.

Ismagilova, G., Gafurov, I. and Safiullin, L. (2015) 'Using historical heritage as a factor in tourism development', *Interdisciplinary Behavior and Social Sciences*, 188(904), pp. 17–21. doi: 10.1201/b18146-5.

Lane, B. (2009) 'Sustainable rural tourism strategies?: A tool for development and conservation Sustainable Rural Tourism Strategies?: A Tool for Development and Conservation', 9582. doi: 10.1080/09669589409510687.

Macdonald, R. and Jolliffe, L. (2003) 'Evidence from Canada', 30(2), pp. 307–322. doi: 10.1016/S0160-7383(02)00061-0.

Okazaki, E. (2008) 'A community-based tourism model: Its conception and use', *Journal of Sustainable Tourism*, 16(5), pp. 511–529. doi: 10.2167/jost782.0.

Ratnasari, S. D. (2015) 'CULTURE Vol. 2 No. 1 Mei 2015 Jejak Hasil Peninggalan Budaya Manusia Prasejarah di Song Terus Pacitan', *Jurnal Culture*, 2(1), pp. 37–53.

Santoso, J. (2009) 'Potensi dan pengembangan obyek wisata pantai klayar di kabupaten pacitan'.

Sidali, K. L., Kastenholz, E. and Bianchi, R. (2015) 'Food tourism, niche markets and products in rural tourism: combining the intimacy model and the experience economy as a rural development strategy', *Journal of Sustainable Tourism*, 23(8–9), pp. 1179–1197. doi: 10.1080/09669582.2013.836210.

Varfolomeyev, A. *et al.* (2015) 'Smart Space based Recommendation Service for Historical Tourism', *Procedia Computer Science*, 77, pp. 85–91. doi: 10.1016/j.procs.2015.12.363.

Vogt, C. A. and Andereck, K. L. (2000) 'The Relationship between Residents' Attitudes toward Tourism and Tourism Development Options', *Journal of Travel Research*, 39(1), pp. 27–36. doi: ER-.

Ward, J. and Peppard, J. (2002) *Strategic planning for information systems*. John Wiley & Sons, Inc.

Wilson, S. *et al.* (2001) 'Journal of Travel Research'. doi: 10.1177/004728750104000203.

Zhang, X. (2012) 'Energy Procedia Research on the Development Strategies of Rural Tourism in Suzhou Based on SWOT Analysis'. doi: 10.1016/j.egypro.2012.01.207.

Development, Social Change and Environmental Sustainability – Sumarmi et al (Eds)
© 2021 Taylor & Francis Group, London, ISBN 978-1-032-01320-6

Author index

Aditya, F.K. 98, 151
Affandi, M.Y. 53
Affriyenni, Y. 66
Afrianty, D. 62
Al Kindy, M.A. 141
Al Siddiq, I.H. 70, 98
Ananda, K.S. 136
Andriesse, E. 8
Anggraini, C. 128
Anzari, P.P. 44, 70, 113
Apriadi, D.W. 44, 102
Astina, I.K. 53, 57
Astuti, I.S. 92
Ayundasari, L. 151, 162
Azzardina, A. 62

Bachri, S. 145
Budijanto 107

Casmana, A.R. 87

Deffinika, I. 62, 107
Demartoto, A. 157
Devy, M.M.R. 145
Dianah, A.F. 141
Dressler, W. 5

Faizal, R. 145
Fatanti, M.N. 70, 118, 128, 136
Fibrianto, A.S. 62, 123

Hadi, N. 57, 113
Hardika 132

Idris 57, 83

Irawan, L.Y. 145
Ishaq, M. 66

Jati, S.S.P. 50

Khakim, M.N.L. 50, 83
Kodir, A. 53, 57, 98, 141
Kurniawati, E. 44, 113

Malihah, E. 23
Masruroh, H. 39
Mawarni, D. 102
Meiji, N.H.P. 18, 141
Muddarisna, N. 39
Mukhlis, I. 98

Nafiah, U. 162
Nasikh, 151
Nurbayani, S. 23

Oktaviansyah, A.R. 39

Paramanandana, S. 98
Perguna, L.A. 79
Prabawangi, R.P. 18, 118
Prasetyo, W.E. 145
Pratiwi, S.S. 70, 74
Purwanto 92
Purwasih, J.H.G. 18, 44, 79

Raharjo, K.M. 132
Rahma, R.A. 66
Ratnawati, N. 57
Ridhoi, R. 14, 162
Rohman, F. 92

Rosyendra, M.G. 53
Rozakiyah, D.S. 74

Sapto, A. 162
Saputra, M. 102
Sayono, J. 14, 151
Silvallana, D.F.V. 70
Subekti, A. 50
Sucipto 66, 132
Sudirman 29
Suhanti, I.Y. 74
Sulistyo, W.D. 50, 162
Sumarmi, 1 141, 145
Susilo, S. 107
Sutanto, H. 79

Tanjung, A. 53, 92, 141
Taryana, D. 57

Umar, R. 29
Utama, A.N.A. 14

Widianto, A.A. 18
Widyaswari, M. 132
Wilodati 23
Wulandari, P. 23

Yuliati 83
Yuniar, A.D. 62, 123
Yuniwati, E.D. 39

Zid, M. 87
Zulkarnain 132

9781032013206